Developing the Craft of Mediation

of related interest

Mediation in Context
Edited by Marian Liebmann
ISBN 978 1 85302 618 8

Advocacy, Counselling and Mediation in Casework
Processes of Empowerment
Edited by Yvonne Joan Craig
Foreword by Daphne Statham
ISBN 978 1 85302 564 8

How Restorative Justice Works
Approaches to Practice in a Range of Contexts
Marian Liebmann
ISBN 978 1 84310 074 4

Working with Gangs and Young People
A Toolkit for Resolving Group Conflict
Jessie Feinstein and Nia Imani Kuumba
ISBN 978 1 84310 447 6

Just Schools
A Whole School Approach to Restorative Justice
Belinda Hopkins
ISBN 978 1 84310 132 1

Reparation and Victim-focused Social Work
Edited by Brian Williams
ISBN 978 1 84310 023 2

Victims of Crime and Community Justice
Brian Williams
ISBN 978 1 84310 195 6

Effective Ways of Working with Children and their Families
Edited by Malcolm Hill
ISBN 978 1 85302 619 5

Developing the Craft of Mediation

Reflections on Theory and Practice

Marian Roberts

Jessica Kingsley Publishers
London and Philadelphia

First published in 2007
by Jessica Kingsley Publishers
116 Pentonville Road
London N1 9JB, UK
and
400 Market Street, Suite 400
Philadelphia, PA 19106, USA

www.jkp.com

Copyright © Marian Roberts 2007

The right of Marian Roberts to be identified as author of this work has been asserted by her in accordance with the Copyright, Designs and Patents Act 1988.

All rights reserved. No part of this publication may be reproduced in any material form (including photocopying or storing it in any medium by electronic means and whether or not transiently or incidentally to some other use of this publication) without the written permission of the copyright owner except in accordance with the provisions of the Copyright, Designs and Patents Act 1988 or under the terms of a licence issued by the Copyright Licensing Agency Ltd, 90 Tottenham Court Road, London, England W1T 4LP. Applications for the copyright owner's written permission to reproduce any part of this publication should be addressed to the publisher.

Warning: The doing of an unauthorised act in relation to a copyright work may result in both a civil claim for damages and criminal prosecution.

Library of Congress Cataloging in Publication Data
Roberts, Marian.
  Developing the craft of mediation : reflections on theory and practice / Marian Roberts.
     p. cm.
  Includes bibliographical references and index.
  ISBN 978-1-84310-323-3 (alk. paper)
  1. Mediation. I. Title.
  BF637.M4R63 2007
  303.6'9--dc22
                          2006102360

British Library Cataloguing in Publication Data
A CIP catalogue record for this book is available from the British Library

ISBN 978 1 84310 323 3

Printed and bound in Great Britain by
Athenaeum Press, Gateshead, Tyne and Wear

Contents

Notes on Contributors	9
Preface	16
1. Introduction	17

The Mediator   21

2. Motivation	23
3. The Personal Qualities of the Mediator	42
4. Attitudes to Conflict	54

Mediation   67

5. The Nature and Purpose of Mediation	69
6. The Principles of Mediation	94
7. Theory and Practice	109

The Task   129

8. Practice Experience: Styles and Models	131
9. Problems of Practice	165

Conclusion   205

10. The Craft of the Mediator	207
Appendix: Topic Guide	235
Bibliography	237
Further Reading Recommended by the Contributors	244
Subject Index	246
Author Index	253

For Jacob

Acknowledgements

The author and publishers are grateful to the proprietors listed below for permission to quote the following material:

Extract from *Elective Affinities* by Johann Wolfgang von Goethe, translated and introduced by R.J. Hollingdale (Penguin Classics 1971). Translation and introduction copyright © R.J. Hollingdale, 1971. Reprinted by permission of Penguin Group (UK). Extract from 'In theory: Bringing peace into the room: The personal qualities of the mediator and their impact on the mediation' by D. Bowling and D. Hoffmann (*Negotiation Journal 5*, 5). Reprinted by permission of Blackwell Publishing. Extract from Stuart Hampshire: *Justice is Conflict*, copyright © 2000 Princeton University Press. Reprinted by permission of Princeton University Press. Extract from *Dispute Processes: ADR and the Primary Forms of Decision-Making (2nd ed)* by Simon Roberts and Michael Palmer (Cambridge University Press 2005). Reprinted by permission of Cambridge University Press. Extract from *A Study of Barriers to the Use of Alternative Methods of Dispute Resolution* by John P. McCrory (Vermont Law School 1984). Reprinted by permission of John P. McCrory. Extract from *Gaza First: The Secret Norway Channel to Peace between Israel and the PLO* by Jane Corbin (Bloomsbury Publishing 1994). Reprinted by permission of Bloomsbury Publishing. Extract from *The Culture of the New Capitalism* by Richard Sennett (Yale University Press 2006), copyright © Richard Sennett 2006. Reprinted by permission of Yale University Press.

Notes on contributors

Andrew Acland
Having studied Russian at university, Andrew Acland subsequently trained in negotiation and mediation with the Harvard Negotiation Project as well as in personnel and financial management and counselling and trainer's training with the Industrial Society. He has Practitioner and Master Practitioner Certificates in Neuro-linguistic Programming. Between 1989 and 2000 he worked as a trainer, lecturer, consultant and practitioner in mediation, conflict resolution and stakeholder dialogue. Examples of recent stakeholder dialogue and public consultation projects include the transport of nuclear waste; disposal of offshore drill cuttings; gas development in Peru; and creating sustainable energy services companies. Since 2000 he has been Director of Dialogue By Design which aims to help people understand each other better through effective engagement and participation, especially around complex or controversial issues such as sustainable development, social responsibility, human rights, the environment, and planning and development. His publications include: *A Sudden Outbreak of Common Sense: Managing Conflict through Mediation* (1990); *Consensus-building: Reaching Agreement in Complex Situations* (1992); *Researching Practitioner Skills in Conflict Resolution* (1994); *Resolving Disputes Without Going to Court* (1995); *Perfect People Skills* (1997); and *Guidelines for Stakeholder Dialogue* (1998).

Yvonne Craig
Dr Yvonne Craig, a practising mediator for 17 years, accredited to Mediation UK, is an enthusiastic, active member of Camden Mediation Service, Church Conciliation Network, Age Concern and various neighbourhood organisations. She has had a lifelong concern for encouraging peacemaking, especially in and by ecumenical and interfaith relationships in diverse communities. She has specialised in contributing to the prevention of elder abuse by mediation and has written *Elder Abuse and Mediation: Exploratory Studies in America, Britain and Europe* (1997). She is also the author of *Peacemaking for Churches* (2000), a practitioner handbook for church mediation, and contributed to many publications on mediation as well as edited various books including *Advocacy, Counselling and Mediation* (1998).

Adam Curle
Adam Curle began his academic career studying anthropology at Oxford University. He then joined the army, serving during the second World War and rising to the rank of Major. After a period at the then new Tavistock Institute of Human Relations (working for the rehabilitation of British soldiers), he lectured in social psychology at Oxford and later held Chairs at Exeter University and the University of Ghana where he travelled extensively helping the government in implementing its educational, social and development plans. There he and his wife joined the Society of Friends, the Quakers. His

Quaker–Buddhist approach, seeking the humanity and potential for good in every person and situation, co-existed with his knowledge and experience of the dark human reality of cruelty, ignorance, fear and greed. In the early 1960's, he was appointed Director of the Harvard Centre for Studies in Education and Development. His experience of this field informed his understanding of the impact of violent conflict on development and of the relationship of poverty and education (or lack of it) on the fuelling and conduct of conflict. In 1973 he was appointed to the first Chair of Peace Studies at the University of Bradford, instituting peace studies as an academic discipline and founding the first university department in the subject.

As an international mediator, he was involved in efforts for peace (often involving considerable personal danger) in conflicts in many countries including India and Pakistan (1965), the Nigeria–Biafra war (1967–1970), Sri Lanka, Africa (Zimbabwe, Rwanda and South Africa where he was imprisoned and interrogated) and most recently, the Balkans. There he worked to support nonviolent grassroots resistance to war in the community in Croatia.

His extensive published works include *True Justice* (1981), *In the Middle* (1986), *Tools for Transformation* (1990) and 'Antidote to Alienation' in *Another Way: Positive Response to Contemporary Violence* (1995). His last book, *Fragile Voice of Love*, was published in 2006.

Adam Curle died, aged ninety, on the 28th September, 2006.

Diana Francis

Dr Diana Francis is a former President of the International Fellowship of Reconciliation and current Chair of the Committee for Conflict Transformation Support – a UK-based network of conflict transformation practitioners. As a freelance facilitator, trainer and consultant, she works with people who are addressing political and inter-ethnic conflict. She has experience in many countries, in the European post-communist world, the Middle East, Africa and Asia. She is Programme Associate with Conciliation Resources and managed their Balkans Programme, more recently working with their Caucasus Programme. She facilitates dialogue of all kinds. In the UK she acts as a facilitator for organisations wishing to evaluate their work, strengthen external and internal working relationships, make future plans or deal with conflict constructively. Diana's doctorate was based on four years of action research into the theory and practice for training for conflict transformation, including conflict analysis, conflict resolution, and strategy for non-violent action for change. This work formed the basis of her book, *People, Peace and Power: Conflict Transformation in Action* (2002). Other publications include *Rethinking War and Peace* (2004).

Fred Gibbons

Fred Gibbons spent his working life on the River Thames until the age of 36. He followed a century's old family tradition and was indentured as a Waterman and Lighterman in 1942. On completing his apprenticeship, he was made a Freeman of the Company of Watermen and Lightermen. Transferring later to a management post, which entailed the organisation of dock labour, he gained personal experience of being a member of both a trade union and management. The volatile nature of the industrial climate led to frequent episodes of closure of the Port of London.

Dispirited, Fred Gibbons left the industry in 1966, trained as a Probation Officer and was promoted to senior management in 1971. He subsequently trained as a family therapist, later becoming responsible for the Civil Work arm of the Probation Service in SE London. This included the provision of reports to various family courts on disputes over children arising from separation and divorce. It was not considered good practice then for the report writer to bring the parties together to negotiate a settlement. To this end however, Fred Gibbons was instrumental in pioneering the first public service family mediation facility in the UK. Sponsored by the Probation Department, he studied mediation practice in New York, Montreal and Ontario. He has been at the helm of the SE London Family Mediation Bureau since 1977. He has been a trainer, public speaker and visiting lecturer, and has contributed articles on mediation to a variety of professional journals.

Mark Hoffman

Mark Hoffman is a lecturer in International Relations at the London School of Economics and Political Science (LSE) where he is Dean of Undergraduate Studies. As head of the LSE's Conflict Analysis and Development Unit (CADU), he has wide practical experience as a trainer and facilitator with the United Nations, the UK Department for International Development (DFID) and other international organisations; and has worked in Moldova, Sri Lanka, Nepal and the Philippines and elsewhere. He has published on third-party mediation, humanitarian intervention and conflict resolution in the post-Cold War world.

Roy Lewis

Professor Roy Lewis is a barrister, arbitrator and mediator, with extensive experience of private labour arbitration and mediation in a variety of industries including oil, banking, insurance, air traffic, railways, education, motors, electrical contracting and media and entertainment. With the late Professor Jon Clark, he co-authored the proposal for an arbitral alternative to the employment tribunals which was taken up by both the previous and present UK governments and has been embodied, in modified form, in the Employment Rights (Dispute Resolution) Act, 1998. Currently Visiting Professor of Law at the University of Southampton and part-time Chairman of Employment Tribunals (assigned to the Southampton Region) he holds a number of other appointments including that of Chairman, Royal Mail National Appeals Panel; Member of ACAS Panel of Arbitrators/Mediators (Trade Disputes); President, Administrative Tribunal, European Bank for Reconstruction and Development; Deputy Chairman, Central Arbitration Committee; and Member of ACAS Panel of Arbitrators (Unfair Dismissals). His publications include *Employment Rights, Industrial Tribunals, and Arbitration: The Case for Alternative Dispute Resolution* [With Jon Clark] (1993); *The Exercise of Individual Employment Rights in the Member States of the European Community* [with Jon Clark and Catherine Barnard] (1995); and 'The Employment Rights Dispute Resolution Act, 1998', *Industrial Law Journal* (1998).

Marian Liebmann
Marian Liebmann has worked in conflict resolution and mediation for 20 years. She was a founder member of Bristol Mediation and was Director of Mediation UK for four years. She now works freelance as a trainer/consultant in mediation and restorative justice, in the UK and abroad. As part of this, she has done work in Russia, Serbia and five African countries. She works part-time as an art therapist in Bristol, and runs 'Art and Conflict' workshops. She has written/edited eight books, including *Mediation in Context* and *Arts Approaches to Conflict*.

Costanza Marzotto
Costanza Marzotto is a Professor of Family Mediation (Theories and Techniques) in the Psychology Faculty and Professor of Methodology and Techniques in Social Work in the Sociology Faculty, at the Catholic University, Milan. She practises as a psychologist and, from 1990, as a family mediator and trainer. She is Vice-President of SIMeF (the Society of Italian Family Mediators), a Member of the Family and Social Mediation Institute in Brescia and is a Member of the Training Standards Committee of the European Forum on Training and Research in Family Mediation. She has presented papers at many international conferences and seminars and publishes extensively on the subject of family mediation.

Philip Naughton
Philip Naughton is a practising barrister and one of Her Majesty's Counsel. He specialises in business law, construction, engineering and manufacturing contract disputes and professional negligence. He is regularly appointed arbitrator in domestic and international arbitrations. In the last 15 years he has been instrumental in the introduction of alternatives to traditional dispute resolution methods and has mediated successfully in many complex commercial disputes in almost every field of business endeavour including oil and gas, aircraft ownership, maritime/insurance, construction, valuation, fabrication/ motor vehicles, supply of goods and services, company acquisition, and patents. He is regularly asked to assist in designing the organisation and preparation of mediations particularly when formal proceedings have not been commenced. Since 1993 he has been active in the promotion of mediation as a means of resolving clinical negligence disputes and has run and participated in workshops and conferences with this objective. He has published papers on alternative dispute resolution (ADR) and mediation which include 'Mega Mediation – a case history', *Arbitration and Dispute Resolution Journal* (1996) and 'ADR and Insurance Law', *Irish Insurance Law Review* (1998).

Christoph Paul
Christoph Paul was born in Oldenburg in Germany in 1950, the second child of a German mother and a Norwegian father. He practises as a lawyer and notary, specialising in family law in the law firm Paul and Partner in Berlin. He has worked as a mediator since 1994 dealing mostly with family conflicts and inheritance issues. He is the Chair of the German Federal Association of Family Mediators (BAFM). Christoph Paul's particular expertise lies in mediation concerning international conflict involving

children, including child abduction and custody and access cases. He works as a trainer and organises the network of mediators collaborating in two pilot projects (one involving Germany and the UK, the other involving Germany and the USA) exploring the potential of mediation in child abduction cases.

Carl Reynolds

Carl Reynolds is an independent mediator and facilitator working in a variety of fields. He provides facilitation services for The Environment Council and has designed and run dialogue processes to engage a variety of national stakeholders in collaborative problem-solving on issues such as the decommissioning of nuclear power stations. He has also worked independently on projects for the Greater London Assembly and Transport for London. He has been a voluntary community mediator since 1993 and has been developing conflict resolution techniques for use in Neighbourhood Renewal Areas for the Office of the Deputy Prime Minister's Neighbourhood Renewal Unit. He was Chair of Mediation UK in 1997/98. Carl Reynolds piloted the use of mediation for employee disputes by designing and co-ordinating a workplace service in the London Borough of Lewisham in 1996. As a result he wrote the Workplace Mediation Manual in 1997 and established a business offering consultancy on mediation in 1997. He has been a member of CEDR's Employment Mediation Group which has worked with the Department of Trade and Industry, the Trade Union Council and the Confederation of British Industries, and other national organisations to influence the Employment Act 2002. He has mediated and consulted on mediation in a number of organisations including the Department of Health, Inland Revenue, the London School of Economics and a variety of local authorities.

Lorraine Schaffer

Lorraine is the Director of the Centre for Mediation and Conflict Resolution at the Institute of Family Therapy (IFT) and Chair of the Postgraduate programme of courses in Conflict Resolution and Mediation Studies run by IFT in collaboration with Birkbeck College, University of London. Lorraine has been a practising family mediator since 1995. She has been teaching the Family Mediation Module at the University of Westminster as part of their LL.M in Dispute Prevention and Resolution since 1999. Lorraine has been an elected Governor of the UK College of Family Mediators since 2001 and is still serving a second three-year term in that position. She is currently the Chair of the Professional Practice Committee of the College.

Lorraine Schaffer grew up in New York City. She did her undergraduate degree at Cornell University and her Masters in Social Work at Rutgers University. Previously she worked as a social worker with adolescents and families and as a tutor on the Diploma in Social Work at Brunel University. She specialised in Groupwork and still acts as a consultant and trainer in this area. She was a Family Group Conference Co-ordinator and a group presenter for the London Information Meetings Pilot Project for the Lord Chancellor's Department. Other professional training includes a two-year course at the Tavistock Clinic – the 'Advanced Course in Consultation to Individuals, Groups and Organisations'. Lorraine Schaffer has written articles for the Journal *Mediation in Practice* and previously for various social work journals.

David Shapiro

David Shapiro, a Consultant at S.J. Berwin, is a member of the Chartered Institute of Arbitrators and accredited as a mediator by CEDR. He was a member of the Commercial Court's Working Party on ADR and the Law Society's Commercial Mediation Panel, and is Chairman of the Panel of Independent Mediators. He is also a member of the Panel of Distinguished Mediators, Conflict Prevention and Resolution (CPR) Institute for Dispute Resolution (New York) and is a Fellow of the International Academy of Mediators. He was formerly Director and Chief Mediator of JAMS Endispute Europe and is currently Visiting Fellow, Department of Law, London School of Economics and Political Science. David Shapiro was a senior founding partner at Dickstein, Shapiro until his retirement in 1996. A mediator and arbitrator for more than 23 years, his appointments in the US include: Settlement Master in both the 'Agent Orange' litigation and the asbestos injury litigation; and principal designer of the national class-action settlement scheme for claims arising out of silicone breast implants. Permanently resident in the UK since 1996, he has developed a successful commercial mediation practice in areas which include advertising and marketing, asbestos, banking, computer law and IT, defamation, fraud/misrepresentation, insolvency, intellectual property, and toxic waste.

He has written widely on ADR; recent publications include: 'Trained Neutrals', *New Law Journal* (March 1997); 'Expert Mediators – Not Experts as Mediators', *16 CEDR Resolutions* (Spring 1997); 'ADR under the New Civil Procedure Rules', *Durham University Law Review* (Summer 1999); 'Pushing the Envelope – Selective Techniques in Tough Mediations', *The Arbitration and Dispute Resolution Journal* (2000); 'ADR and the Environment', *Journal of ADR, Mediation and Negotiation*, Vol. 1, No. 3 (September 2000); 'Compensating the Consumer – Mediated Solutions under the New Enterprise Act', *New Law Journal* (March 2003).

Tony Whatling

Tony Whatling is a self-employed trainer and consultant in mediation and management development with 20 years experience as a family mediator. He is Director of TW Training Works and an Associate of Key Mediation Training and Consultancy. He has trained hundreds of mediators throughout the UK during the past 20 years, in family, community, health care complaints, and victim–offender mediation contexts. Prior to establishing his own business 12 years ago, he was Head of the Department of Social Work Education at Anglia Polytechnic University Cambridge, with a professional background in social work (child care, family therapy, adult psychiatry, social work management and social work education).

He is a Governor of the UK College of Family Mediators, an independent founder member of its Professional Practice Committee and a Competence Assessor for the UK College. Over the past five years he has designed and delivered foundation training programmes to Shia Imami Ismaili Muslim mediators in the UK, Pakistan, India, East Africa, Portugal, the USA, Syria and Afghanistan. He is Professional Practice Consultant to services in south Staffordshire, Nottinghamshire, Leicestershire and to the African Caribbean service in Brixton, where he also mediates. He has published several articles on mediation practice.

Tony Willis

Tony Willis was, until his recent retirement, a litigation partner in Clifford Chance. He was joint Managing Partner for two years (1987–88) and led the litigation practice up to the end of 1995. He then led the Commercial and Investment Banking Litigation Group. His career has been in the field of dispute resolution in business and financial matters, including all forms of resolution – arbitration, litigation and ADR. He has experience in the UK, USA, Asia and elsewhere. He became a CEDR-accredited mediator in 1991–92 and is now a member of the CEDR training faculty. He has also been associated for some years with the Conflict Prevention and Resolution (CPR) Institute for Dispute Resolution in New York and is a member of their international Panel of Distinguished Mediators serving on their European Advisory Committee. He is a member of LEADR (Lawyers Engaged in ADR) in Australia and New Zealand.

He is also a member of the Commercial Court Working Party under the chairmanship of Mr Justice Colman, set up in 1995 to study the use of court-annexed mediation and evaluation techniques in Commercial Court cases. He is a Fellow of the Chartered Institute of Arbitrators and is a member of several arbitral panels. He acts as a mediator, usually in business and commercial disputes, and acts for parties engaged in all forms of ADR processes.

Preface

Mediation is today an institutionalised, officially endorsed and expanding mode of decision-making in many areas of social life. This extraordinary development, along with the rise of other alternative dispute resolution processes in western civil and family justice systems, has spawned an extensive body of writing and research. However, the voice of the mediator is seldom heard. Here the mediator has a say.

The aim of this book is threefold: first, it seeks to provide a unique and current opportunity, for mediators to reflect on their experience and understanding of their work – and for readers to attend to these actors' perspectives. Second, it is hoped that an exploration, and also a communication, that would not otherwise have occurred, is made possible within and across diverse fields of mediation practice, revealing important differences and unexpected commonalities. Third, it is hoped that the reflections of seasoned practitioners will contribute to more informed, and therefore more effective practice, as well as to more grounded, and therefore more relevant and rigorous theoretical understandings of the nature of the task.

I know, as a practising family mediator, how much I learn from colleagues. Listening to the contributors to this work has been a privilege and an education and my thanks go to them for the generosity of their participation. This book would not have been possible without that. My sincere hope is that I have done justice not only to each contribution, its accuracy, meaning and spirit, but also to their significance as a whole. I feel honoured, in particular, to have interviewed for this project Professor Adam Curle, international mediator and scholar, who died on 28 September 2006, aged 90. His immediate enthusiasm (he telephoned me the moment he received my letter) encouraged me hugely. My good fortune, too, was to meet him, immensely experienced, gentle, self-effacing, and clearly courageous and compassionate. His contribution, to the practice and to the scholarship of peace studies, is unique.

Thanks go to Susan Hunt for her help with the painstaking task of transcribing the interview tapes. I am grateful too for the expert assistance of Stephen Jones at Jessica Kingsley Publishers. As ever, Simon Roberts' knowledge, advice and guidance has been invaluable. Responsibility for the general views expressed in this book, any errors and all its limitations, remains mine.

Marian Roberts
November 2006

1

Introduction

> Can two walk together, except they be agreed?
>
> (The Book of Amos 3.3)

The modern emergence of mediation represents the new and evolving application of an ancient and universal method of settling quarrels. The re-emergence of this mode of dispute resolution in the 1970s embodied, certainly for its pioneers, two explicit and distinguishing features. First, the objective of mediation, of retaining decision-making authority with the parties, was founded on certain core values, held to by the disputants as well as by those who chose to become mediators to justify its use. These derived from a humanist tradition informed by ideals of autonomy and respect (Lukes 1973). Second, in pursuit of that objective, the intervention of the mediator, however varied and powerful its impact, was different from that of the usual role of the professional, that of the dominant expert.

The values of mediation have exemplified, above all, a fundamental ethic of respect, for the parties' autonomy and for their authority to make their own decisions. These were, and still are, seen as essential if the mediator were to have proper regard for the right of the parties, whatever the difficulties, to be the architects of their own agreements and if party authority and control were to have any meaning. Norms of fairness, mutual respect and equity of exchange informed the expectations of adult behaviour that party decision-making involved (Davis 1984; Fuller 1971; Rubin and Brown 1975).

The professional skill of the mediator has been seen to lie, ideally, in acting in a manner that reflects an understanding of what has been described as 'the subtleties' of respect – 'acts of recognition and regard that orchestrate the experience of respect' (Sennett 2003, p.149). Expectations such as these can be seen to be of most value precisely because of the recognition that the circumstances necessitating mediation, of political, social and personal conflict and dispute, and of stress, distress and suffering, could be bringing out the 'worst' in people.

It is well recognised too, that the minimal numerical transformation that occurs in mediation, of the dyad into the triad, can have radical, complex and paradoxical effects – intellectual, social, psychological and negotiation effects. The presence of the third party qualitatively transforms the interaction. On the one hand, merely by being there, the mediator alters the relationship between the parties and exerts influence. On the other hand, the third party in any dispute resolution process, not only mediation, transforms the interaction in another important respect, by embodying the principle of objectivity and reasonableness in decision-making – 'the non-partisan tempers the passion of the others' (Simmel 1908a, p.152).

With aspirations as ambitious as these and in circumstances as difficult, the scale of the task requires the mediator to adopt a modest approach, with full awareness of the limits and obstacles. In many instances, mediators hope to do no more than provide disputing parties with a calm, safe forum for reasonable exchange, and the opportunity to have a conversation that they may not be able to hold on their own.

These dimensions of mediation and the development of dispute resolution in its wider aspects (recently, the field of alternative dispute resolution generally, known as ADR) have been the subject of scholarly study and research to an unusually large extent since the early 1980s. A large, cross-disciplinary body of literature, much of it North American, valuably informs understandings both about the nature of ADR and of mediation in particular. This literature encompasses a range of perspectives and conclusions, some of which raise serious questions about the political implications of informal justice, about power, neutrality and coercion, about styles and models and the assessment of effectiveness. Another literature resource, including handbooks on training and practice approaches, focuses primarily on introducing the subject of mediation (its nature, principles and techniques) to students, lawyers and ADR practitioners.

There has been an acknowledged dearth of opportunity (more so in the USA than in the UK), for researchers and practitioners to converse together and explore the practice implications of research studies (Rifkin 1994). There is, too, an extraordinary absence in the literature of the practitioner perspective, particularly one based on actual mediation experience, let alone one informed by different fields of practice.

This book seeks to fill that gap. Mediation is now an established and expanding mode of dispute resolution in a growing number of practice fields – in spheres of the family, the community, the elderly, victim–offender, civil and commercial matters, the environment, and the workplace and public policy fields, as well as those long-established areas of practice in labour and international mediation. Mediation is increasingly being applied to new areas such as child abduction, child protection, housing, and medical negligence, to name but a few. There is now a rich reservoir of practice experience and knowledge. This book hopes to bring to life, through the voices of accomplished and articulate practitioners speaking for themselves, and based on their individual knowledge and concrete experience, vivid representations on the nature of their task. The book aims too to contribute, through enhanced understanding derived from an original practitioner perspective, to some of the major theoretical and practice issues, debates and dilemmas, that inspire and beset the mediation world.

The book presents – in some cases at length – the experiential reflections and the fresh insights of the contributors and draws on these to explore fundamental themes – of the mediator, of mediation and its principles, and of the nature of the task.[1] A detailed picture emerges – of personal motivation and attitudes to conflict, personal qualities, of the impact on practice of political, social, and institutional structures and constraints, and of the professional demands and problems of practice – which reveals some of the complexities, difficulties and stresses as well as the satisfactions and even excitement of the work of the mediator.

A further aim of this book, as in mediation, is to open up a conversation that would not have taken place otherwise amongst practitioners who have no other means of learning about different ways of thinking, alternative approaches, models, styles and techniques in a variety of fields of practice. As these fields have developed separately and autonomously from one another with minimal opportunity for mutual exchange, this book aims to provide a new conduit of communication amongst practitioners.

A number of guiding principles, rather than any systematic method of selection, influenced the identification of contributors. It was necessary, obviously, for the major fields of mediation practice to be included and for there to be as balanced and representative a mix as possible, of genders, professional backgrounds and ages (which, in fact, ranged from the 30s to the 90s). The incorporation of the German and Italian contributors, both amongst the pioneers of mediation developments in their own countries, placed the predominantly British experience in a broader European frame. Two of the contributors (a family and a commercial mediator) happened to originate from the USA which added, fortuitously, a helpful North American comparative cast to their reflections. The cross-cultural dimension proved to be significant in several areas of practice, yet it was not possible, regrettably, to match that in terms of the representation of the contributors.

The primary guiding principle for identifying contributors was that each should be an accomplished mediation practitioner, highly regarded in his or her own field of practice and therefore seen to be a representative member, however idiosyncratic, of their particular community of mediators. All the contributors are considered to be influential and have, in their own ways, made a special contribution to developments in their fields of practice and, in some cases, in other fields as well – whether in theory, research, training, teaching and writing, innovative professional initiatives and practice developments. The capacity to reflect in a thoughtful and critical way, about mediation practice as well as about larger issues, including the context in which they worked, proved valuable.

This is not to say that there are not other distinguished practitioners and contributors to their fields who could have equally satisfied the identification principles. Some with published writings have already had the opportunity to express themselves. Ultimately a project of this small size imposed its own constraints. Inevitably too, an element of subjectivity based on the author's own direct personal knowledge and experience was bound to have influenced the final choice of contributors.

One of the central questions this work considers is whether, in the light of the richness of differences – of approach, of model, of style, of subject matter and of context – it is possible to identify a common perspective in mediators, wherever and however they practise, about their work and about its essential nature. Another central question is to what extent it would be accurate to describe this activity as fulfilling the requirements of a craft, constituted of those recognisable general attributes, rather than either the successful exercise of technical expertise or the practice of a mysterious and elusive art.

It is not the intention of this work to form definitive conclusions about the many central questions asked of the contributors. This is the opportunity for mediators to reflect on the nature of their practice and on the major debates and concerns of the field at a particular moment in time. The diverse views reflect the many influences that create the heterogeneity and eclecticism as well as the coherence of the theory and of the practice of mediation in various spheres in the early years of the 21st century.

Attending to the practitioner perspective makes possible, too, an exchange of communication across disparate fields of practice illuminating cross-disciplinary understanding that would not have occurred otherwise. If this work provides a conduit of learning and discovery, enabling mediators from all fields to participate in the same 'exploratory interaction' (Gulliver 1979, p.89) that the parties themselves directly engage in during any process of mediation, it will have served its purpose.

Note

1. This is a different approach to that adopted in the vivid, interview-based profiles of 12 exemplary North American mediators who contributed to their various fields in individual ways in the 1970s and 1980s (*When Talk Works: Profiles of Mediators* (Kolb *et al.* 1994).

The Mediator

2
Motivation

> [mediation] ... this oddest of vocations
>
> (Goethe 1809, p.34)

The radical and general transformations associated with the emergence of the alternative dispute resolution (ADR) movement in the West in the early 1970s – transformations of language (e.g. from 'cases' to 'disputes'), of focus of discussion (e.g. away from formal justice towards the possibilities of alternatives) and of policy and practice developments – have been well elucidated by scholars (see Astor and Chinkin 2002; Menkel-Meadow *et al.* 2005; Roberts and Palmer 2005).

But what has transformed individuals' practice towards alternative processes? Did they choose to become mediators, and if so, why? Contributors' answers to these questions reflect a picture as complex, diverse and overlapping as that of the field iteself. Simple categorisation, for example, of subject matter, gender difference and professional boundaries conceals the rich variety of influences and their combinations in some cases. Several general threads emerge however.

Direct experience of political or industrial conflict and violence

Contributors representing a range of professional fields – a family mediator, an environmental mediator, a commercial mediator and a mediator in the field of international relations – all recount the considerable impact of their early direct experience of political and industrial conflict on their gravitation towards alternative processes. For an international mediator it was an experience of war itself:

> **Professor Adam Curle, international mediator:** The Biafran war – this changed everything for me. It was no longer romantic and interesting and ego-enhancing. It was a really horrible slaughter and famine – and it lasted a few years and I was in and out – and that was really the beginning.

It is probably unique in the sphere of family mediation, that experience of industrial strife in the Thames River barge industry was a critical factor influencing one contributor in becoming a mediator:

> **Fred Gibbons, family mediator:** I suppose the overriding factor of my interest in mediation stems from the 20 years that I worked on the London river as a Thames lighterman. I was involved in many industrial conflicts in which there were long periods of unemployment and the labour force was out on strike and [there was] loss of income and I saw a lot of my colleagues having to sell their homes to actually maintain the life of their families. A very difficult period. It never changed in all that time. In 20 years it never ever changed. The two sides were absolutely polarised in terms of never reaching agreement or a solution. Somebody had to win and somebody had to lose. In almost every case it was the labour force that lost because they didn't have the resources to cope with weeks of unemployment. The basic argument actually got lost in the two sides actually taking up their stations. Nobody had the respect of both sides, no intermediaries, nobody able to bring the temperature down.

Experience of international conflict was a decisive influence in a later evolutionary move towards commercial mediation.

> **Tony Willis, lawyer and commercial mediator:** So I was exposed in a way others weren't. If there was one seminal event which set me off in a rather more consciously structured way it was the Iran hostage crisis where I was with the American banks ... and of course the release of those hostages was brokered by Algeria which acted as a mediator. And I was very, very closely involved in those negotiations, for five days in a bunker, and the White House on one line, and the Treasury on another, and Iran on the other and Algeria and so on. So although a passive observer of that, I wasn't passive in the sense I was concerned with the documents – the money flow. I had suddenly been interested in an actual example, I suddenly had a real concrete example. So it made a big impression. That was 1981. That increased my interest and I did some more reading.

A similar exposure to international conflict was instrumental in awakening a lifetime's involvement in mediation in the environmental and organisational spheres.

> **Andrew Acland, mediator in environmental and organisational issues:** It was a mixture, really a combination of chance and circumstance. In the early 1980s I worked for the Archbishop of Canterbury for about four and a half years as a research assistant and speechwriter and general dogsbody really. Previously to that I had been a political analyst working mainly on East–West relations and issues like arms control. I went to Lambeth Palace and did this fascinating job for about four years in the course of which, as you might remember, the office became involved in trying to get British hostages held overseas back, in particu-

lar the efforts of Terry Waite, the Archbishop's envoy. And on one of these trips to Libya, Terry needed another pair of hands so I got sent along too and had not the most relaxing week of my life trying to help sort out this little local difficulty. And I got fascinated in the role which third parties played. So that was really my first experience of this field and this was in 1985.

Then I went to South Africa to work on a Swiss-backed project. We were there for about six months and the idea was to look at the potential for using intervention around the possible constitutional options to try and see what might be helpful for the country's future shape. This again was 1986 so Nelson Mandela was still in prison. And we spent six months there talking to lots and lots of people on different sides of the political divide. So that was really my baptism of fire. It was very much at the sharp end. It was awful actually. Because I was going into a local township, which was dangerous in itself, and talking to people who had been appallingly used and abused by the South African government.

As a mediator, the first thing you get drummed into you is the need for impartiality and independence and neutrality and all those words which are very difficult to maintain when you are in a situation where you can see the evidence of really the most appalling violence in front of you. So it was not the easiest place to be. Whether or not we did any good I don't know. The only concrete thing I sometimes point to is a particular meeting involving some of the churches which brought together people in a way I think they probably hadn't spoken together before and coincidence or not, it was not long after that that the Dutch Reformed Church actually really removed its support for apartheid.

Intellectual curiosity

Several informants ascribed their introduction to mediation to an intellectual curiosity in new forms of dispute resolution. This early interest preceded any involvement as a practitioner though it coincided, in some cases, with a professional readiness to adopt new methods.

Christoph Paul, German lawyer and mediator in family and commercial disputes: The initial word I would say is curiosity. I worked as a lawyer for 14 years before I got to know that something like mediation existed. Obviously I was ready for it. I was interested in finding something more than just the ordinary work as a lawyer. I was so much more interested in how people got their resources to resolve conflicts themselves. I often talked with friends about it and it was such a new field. The more I read about it, the more curious I was about it. I said I wanted to try it. They said there is no funding with it. A thing like mediation, if you do it you don't do it at the very moment because you want to earn a lot of money. You do it because you feel this is something that fits into your personal attitude towards your work. This gave me the idea that I should somehow start. Then I took courses and from the first moment, I still know the moment when I came into this teaching room – and I said 'This is just exactly the thing I wanted.'

For other lawyers the intellectual curiosity in mediation derived from innovatory developments in their legal practices.

> **Philip Naughton, lawyer and commercial mediator:** How I came to mediation? I did a mini-trial in about 1987 and it was the first mini-trial that was known to have been undertaken in the UK and I was asked to speak about it. And in order to speak about it, I made enquiries about its provenance and became interested in alternative dispute resolution as an alternative at a time when there was much talk about all sorts of different techniques in the States. But the Americans were trying out all sorts of things. And I became frustrated with how much I didn't know. I think in 1988 or 1989 I went to the States to talk to the people that counted. I talked to specialist mediators in Washington, New York, San Francisco, Seattle and I learned a lot more. The reason why I was doing this was because I was interested in the subject. And it seemed like a good thing. But I had no intention at all of practising as a mediator. It was in order to promote an idea that I went to the States. Of course, what in fact resulted was, because I now knew more, I was asked to speak more. That and other talks that I gave led me to start meeting people and in 1990 I called a meeting at King's College, London between all the people that I understood were interested in the subject. And out of that grew the proposal to put together CEDR [Centre for Dispute Resolution]. But having said that the principal actors at that time in getting CEDR on the road were David Miles, Karl Mackie and Eileen Carroll, deputy Chief Executive of CEDR. They, and I think others, took the idea and turned it into reality. I didn't participate in that, other than being around. I didn't do the leg work. And I was, thereafter, a Director of CEDR in 1999.
>
> And of course I was asked to talk about it more and I went to the States again and learnt more and got myself mired in the idea. And the time came really when it became impossible to talk about it without actually having done it. And so I started doing it. And I think I did the first mediation in 1992 and a few mediations each year thereafter, and one thing led to another. And now it depends very much on what comes through the door [i.e. mediation, arbitration or commercial litigation].

Another successful litigation lawyer, also unusually for the time, allowed his intellectual curiosity to lead him towards new forms of dispute resolution.

> **Tony Willis:** Litigators are always settling things. I suppose that's the simplest answer [to what brought me into mediation]. And if you're always settling things and you're always negotiating, then anything which helps you settle and helps you negotiate, and the discipline which is relevant to how you go about that and how successful you are and how bad you are at it, and so on, helps. So I got interested in mediation way back. And of course I read a bit about it. I didn't know a great deal about it. And I spoke to lots of people, so I was exposed in a way that others weren't.

Professional innovation

Developing interest in new dispute resolution approaches coincided, in several cases, with a recognition of the limits of current practice, whether of adjudication, litigation and arbitration, of welfare interventions in family situations or of the criminal justice system. At the time this new thinking about practice was radical and pioneering in this country.

Marian Liebmann, mediator, restorative justice practitioner and trainer, and art therapist: It was really through doing work with victims and offenders or rather, to be specific, first offenders and then victims and realising that they were kept apart by the criminal justice system and that the criminal justice system was really based on 'never the twain shall meet'. So when I heard about mediation, I just thought what about this? I came to London for a weekend [in 1984] being run by two mediators from the Friends Suburban Project, Philadelphia and all the lights went on in my head. And then when I went back to work with offenders I really wanted to try and help people put things together. It was slightly odd in that the offenders that I was dealing with were on probation at a day centre and I was on the education side [having trained as a teacher on graduating]…running numeracy and literacy and small group problem-solving and video role plays, everything with offenders. Then I went to work from the day centre to victim support. And then I trained as a probation officer and went back to work with offenders but on the whole, they weren't the same victims and the same offenders even, because the victims of crime that we visited were mostly of a more serious sort, they were mostly burglary victims, assault victims, occasionally rape and murder victims or their families. We didn't deal with the sort of minor things that the people that I worked with on probation [had done], which was mostly shoplifting or stealing from garden sheds, or stealing bikes or being drunk or getting into a fight with someone. And it didn't match up but I could see that there was a need to somehow get this whole thing together.

Another probation officer also working initially with criminal offenders and later in the family divorce courts, came to a similar realisation about the possibilities of mediatory intervention but via a different path.

Fred Gibbons: The other thing which happened was I then moved into probation and I found there, that I could really provide the kind of intermediary function which was missing from my previous employment [now on the management side of one of the last of the largish companies running Thames barges] in that I was a buffer between the community, and the punishment that one side might demand or expect, and the offender, who was an inadequate person usually who really needed support to be picked out of the gutter and really needed help to establish themselves in society, find a job, etc. So I suddenly felt released and very free to take the kind of action which I thought was required, and which gained support [from the Probation Office] as appropriate action...and [I] could see the power of moving across between the two sides. In early 1977, I think the pivotal point was I moved out from probation into court welfare, the same service, a different section. I still had responsibilities in criminal activity but in taking over the family work and the family courts, one of the things that was brought to my notice in the family court system where court welfare was concerned, was the repetition of reports that were made in respect of the same family and the same conflict. There was a particular case where a welfare officer, over five consecutive years, had produced the same report. And what that person had done was report on what they saw. So the judges were absolutely blocked off from taking any positive action to help the family because the report writer was presenting the very information they'd brought before.

Ironically, a change of direction towards mediation arose in the following case from the mediator's very success as an outstanding North American litigator and negotiator.

David Shapiro, lawyer and mediator in commercial matters: I had a major case against the telephone industry in 1980 and the case was settled for a tremendous amount of money, an unbelievable amount of money right before trial. A couple of weeks later I got a phone call from the new general counsel to ATT [an American telephone company] who had been a lawyer I had been litigating against way back, as early as 1957. He said to me, 'Look, we have something like 300 anti-trust cases arising out of the break-up of the Bell system. My lawyers are crazy, all the plaintiff's lawyers are crazy. You are the only guy I know who can talk sense to the plaintiff's lawyers and they will listen to you. Do you want to undertake the job of, in effect, becoming a settlement counsel?' I said, 'Howard, I've got three other anti-trust cases against you right now, I don't know what I'm going to do with those.' He persuaded me to take on this job. It was a mix of negotiation and litigation.

I was recognised in the States back from the mid-60s until 1980 as maybe the toughest plaintiff's lawyer in America at that particular time. I took no prisoners. There were several cases where people know that if I couldn't settle them, there was no point in trying. And I had a pretty good success rate. So the other side knew that either you are going to settle with this guy or you are going to trial. And so for the next 11 years I was in effect, I suppose, the Ombudsman for the telephone industry.

While this was going on, I got a request from a judge in the southern district of New York by name of Jack Winston who was handling all the Agent Orange class actions. This was, I think, probably in 1985. He said, 'Look, I've got this settlement master, but he's not all that experienced in this sort of thing. Would you come on board as the other settlement master?' And in six weeks we managed to settle that whole Agent Orange thing. It got a lot of press, and the word got around that that was what I was doing.

Concerns about current approaches to dealing with conflict in another legal capacity, that of the adjudicator, determined recognition of the need for change.

> **Yvonne Craig, mediator in community, elder and church disputes:** Conflict unresolved was a problem that I wasn't dealing with adequately... [as a social worker]. It was even worse when I was a magistrate for 20 years and found that I didn't like judging, particularly neighbours, each of whom had contributed to conflict and one of whom had to be regarded as guilty and the other as innocent. And I found, therefore, the judicial skills were not sufficient for the social problems that I saw in the very poor community where I was a magistrate for 20 years. Then, of course, I began to hear, in the 60s, about mediation and that this was the thing to do. And I came off the bench at [the age of] 70. I was able at once to join the beginning of the mediation movement in Britain. I started off before ADR began to flourish, I started off by editing, for eight years, mediation's first journal *Mediation* [the organ of FIRM (Forum for Initiatives in Restoration and Mediation)]. There was a lot of the preparatory thinking and co-ordinating work. But then I helped to start the first community mediation service in Camden and immediately became a community mediator.

Industrial relations has the longest practice history of official conciliatory process in Britain. The Conciliation Act 1896 provided the recognisably modern statutory framework for state-sponsored conciliation and arbitration of collective labour disputes, although such forms of intervention existed for several decades prior to the Act of 1896. The current legal framework is contained in section 212 of the Trade Union and Labour Relations (Consolidation) Act 1992. Within this legal framework, the public agency, the Advisory, Conciliation and Arbitration Service (ACAS), sponsors conciliation, mediation and arbitration.[1] This long-established, dominant institutional context determines the way its practitioners enter the field.

> **Professor Roy Lewis, arbitrator and mediator in industrial and labour relations:** I was an academic in the field of industrial relations and labour law. The people who do arbitration and, as far as it exists, mediation in the field of industrial relations, especially the ones who are asked to do it through ACAS, which is the primary provider, are academics, typically in the field of industrial relations and/or one of the satellite disciplines like labour law, industrial sociology and labour economics. At that time I was a career academic in that field and also one that was always interested in public policy and doing things outside the university as well.
>
> I got involved in ACAS as an arbitrator and even before I was asked to be an ACAS arbitrator, which is over 20 years [ago] now, I actually did some arbitration in the labour field, that is to say, arbitrations where the parties are predominantly the collective parties as I say, the employer and the trade unions. Even though there may be individual issues, the typical parties are the collective parties in industrial relations. So that is the origin of my involvement.

I became a member of the ACAS Panel of Arbitrators when I was at the University of Warwick. At that stage I held the post of Principal Research Fellow in the Industrial Relations Research Unit. [I became involved in mediation] at the same time, simply because there is a slightly blurred line in that if you are appointed as an ACAS arbitrator, the normal brief is that you are expected to make a decision like any other arbitrator on a dispute and your decision in the form of an award is then binding, though in that sphere – industrial relations – binding in honour on the collective parties.

However, there are situations where the parties don't want an actual binding award. What they prefer is someone to hear what they have got to say and then to make suggestions or even recommendations as to the way forward. So some of the so-called arbitrations are really closer to mediations. In fact ACAS recognise that and call those things mediations. So right from the outset, although it's only a minority of cases that are dealt with in that way, if you are an ACAS arbitrator, you do some mediations and not only that. Sometimes things that are, in terms of the terms of reference, straightforward arbitrations end up as something more consensual. Because during the course of the arbitration, you see an opportunity to say to the parties, 'Well, X and Y, isn't that your position?' And they say, 'Yes,' and ditto with the other party. 'Wouldn't the way forward be the following?'

And there have been cases I've helped in and others, in that position of ACAS arbitrators, where you start off with an arbitrator's terms of reference and you end up doing a mediation. So that's the origin of it. Because of my legal background I'm always terribly conscious of my terms of reference, so if I've got an arbitrator's terms of reference and it's going in a different direction, I get the parties to agree to whatever is happening in a formal sense. I make a note of what they agree to.

Values and ideology

A spiritual dimension, whether influenced by Quaker and Buddhist values or Christian pacifism, characterises the involvement in mediation of two mediator contributors, both distinguished in their roles as intermediaries in situations of international conflict – 'outside interveners in the pains and problems of other countries and other cultures' (Curle 1990a, p.2). Both would agree that by its nature, their kind of intervention is necessarily slow and difficult. In the field of international mediation, Princen (1992) identifies two different ideal types of mediatory intervention, each with specific characteristics and distinctive advantages: 'principal' mediators who have clout and their own interests in the dispute (national or regional) such as Jimmy Carter mediating between Egypt and Israel at Camp David in 1977; and 'neutral'[2] mediators whose very lack of power affords opportunities for demonstrating their neutrality and building trust by creating 'realistic empathy' through direct interaction (Princen 1992, p.27). The contributors would regard themselves as 'neutral' mediators according to this classification.

Professor Adam Curle, veteran mediator in the Nigeria–Biafra civil war (1967–1970) and in conflicts between India and Pakistan, in Sri Lanka and in the Balkans, has written extensively of the values that inform his prescription for the 'tools for transformation' necessary in situations of international conflict. These are deeply influenced by Quaker and Buddhist principles. Adam Curle describes Quaker mediators who have adopted a particular approach and style to their work. Its main characteristics are that it combines psychology with diplomacy and it tends to last a long time, years rather than months. Wars may drag on because each combatant has so distorted a perception of the other's character that a non-military resolution seems impossible. That is the reason – when the time has come – mediators tell each side about the grievances and suffering of the other side – this is their attempt to bring about a change in understanding and includes continual interpretations of what the other side is saying, explanation of their attitudes, therapeutic listening and the development of a personal relationship of truth and friendship with the people they listen to on both sides. By such means tensions from hostility and anxiety may be reduced to a point where cautious hope prevails. He considers the task for would-be peacemakers/listeners to be on two levels. They must dig out the roots of unpeacefulness within themselves: the blindness, the illusory sense of 'I', the cravings, antipathies and guilt. Without this effort, however partially successful, they can never hope to have any real effect on others (Curle 1990b).

> **Adam Curle** describes his personal experience in this way:
> I actually met Indira Gandhi [shuttling between India and Mohammed Ali of Pakistan] but I have to say that my main feeling about this was one of conceit and pride to be chosen to do international mediation which didn't work out really very successfully although we had two constructive talks. But I was mainly concerned with the excitement of doing this…[until] the Biafran war – and then this changed everything for me. It was no longer romantic and interesting and ego-enhancing. It was a really horrible slaughter and famine…and it lasted a few years and I was in and out…and that was really the beginning.

For another contributor involved in international conflict, the influence of her parents who were actively committed to the values of peace and justice informed the direction of her life's work.

> **Diana Francis, freelance trainer and consultant, mediator and facilitator in situations of political and inter-ethnic conflict:** I came from a background of being a campaigner for peace and justice issues. My parents were both Christian pacifists and took both peace and justice very seriously, as a matter of faith. And I was brought up in that approach and from my teens I was involved in movements for peace, and particularly, economic justice. And I was a member of

the Fellowship of Reconciliation, which was the ecumenical Christian pacifist organisation. I campaigned for nuclear disarmament and so on and was involved in all kinds of direct action and the like. I eventually became President of the International Fellowship of Reconciliation [IFOR], which is an intercultural, inter-religious, transnational organisation of people working at the grassroots, for change through non-violent action. The notion [of] reconciliation clearly was fundamental to that movement, but that the focus among the left was on non-violent action for justice, and having always had to rely on Martin Luther King and Gandhi, as it seemed the great gurus, the great exemplars of non-violent action, we suddenly saw a lot of widescale political change happening through non-violent, so-called people power – first in the Philippines and then across the former Soviet world. So that was big good news, although the world didn't seem to take very much notice of it in terms of rethinking the need for war or the justification for war. But at the same time we began to see that getting rid of injustice didn't necessarily make for peace. And that there were many, many internal wars taking place, as people desperately sought some kind of new identity and hope, with economic suffering that hadn't necessarily been there lots before.

And I began to think much harder about the need for accommodation, the need for stability for people to thrive, and very much seeing that a constant state of stand off, often accompanied by violence, didn't produce justice. So this coincided with the time of my stopping being President of IFOR and having more time, and I very much wanted to be involved in peace work at home and got involved in the mediation movement. [In the] early 90s...in particular I got involved with Bristol Mediation, which was just beginning to form itself and establish itself. I did training as a neighbourhood mediator and became a trainer of mediators.

I also got involved in the early days setting up the Committee for Conflict Transformation Support, which was a gathering of people to reflect on practice in supporting efforts to transform conflict in non-military ways... you know that conflict transformation and conflict resolution are sometimes competing terms in indicating approaches. There have been others, notably John-Paul Lederach and probably others before him, [who first deployed the term 'conflict transformation']. But within the conflict resolution, the growing field, there was a collection of people who didn't want to lose sight of the notion of justice and, of course, mediation is typically non-judgmental and [there was] talk of the term 'objective justice', which is an intriguing idea. Although I think there will always be disputes about what is and what isn't just, I think most people would agree that injustice takes place and there are structural injustices, for instance. Some people are excluded, oppressed, etc. The theory of active non-violence is that there are oppressive situations and that they can be addressed in ways that respect all parties to the conflict. So the value of respect is there, even in a non-violent struggle for justice. And the value of inclusion, because although you may have a partisan struggle, the goal of a non-violent struggle is that all parties to the conflict shall be included in the solution of the conflict.

And what I wanted to do, and I suppose this is what I tried to contribute when I was fighting to contribute at a theoretical level, was to put together the field of active non-violence with the field of conflict resolution, to try and understand how these two fields were complementary in producing a full menu for conflict transformation – conflict transformation which upholds the usefulness as well as the inevitability of conflict. And that is saying what matters is *how* we handle conflict. It is not about conflict prevention which is a term we detest.

I didn't initially move away [from the local neighbourhood mediation movement]. I initially was working on both. It was very important for my international work, both that I had done the local mediation and that, as long as I could, I continued it. It became impossible, partly because I moved temporarily to London and partly because I just was away too frequently to be able to take up local cases which needed continuity. It just became impractical. But my intention was to work at home. I tend to respond to requests rather than going out and making my life happen. Where I was asked to work was in the international field. Really, international work is my professional work. I do a lot of campaigning, lobbying, public speaking and so on in the UK, particularly on policy issues. Because I see that unless we can sort out global issues of power and political agenda, the ground for violence will remain endemic. So it matters to me in terms of personal integrity that I am really making every effort in terms of policy in my own country. But my professional work is almost exclusively in the international field, not entirely – I facilitate team building and strategy and so on, workshops within related organisations in the UK.[3] So that is almost on the basis of my international work.

Concerns about the ethical and relational implications of family break-up in the aftermath of the rising incidence of divorce and separation, led an Italian psychologist to consider new approaches for addressing family conflict in Italy.

Professor Costanza Marsotto, psychologist and mediator in family disputes, professor in family mediation (theories and techniques) and tutor in the Masters course on family and community mediation: I decided to address my professional interest to family mediation, at the time of my second degree: I was already 32 years old, I had worked for seven years in public services for families and I was trainer for social workers at the University.

I had noticed the increase of divorce in our country and the necessity to find new ways to help fathers and mothers pass through this crisis [while] saving the faith in bonds and the hope to build new relations. In Italy the price of separation is very high: the members of the family – during the divorce time – risk destroying not only the couple bond but also the parental tie. My hypothesis is that family relations consist not only in sentiment and love, but also they have an ethical dimension. My responsibility, as a psychologist, consists in offering a different context in which the parents can discover a personal way to remain parents and to allow the children access to both branches of the family.

> So I decided also, on behalf of the group where I was engaged for research and training courses, to find out more about family mediation and to do personal research and a thesis.[4] At the end of 1980, I started to work privately as family mediator and from 2003, I have been a family mediator in a Service for Couples and Families at the Catholic University [Milan].

Personal and life experience

Childhood and adult personal experience – positive and negative – accounts for an interest in and desire for more constructive approaches to dealing with difference. Positive role models, for example, of a pacifist parental influence – 'my mother was a very remarkable woman and she was a natural pacifist. [Which] I became and I'm still really becoming … I can't kill an insect' (Adam Curle) – are as powerful in their impact as negative experiences of family conflict.

For one contributor, family life created its own demands for third-party intervention.

> **Yvonne Craig:** My personal reason [for turning towards mediation] was I think because as a mother, bringing up children and having an academic husband, I was always mediating about noise between them. I found myself mediating between my friends. I found myself mediating informally and of course not consciously then, all those years ago of what mediation was. But therefore I have always unconsciously practised from early years a conciliating role in life.

Having to stand up for herself as the middle of seven children had beneficial results for the next contributor:

> **Costanza Marzotto:** I bring to the mediation practice my family experience as the fourth of seven children; my pleasure in being in the middle, at risk of being smashed but also being able to come out of the conflict.

The impact of early childhood experience may not have been explicitly understood initially. Childhood exposure to family conflict resulted in a deliberate search professionally for new and constructive approaches to managing conflict for the next contributor.

> **Tony Whatling, trainer, consultant and mediator in family disputes:** It was a long time before I uncovered that driver I suppose. It happened to me in family therapy that I realised why I was involved in families in trouble. Because I came from a background of family feuds which were tremendous family feuds. I often say my family could feud for Britain. I mean serious, major family rifts. My father fell out with his father just after I was born and they never spoke to each other again. The consequence of which was I grew up with no experience or knowledge or awareness or contact with the paternal side of my family at all. When I did my family genogram there was no paternal side. Vague ideas about aunts and uncles but no contact. Complete shut off.

> About 25 years ago my mother fell out with my grandmother. My grandmother was terribly important to me. I think I spent more time [there] as a child. They lived just up the street and I spent more time as a child with my grandmother who lived with her married daughter and son-in-law and my unmarried aunt and they all lived in the same house together. They all lived in this rather small cottage as a family, a grandmother, two aunts and an uncle all living together. And I spent a lot of time there. I had little time and attention from my parents. My father was a builder. They weren't very good with children. They were decent people. They were not bad parents, they just weren't terribly involved with their children. My mother fell out with my grandmother. They never spoke to each other again. So for the next generation of my sons, if we hadn't worked there, it could have been the maternal side [as well]. My wife and I insisted on walking between the two. They never came back together. My grandmother subsequently died but whenever we visited and wherever we were living, we spent equal time with each side.
>
> So I think all of that is really behind my work for a while in family therapy, an unconscious driver was to get the families back together. I think I got through that to the point where I was driven by a wish to help families break up constructively, if that's what they were really interested to do. So I think there is a connection really with mediation. And that combined with a poor childhood experience of constructive conflict.
>
> We found over and over again with training mediators, when we get them to talk about it, that a very high percentage, from my experience of doing exercises on that, come out with very negative experiences of constructive conflict in their childhood. There are always some who have had that. The majority are quite worried by it, frightened of it. I think something about coming into mediation is about trying to deal with that tension. I had this conversion I suppose.

Personal appearance as well as circumstances of upbringing determined subsequent attitudes and career choices.

Carl Reynolds, independent mediator, facilitator and consultant in community, workplace and public policy fields: I think I work in it because there's history for me. Being a redhead firstly. I was constantly in scraps when I was a child from the age of about 9, until about 16. And I was also at an all boys' school. So the notion of violence was kind of a daily occurrence. I think [as a redhead] you are perceived to be more fiery. [It did provoke violence] so I rarely initiated [it]. It was always towards me. I never came off really badly, it was a kind of two-way process really. But at the age of about 15, someone taught me how to hit somebody properly so to speak, to defend myself. And I've never been attacked since. In a sense it's partly a presence of mind. Since then I've done a certain amount of aikido and tai chi and so on. So I think partly it comes because, personally, I've seen how violence is really destructive, [how] it gets in the way. On a daily basis I can have the memories brought to mind now, of thinking [that] being in an environment where there is the potential for violence all the time, is

> not very pleasant basically. So the notion that you can spend your life and earn a living from helping people to be non-violent, whether it's physical or emotional, is actually quite a blessing. And I suppose I've been influenced, to some degree, when I was younger, by non-violent direct action as well. Because I was involved to a degree with Campaign for Nuclear Disarmament (CND) and the peace movement as a teenager. So the notion of protesting in non-violent ways I find that quite interesting. And of course since then, the whole notion of non-violent resistance, I find quite appealing. I wouldn't say that I'm a pacifist but I would be very close to one.
>
> If I see violence on the street I often intervene, not necessarily physically, but it appals me. My father was in the Air Force, so I lived on airbases. Jets would take off that were capable of wiping out several hundred thousand people in one go. So I think there's that psychological thing of growing up in the Cold War as well, which is interesting, the notion of nuclear annihilation. And I think that would be my attitude to disputes and violence and what's motivating it. I think also, I'm motivated to do this work because I'm not entirely clear about myself all of the time. We have this great rational awareness of ourselves and can explore our own unconscious motivations. Because they're unconscious, it's very difficult sometimes to spot them all. I'm sure if somebody attacked me, because of the tai chi and stuff like that, I'd just probably automatically respond without thinking about it. But I've been taught to do that so I don't hurt.

Another contributor with childhood experience of conflict became both a combative litigation lawyer and a successful mediator.

> **David Shapiro:** [My family background was] very aggressive, very confrontational. This guy was going to write a book. The same guy wrote this profile. He came up with stuff that I never heard about, never knew about. He got it from my kids – OK, wild stuff. My father was the kind of guy that went to a restaurant, even with one of his grandchildren – my son, Tony, tells this story – he waits too long for service, they know him and he's been in there many, many times, he will stand up, take the tablecloth, rip it off the table, everything on the floor, stalks out, won't pay a dime. That's a nut case. The same guy would never be able to stand in a queue. He'd always have to bust to the head of the queue. And he was a very large man, a six-footer. He weighed about 220 [pounds]. Very imposing man and with very sharp elbows. This was him. So it is fair to say I come by it naturally.

It appears that a common experience of family conflict influences many who chose to become commercial mediators.

> **Tony Willis:** I recently did a session/workshop with American mediators and asked why they wanted to become mediators. [I] asked what was intended to be a light-hearted question: what was the single worst fault that they thought was material to their becoming mediators and nearly all had come from dysfunc-

tional families. And this was quite interesting. Fairly dysfunctional, not dramatically so. This has something to do with it. I think a background which includes some personal experience of conflict and possibly leading to a distaste for it, or a wish that it didn't happen, affecting me personally, I think, that is a component of *my* background.

Traumatic family circumstances exacerbated by the impact of the Second World War shed poignant light on another contributor's powerful motivation to work towards the mitigation of the pain of family separation and loss.

Fred Gibbons: I think in terms of working with families which is, I think, the great attraction, my own childhood played a very important part because, in trying to understand the trauma of separation, I had a double blow in my own childhood. My father and sister died within the space of six months when I was six years of age – the dreaded disease of tuberculosis and meningitis. It devastated the family. Suddenly my mother had to do three jobs to try and keep a roof over my head, the only child.

She [my sister] was three. My father was 31. My father died of tuberculosis, my sister of meningitis. So my mother was in the middle of that and had to try and cope. So the sense of loss. And I think the overwhelming concern for me was that, when my mother went away – I was six years of age – was she coming back? Because in a short space of time, two losses, three, so you look out the window and think, is she coming down the road? Although you can't be subjective, it does give you a feel of what it may be like, in my view, for youngsters who have to cope with a parent leaving the home. Uncertainty in that sense. Different circumstances. But if you asked me the question what shaped my life, that would be important.

[At] 70-odd years of age, it's still an overwhelming thought. It stays with me. Everybody has a significant experience which stays with them.

[Do] any two children have the same experience? In fact, a child of six, compared with one of two, has a totally different experience. At six, I think I was in the latency period, which as I understand it is *the* most difficult time to come to terms with that. Then I was evacuated in the war and I lived in four different homes, moved all over the country. So I had to adjust, adjust, adjust, separated from my mother. In terms of formal education, it was non-existent because I just kept moving from one area of the country to another. I was sent to Folkestone which had the first air raid.

[My mother had a tough time] in terms of finance, economically. Fortunately she was one of 15 children so her sisters and brothers all helped to keep me. The change for me was enormous. [She married again] and then she had another girl. In some ways that would restore a very happy time. A great sense of loss. As a child you don't appreciate what is happening to the person who is going to be you.

It's [an experience] that will shape your future. Not everybody has that. The question was, is there a significant aspect to your childhood? And that would have to be [another] one – I think I saw something of the problem of the step-parent coming into the home and the natural resentment of the territorial rights. That this new person was taking up ground that should have been the father's. The predicament of the mother to cope with life, the pressures on her. And it wasn't until I was 22 years of age that I realised what a nice man he [my stepfather] was. When I married I went for a quiet drink with him and I suddenly got to know him in a totally different way and formed an entirely new opinion. I was deeply resentful through all my childhood.

Serendipity, fate and chance

A minority of contributors have found themselves involved in mediation fortuitously, rather than having chosen it deliberately – though this is not always, of course, the whole picture. For the next contributor, professional advance to a managerial and teaching position resulted in a sense of being cut off from the world of practice. That the practice opportunity lay in mediation was not anticipated.

Tony Whatling: I had a background in social work and initially in family child care and then in adult psychiatry. I was in three or four management positions. All the way through that I was working as a family therapist. That was my professional practice interest. So when I was a manager I wasn't being cut off from practice because I was always involved with a thing called the Cambridge Family Therapy Workshop. We [were involved in] supervision and then started taking case referrals. I then became head of the Department of Social Work Education at a Cambridge college and I had always said that social work lecturers should not be out of practice for too many years. And I found that the department had got lecturers who had been out of practice for 20 years.

But then this thing kept coming back to me, here I was doing what I said I shouldn't do. So I looked around for some kind of practice opportunity, possibly in family therapy. And I saw this advertisement for the Cambridge Mediation Service starting up. I started in family therapy in the days of family psychotherapy – I took a masters degree in 1990 – where they were practising a particular focused, time-limited behavioural approach to family therapy. And I liked it. I liked it a lot. The interventions with families in trouble were much shorter. It had echoes of what had been around since the 70s, and that appealed to me then. So I think that's where [I got into] this style of family therapy, as opposed to therapist-led [approach]. Power has to be there, as far as possible, in the hands of the client. And the Cambridge [Mediation] Service starting up had the first pilot training programme. I was part of that first experiment. And in a couple of years they were selecting for trainers.

In an entirely different area of work, promotion also led to a fresh avenue of enterprise.

Carl Reynolds: I didn't know the term 'mediation'. I had been a trade union activist in a local authority and I had been a convenor there. So I had done a lot of negotiations, a lot of representing people in groups, and disciplinary hearings, and negotiating terms and conditions. So I understood, in a sense, the notion of negotiation. After a while I got promotion, I could no longer be a trade unionist and I've always had an excess of energy I suppose, so I saw an advert for a community mediator. I had no idea what that meant but went along anyway and fell in love with it. So that's really the story. I had been so embroiled in adversarial type work where I was constantly thinking of negotiated strategies to, in a sense, best the other side, that it was so refreshing to be exposed to a different way to bargain, I suppose, for want of a better word.

To a degree, as a trade unionist, when I became a mediator, it was also interesting to see that difference between being somebody who has an opinion and is involved and is in a sense advocating or representing, to being somebody who is actually looking at communication between people. And also the interesting intellectual, I suppose, and, to a degree, emotional state of saying, 'My opinion doesn't matter. My opinion about process matters, but my opinion about who's right, who's wrong, what I think about it, is marginal, and, ideally, is not pertinent at all.'

Another chance event brought mediation to the fore, although there was an existing though hitherto unrealised family connection with mediation.

Lorraine Schaffer, family mediator and Director of the Centre for Mediation and Conflict Resolution: My career was as a social worker. I trained in 1973 in New York as a social worker, and I practised social work for a few years there before I came to England in 1976 and I practised social work here for another 20-odd years. The way I came into mediation was really a tribute to my father. My father was a guidance counsellor and a teacher. When he retired and my parents moved to California, he became a volunteer community mediator in his late 60s, early 70s. And it was from him that I actually heard the term 'mediation'; I don't think I'd even heard the word mediation before that. So in 1994, I was working at that time as a group work trainer and consultant for a London borough Social Services Department, but my specialism was group work facilitation. They were making changes and cutting [jobs] and I was going to be made redundant and, by a complete fluke, I was sitting in a petrol garage locally, and saw in a local paper that would not have been delivered to my door, so I consider it quite fateful, I saw an advert for training mediators. It caught my eye because I had heard about mediation from my father; I knew, really, very little about it. I applied and was accepted as a trainee. I consider it fate really because I would never have seen this advert otherwise if I hadn't been there that day.

> I started working as a sessional mediator ten years ago. I got a job here [at the Institute of Family Therapy Mediation Service] in July 2001 and since then it's been my full-time occupation.

No conscious decision to be a mediator was involved either when, unexpectedly, a 'serendipitous' invitation came in 1993 from colleagues in the United States looking for people to assist in 'second track'[5] facilitative processes in Moldova. For this university teacher, this was the opportunity for the practical application of international relations theory (needs theory as a basis for understanding conflict and the work of Banks, Burton and Habermas in particular).

> **Mark Hoffman, mediator and facilitator in international conflicts:** I said yes, but had no idea where it was or what it was and this was my first hands-on experience in terms of doing it.

Although so far as any training was concerned, there was 'absolutely none', the process of formulating questions which was central to the form of practice experience involved in the Moldovan experience bore for him a strong similarity to that of the questioning approach of the post-graduate masters seminars conducted at the university. That first occasion led to further commitment of time and energy, a growing reputation and further work in conflict situations in Northern Ireland, Cyprus, Sri Lanka and Nepal, underpinned by the core principle that mediatory intervention must be by the invitation of someone involved in the conflict.

Summation

The reasons – a combination in some instances – for the contributors becoming mediators are as varied and rich as their fields of practice and their individual circumstances. Whatever the route into mediation, there was the hope that this new direction of interest and practice would lead to greater intellectual, professional and personal satisfaction. Expressly articulated ideals – particularly for a 'better' way of addressing conflict and disputes – virtually unanimously inform the motivations.

Notes

1. ACAS distinguishes between arbitration, mediation and conciliation. Conciliation is conducted by an official directly employed by ACAS, who follows the dispute carefully and, if appropriate, seeks to intervene to promote a settlement – a process termed 'running alongside a dispute'. ACAS does this on an entirely voluntary basis within the legal framework. For its arbitration and mediation work on the other hand, ACAS has a Panel of Independent Persons, ex-academics mostly, though more recently also ex-consultants and lawyers, who are appointed to act as arbitrators and mediators.

2. Princen draws a distinction between impartiality, which refers to questions of acceptability, and neutrality, which applies to the effect of the intervention on the parties' interaction –'this distinction appears more useful analytically than those that equate the two or that simply claim intermediaries *are* impartial and neutral or that the intermediaries are never impartial or neutral' (Princen 1992, p.63).
3. This includes support for local actors (or mixed groups, organisations or people from different countries) through training in the concepts and skills of conflict transformation; training trainers; dialogue workshops and strategy workshops. An example of international work (facilitating strategy workshops and training in particular skills in relation to a specific situation) is that with internally displaced people in Tbilisi and other parts of Georgia, to see how they can exert the most influence as a peace constituency for a peaceful resolution of the conflict in Abkhasia where they lived before being displaced.
4. Marzotto, C. *La mediazione familiare nella separazione e divorzio. Una riflessione su alcuni aspetti teorico organizzativi di due esperienze francesi*, Università degli Studi di Milano, aa. 1989–90.
5. 'Second track' negotiation is a term of art in the literature that describes the informal negotiation and facilitative process that can occur in parallel with and complementary to the formal negotiation process, where decision-making authority lies. In Moldova, the same actors, taking off their formal hats, participated in both processes. 'Second track' negotiation, as well as encouraging informal exchanges and explorations, has the advantage of enabling linkages to be made across political levels, from the elite decision-making level, to the mid-level political actors and structures, to the grassroots and civil society level of the non-governmental organisation.

3
The Personal Qualities of the Mediator

> 'Centering' is a process familiar to anyone who has ever tried to throw a clay pot on a potter's wheel; the first step is to press against the clay from each side until the spinning mass rotates smoothly and can then be shaped. Centering the clay is similar to what we as mediators do when we begin a mediation: we bring a certain atmosphere into the room, through our personal presence, which has the effect of centering the mediator and the others in the room.
>
> (Bowling and Hoffman 2000, p.26)

A large body of literature illustrates the complex and subtle ways in which the mediator, notwithstanding adherence to the minimal functions of catalyst and facilitator of negotiations, is acknowledged to exercise influence within the process (see Simmel 1908a; Deutsch 1973; Rubin and Brown 1975; Gulliver 1979; Pruitt 1981; Stulberg 1981; and, for a comprehensive account of recent empirical research findings and researcher/practitioner exchanges on this issue, Conneely 2002).

It is already noted that the minimal numerical transformation that occurs in mediation, of the dyad into the triad, qualitatively transforms the interaction between the parties. On the one hand, merely by being there, the mediator alters the relationship between the parties and exerts an influence: 'I [had] contributed nothing but my presence' (Meyer 1950, p.6). Minimal, non-verbal behaviour can have a significant effect:

> A gesture, a way of listening, the mood that radiates from a particular person, are enough to change the difference between two individuals so that they can seek understanding, are enough to make them feel their essential commonness which is concealed under their acutely differing opinions, and to bring this divergence into the shape in which it can be ironed out the most easily. (Simmel 1908a, p.149)

In addition, representing the principle of objectivity and reasonableness, the mediator transforms the interaction:

> The diminution of this personal tone is the condition under which the understanding and reconciliation of the adversaries can be attained, particularly because it is only under this condition that each of the two parties actually realizes what the other must insist upon. To put it psychologically, antagonism of the will is reduced to intellectual antagonism... no matter in what form the conflict enters from one side, it is transmitted to the other only in an objective form. (Simmel 1908a, p.148)

While it is acknowledged that the physical presence of the third person itself influences the interaction, for good or ill, relatively little has been written about the personal attributes of the mediator. One reason for this is that dispite the weight that has long been attached to the personal rather than the processual aspects of the role, personal qualities, in their nature elusive and idiosyncratic, are not easily susceptible to analysis. So the catalogues of qualities that have been devised are anecdotal rather than scientific. The most useful approach to an understanding of what qualities make up the 'good' mediator has been to adopt the perspectives of the parties to the dispute. In such studies (e.g. Landsberger 1956; Stulberg1981; Raiffa 1982) a list of preferred qualities emerges, for example:

- originality of ideas
- sense of appropriate humour
- ability to act unobtrusively
- the mediator as 'one of us'
- the mediator as respected authority (that is, personal prestige)
- ability to understand quickly the complexities of a dispute
- accumulated knowledge
- control over feelings
- attitudes towards and persistent and patient effort invested in the work of mediating
- faith in voluntarism (in contrast to dictation)
- physical endurance
- the hide of a rhinoceros
- the wisdom of Solomon
- the patience of Job

- capacity to appreciate the dynamics of the environment in which the dispute is occurring
- intelligence (both 'process' skills and 'content' knowledge).

What emerges from this catalogue approach is a consensus about a combination of attributes, intellectual, moral and personal, that goes towards the making of the ideal mediator.

More recently attempts have been made to explore 'some deeper and more fundamental quality that the most effective mediators, have – a quality that may include such attributes as patience, wisdom or wit, but which involves other attributes that are not on the above lists' (Bowling and Hoffman 2000, p.9). It is contended that where empirical studies of mediation show favourable results, including high levels of party satisfaction, these occur regardless of the individual style or philosophical or professional orientation of the mediator, or whatever practice skills or models are adopted (Bowling and Hoffman 2000). It is asserted too that it is 'a mediator's "presence" – more a function of who the mediator is than what he or she does – [that] has a profound impact on the mediation process' (Bowling and Hoffman 2000, p.5).

What are the personal qualities of a mediator?

This familiar question elicited a circumspect response from contributors. This, from the environmental and organisational field, was typical:

> **Andrew Acland**: In some ways one can go on about endless qualities like patience and listening and all the skills which do frequently get cited and with which you are familiar.

A similar view comes from the field of commercial mediation:

> **Tony Willis**: It's terribly difficult to answer this question because everyone's degree of insight into their own structure is variable, to put it mildly. And you could trot off all things which are, no doubt, necessary like patience and the hide like a rhinoceros.

More surprising perhaps, very few contributors referred to those qualities (catalogued above) traditionally identified as essential for effective practice – with the exception of the quality of patience. Intellectual capacities (analytic and creative), a sense of humour in difficult circumstances, and the capacity to listen attentively were cited – in particular, the ability to listen in a way that 'would make [the parties] feel, as you left them, that you really have taken note of what I said, really tried hard to see my point of view' (Fred Gibbons).

Three unanticipated answers to this question emerged, irrespective of the area of practice, professional background or gender of the contributor. The first perspective highlights the requirement for the mediator to have a genuine interest in, liking and concern for people.

The comments of this German family mediator are typical:

> **Christoph Paul:** I think you have to be curious, you have to be interested in people. I think you should not be too competitive. I think it is helpful that you don't want to compete with the clients. Personal authority I would say helps a lot. I think getting older helps a lot. It is one of the few fields where getting older helps. Patience. A good sense of humour. And a general respect – interest and respect for people, what are their resources, what are their conflicts.

A British family mediator had a similar answer:

> **Lorraine Schaffer:** I think you have to enjoy working with people, you have to care about people and I think in mediation what I really find very fascinating is just hearing people's stories. There are many common themes, also every person is an individual and brings their own take to it. So I find it endlessly fascinating and I never get bored. That's what I like about it.

A third family mediator highlighted the combination of personable qualities with a necessary acuteness of focus:

> **Fred Gibbons:** I think that warmth and friendliness are absolutely crucial, to have tolerance *and* to be able to focus. I think putting people at their ease, to help people see the opportunity they have been presented with.

Work in community mediation and with the elderly evoked a view that accorded importance to an appreciation of the heterogeneity of society, and the responsibility that imposes to attend and to avoid the making of assumptions about others.

> **Yvonne Craig:** [The qualities needed are first] a deep understanding and appreciation of the rich variety of human personalities and a gratitude for the different social and cultural contexts in which we are all fashioned and developed. And I feel it is increasingly important, in our multi-ethnic society, for mediators to have this empathetic awareness of the richness and diversity of life. And I think the second one is the ability to listen attentively, with care and compassion, to those with whom one is working. And that one's concern for them overrides one's own self-interest or desire for self-expression. There is, I think, a great need to have an ability to continually learn, for me to consider that each case is unique, each individual is unique and to be able to come to each person and each situation and each relationship [and] to learn from that, and to integrate the new learning with what one has learnt in the past. So this is, to me, the excitement of mediation. It offers the opportunity for continually learning from people and about people. And about life's journey.

This curiosity was echoed by another contributor involved in public policy, workplace and other mediation fields.

Carl Reynolds: I am intrigued by people as well. I suppose what also influences me is that Carl Rogers thing about 'unconditional positive regard'. I don't think I'm capable of that but I think it's a great aspiration.

Another view, more understated, highlights the same critical importance that the contributors attached to the requirement for personal warmth and approachability in a mediator. The meaning and purpose of this requirement is explored further in relation to its potential to meet the needs of the parties in the difficult circumstances of the negotiations – in particular the need to feel safe in the midst of conflict. And that requires of the mediator, too, a certain brand of toughness.

Philip Naughton: Well it's clichéd I suppose, but I think that, as far as parties are concerned, it is inevitably important that I'm perceived to be a nice guy. People need to get on with mediators. And therefore need to be able to easily forge a relationship with those with whom they're working. And it's not always the case but sometimes it's necessary for a mediator to be quite tough and quite aggressive and I think I can do that too. I could be trusted and austere but if I was too austere then I would never get people to participate. I am afraid I do [think that approachability is an essential quality]. I think that is much more important than ability. [Though] I've obviously got to be able to understand complicated cases.

This perspective sheds somewhat paradoxical light on another aspect of the subject of personal qualities – those same attributes recognised to be virtues in a mediator, are perceived also to be personal failings in everyday life – as one contributor put it: 'my consciousness of not being able to resolve the problems of people' (Costanza Marzotto). While a liking for people continues to be a paramount condition for engaging with the parties, this is recognised to be hugely demanding in practice, requiring the mediator to like (and be perceived as likable) not only by one person but also at least two or more people who are, in the circumstances, in conflict with one another.

The interaction of these factors is highlighted by this community mediator:

Marian Liebmann: One of the biggest and best qualities is something I always used to feel was a kind of failure in myself. I always find myself sitting on the fence with issues and able to see both sides. I was very rarely able to plant my standard on a particular pole and be wholehearted about that side. And that's a positive advantage as a mediator. It's one of the best qualities to have. I have sometimes been out with fellow co-mediators and they rush to judgment over some case. They say, 'It's obvious, its blah, blah.' I say, 'Is it? Isn't that a bit soon to make that kind of statement?' This kind of slowness to reach judgment is actually, being very patient, persistent, dogged even, is actually a real virtue. Just keep going at it really. I think liking people helps. I don't see how you could do it otherwise. I think one of the hardest things is this business of holding two people in focus rather than one. So much work in social work and people fields or counselling, is that you are there for that one person. In mediation you can never be there for that one person. You've got to be either not there for either of them or, as I like to put it, there for both of them, or all of them if there are more than two. I think to be able to frame things up in non-aggressive type language or non-blaming type of language and to practise that for quite a number of years. It is quite helpful. Creative thinking, thinking outside the box is sometimes very useful. To be able to see patterns I think is really useful. You kind of see a pattern of relationships.

Very often in neighbour mediation, and other mediations as well, sometimes people are mirroring each other. You go to a family who will say, 'Well, you know we are flexible and accommodating. But then next door, and their kids are dreadful, they do this, this, this and this. And of course we're very accommodating but they are just terrible.' You go next door and they say, 'Well, of course, we're very flexible and so forth. It's their kids.' It is interesting to notice the kinds of patterns of what people say.

Another view, this time from the international field, exemplifies these conjunctions.

Diana Francis: It's interesting, I think: when anybody does work in relation to something, you, they, have to ask yourself why are they drawn to that. I do care very passionately about people. I think I am a very compassionate person and therefore the desire for violence and cruelty not to happen is a very strong desire I have. So that's a strong motivator. But I also think that – well I know – I'm quite an aggressive person by nature, particularly when I view myself from a gender perspective, I know I was always too rough to be a 'proper little girl'. And that probably makes me see myself as more aggressive than I would if I were male. But, I think the plus of that is that I am not uncomfortable with conflict. And I think one of the things you have to learn to do as a mediator, and which some people will find more difficult than others, is at some level not to mind that the micro-conflict that is taking place within the mediation *is* taking place. *That you are there for it to be able to take place.* And I think I am relatively not phased by hot interpersonal exchanges. I think that's useful.

And I think the other reason why I am comfortable in the facilitator role is because I always have a sense of taking up too much space in the world, in terms of sound time or, even more, in terms of energy, of being too liable to be dominant. And if I am in a mediator/facilitator role I have a framework, in which I feel both that I do contain myself in a very conscious way and as a matter of habit now. Because I know that my job is not endlessly to be coming up with or holding forth opinions, but is to create space for other people to think and express themselves. So that gives me a kind of sense of OK-ness in that role.

I actually think I've developed good listening skills, anybody could, and I'm very interested in levels of awareness of what's going on, both in myself and in other people. And I can be assertive when assertiveness is needed – and it certainly is if people are going to feel safe. Then they need to know that the room is being held and I'm confident at doing this 'aggressive' bit. It comes out as assertive and it's useful. I'm full of angst. I can be very nervous but in the moment I'm not going to find it impossible to do what has to be done.

Working with translators, frequently necessary in international work, brings complications and advantages.

Diana Francis: I have to work with interpretation. I have some Russian but not enough to work in. I can tell when the interpretation is not working. It's a barrier in that I can't talk with people between sessions. It really is like that. In a curious way it helps me to stay absolutely functional and focused. And it certainly should be translated consecutively. You have time to collect your thoughts and be more economical and more straightforward. You have to cut out some of the more difficult ways of saying things. So it has a streamlining effect. I feel real frustration in coming out as somebody other than me, because I am quite strict in groups, particularly in Georgia, because, for instance, talking for the sake of talking is culturally normal. And trying to ensure that actually communication is pointed and efficient really matters if you are going to achieve something. So I have a somewhat dragon profile, and I think people appreciate it, but I don't like being perceived that way.

I think, yes, [it is seen as a strength]. But if I were working in my own language or for myself I am actually quite funny as a facilitator, so it balances out the strictness. But I can't be funny. It's part of who I am because I do find everything very funny.

In order to mediate, some degree of self-knowledge of one's failings is necessary if there is to be an understanding of what is required by others, those in conflict in particular – a viewpoint, in this case, from a mediator working in different fields (the community, workplace and public policy).

Carl Reynolds: But I would say that the qualities are [that] I think you need to have a certain self-confidence to do this work. You have to know yourself in the sense of knowing how you react to stuff that people say. So you are able to understand the mechanics of being impartial. You are able to understand stuff, even if intellectually you are not reacting, are you aware of how your body [reacts], a somatic response to what you are hearing. So I think qualities are an inquiry about self, an inquiry about how we are as human beings, so whether that's having some models of psychology, for example, the Gestalt and Jungian approach inspires me. The point I am trying to make [is] to have an eclectic approach, and to not be dogmatic, to say, actually, at the end of the day, a mediator or facilitator is a designer of a process, and that one size doesn't fit all, and that you need to adapt. So there are certain basic practices but then you need to adapt.

I've always thought that, on a training group, what is the most important thing for you to learn is to understand, to some degree, what it means to be impartial and what it means to be neutral and to be able to understand, when people are talking, what it is that they are *omitting*, what it is they are *intimating*, what it is they are *avoiding* and to be able to ask them questions in a way that doesn't challenge them but enables them to speak more about everything.

I think to be a good mediator, I think it's like any profession really – the notion that you are never good enough, you've got to be better than you are. Which is sometimes an odd thing to mix, between the notion of being very self-confident and saying I am flawed. So to have a reflective practice, I suppose.

The identification of the requisite personal qualities of a mediator was premised, for several contributors, on what *the parties* in mediation most required in order for their conflict or dispute to be mediated successfully.

Andrew Acland: In some ways I think 'unflappability' is the most important thing. People, in going into a mediation in a conflict situation, have to feel safe. So to instil in them a sense that you are utterly calm about it, the situation does not throw you, and that you are going to make it safe for them to expose themselves in a way they wouldn't normally do, I think in many ways is the most important thing.

This capacity to create a safe forum for the parties is echoed by others, in this instance a family mediator for whom expressed conflict is not personally frightening.

Lorraine Schaffer: I do think that people who are attracted to mediation have to in some way be interested in conflict. I know from hearing other stories, that some people are attracted to it because they find it difficult. I don't think I find it difficult. I grew up in a family where there was lots of outward conflict, lots of shouting, yelling and emotions expressed. So I don't have a difficulty with that. And I think it's actually a positive quality really. Because if you are working with people who are in conflict, there are bound to be a lot of feelings associated with it. And I'm not at all frightened of people raising their voices or expressing themselves. So I think you have to be able to deal with that and not be frightened of it, as a mediator.

I think the other thing is just a very strong belief, which obviously you use in social work as well, that people can resolve differences by talking to each other, by communicating, and that they don't resolve things if they avoid it or leave things in a state where it is just anger expressed and nothing done to relieve that.

Patience

> [T]here must be an endless supply of patience and perseverance. Sometimes the mountains seem so high and rivers so wide that it is hard to continue the journey... Seeking an end to conflict is not for the timid or the tentative...We had 700 days of failure and 1 day of success. (Menkel-Meadow *et al.* 2005, quoting George J. Mitchell [describing negotiations in Northern Ireland], p.326)

Patience has long been recognised as a fundamental attribute of the mediator, and was certainly considered so by most of the contributors. Fresh insight emerged, too, into the nature and function of patience as an attribute of the mediator and the relationship of patience to the purpose of mediation. The association, for example, between the personal characteristic of being slow to reach judgments in everyday life, and the professional attribute of patience in mediation, has already been alluded to in the context of community mediation (see Marian Liebmann above).

The comparison between the 'outcome-driven' and the 'process-driven' approaches in international mediation points to the patience necessary for the latter approach.

> **Mark Hoffman:** I call myself a facilitator rather than mediator. The difference I think is partly again something that the literature teases out – and it sets up almost dichotomous ideal types that probably break down in actual practice. The main distinction would be that mediation often [follows] a more formalised, tighter structure: mediators often, at least at the international level, are presumed to bring with them certain kinds of resources that they can use. They often have interests in an outcome, a particular kind of outcome to the conflict, and so to that extent, a mediator, at least in the international conflict, would be deemed to be somebody who is outcome-driven – they know more or less where they want to get the parties to, and how to assist to get the parties there.
>
> Whereas the facilitator is more process-driven, and to a certain extent may have particular ideas about what might be useful or appropriate outcomes but, in a sense, isn't wedded to a particular outcome and indeed part of what they are trying to do is to explore a whole range of possible outcomes and foster a process of creative thinking on the part of the parties to the conflict. But from our point of view – and the principle is in a sense derived from people like Burton and Curle – *the solution has to lie with the parties themselves.* It is not something that can be imposed from outside and so rather than bring them the solution and how to get them to it... *it is drawing out of them what would be an acceptable solution between the various parties involved in the conflict that would make it work.* [Emphasis added.]

In the context of commercial mediation, experience confirms the importance of patience *and* toughness.

Tony Willis: Endless patience. Tough as several tons of bricks and there's a difference between qualities and experience. The experience that I bring to it is *very* heavy commercial dispute resolution. I've a lot of experience which I have been extraordinarily lucky to have had; it took me to all sorts of places and taught me all sorts of things. It's not the qualities so much as the professional experience. [So] I do [bring patience and toughness] because in a mediation context, I am sometimes possibly even too patient. One of the long list of failings – this is the counterpoint to your question – what qualities do I *not* have? What are my failings that make me a worse mediator than I should be, is probably being endlessly patient with people to the point where in the end frustration overcomes me. Professionally I am very patient – *I give them time and I give them space and the opportunity to understand themselves. I don't impose my view on their position and... what's been happening.* [Emphasis added.]

As these examples make clear, where the primary objective of the mediator is perceived to be that of enabling *the parties themselves* to reach their own agreed outcomes, a high degree of patience is also recognised to be a concomitant requirement. As the renowned labour mediator, Meyer, expressed it as early as 1950:

> The final demand is still for patience and endurance. Be patient, be patient and evermore be patient. Be not too patient! Never tire, but watch for the gathering signs of fatigue in others. Then push over the pins that are already trembling. How? I cannot tell you. A sudden change in attitude, a deepening of the voice, a strident, unexpected urgency ... but no two cases are alike and even if they were, no two mediators would attack them on parallel lines. (Quoted in Douglas 1962, p.108)

It is clear though that there are differing views (certainly within the commercial mediation field) about the relative significance to be attached to the contribution of the personal attributes (for example, 'being perceived to be a nice guy') or of the ability of the mediator. Professional experience and personal preference may push the mediator towards a particular practical approach, as illustrated in the industrial relations field, where the mediator and arbitrator roles may both be conducted by the same person.

Roy Lewis: I'm probably unconventional I suspect. I'm really quite directive. As I say I'm quite prepared to put pressure on the parties and even, if necessary, to bully them into positions. And I don't think that conforms very easily with some of the conventional theories of mediation, which are much less directive, where you simply ask the parties what the alternatives are and what options they want. It's not that I don't do that. I do do that. It's just that perhaps because I've got more experience as an arbitrator, I tend not to stand on ceremony too much. I make positive suggestions once I'm fully confident I understand what's going on.

Now there's a way that is almost institutionalised in the industrial relations field. Some of the mediations you do may actually be with the assistance of full-time industrial relations officials from both sides of whatever industry you are talking about. And the expectation there is, although at the end of the day you can't actually make any kind of binding award, you can work through the two sides' institutions to get them, as far as possible, to encourage a serious consideration of ideas that will be most likely to resolve a dispute. As I say, I think what I've just said probably goes completely contrary to the normal theory of mediation.

It's easier to do that [adopt a more directive approach] if you are dealing with collective labour relations. If you are in an individual employment dispute, of course, like everything else, it depends on your terms of reference. And some of the terms of reference can really tie down the mediator to the point where they are almost prevented from making positive suggestions unless the parties are very explicit in asking for it.

[The more directive style] just suits me really, it suits the way *I* do things. But there will be other people who work either in the collective labour relations or the individual employment dispute field who will probably be less directive than I am. And it can be just as effective, obviously more effective perhaps depending on the circumstances. You have to do something that is consistent with your own way of doing things really, your own personality.

The contrast would be with an ACAS conciliation undertaken by direct ACAS employees. In collective labour relations, you don't get any kind of direction at all. They run alongside the dispute – listen, listen, listen. They don't really say to a party at any time, look, are you going to settle this or not? What's your bottom line? Whereas the individual mediator that is appointed to do that kind of thing can do it, assuming the parties want that to happen, or allow it to happen. It has to be obviously consistent with the terms of reference whatever the terms of reference are.

Professional experience in another context and country, as a settlement master in the USA following extensive litigation and negotiation experience, inevitably influences this mediator's views of what personal qualities matter most.

David Shapiro: Somebody asked me that [question] a long time ago. I think it was a Professor Peter Schuck writing a book called *Agent Orange on Trial*.[1] And if you want to find out exactly what I did in the Agent Orange case you want to get hold of Chapter 8 of his book. My answer to him was, that I think my greatest skill wasn't really as a trial lawyer, but basically, if you really come down to think about it, it is getting a whole bunch of people with different interests to march in the same direction. That was probably my greatest strength.

Perhaps the well-recognised requirement of 'personal authority' cited by contributors sums up that combination of attributes – individual qualities (intellectual, moral and personal), professional experience (analytic, substantive and practice knowledge and skills) and ability (capacity for critical and creative thinking, understanding and engagement) – that make the practice of mediation a demanding and creative task.

Notes

1. 'Shapiro's assignment [as one of two special masters for settlement]...was to actually negotiate the settlement (in Shapiro's unvarnished words, to "get a deal done"). For this task, he was an ideal choice. In his mid-fifties, Shapiro was a feisty, shrewd, colorful man, given to scatological stories and deadpan humor. Corpulent but fastidious, he resembled a bullfrog in a pin-striped suit. He had begun his career in an office over a delicatessen on 91st Street and Broadway: "I got my first trial experience defending whores in women's court," he fondly remembers, "before going to work for the CIO." During the 1960s and 1970s, Shapiro had been celebrated by many in the plaintiff's bar as "the father of the consumer class action"; this reflected his ingenuity in engineering massive antitrust actions on behalf of state and local governments against the drug and other industries, winning enormous recoveries for his clients and lavish fee awards for himself. No one was more knowledgeable than Shapiro about the design, trial, administration and settlement of complex class actions. In addition, he was an exceedingly skilful, experienced negotiator and mediator. (His bookshelves are lined with works on the subject.) "What I do best and have done for twenty years," he says, "is to get a diverse group of people to march in the same direction."' (Schuck 1987, pp.145–6)

4
Attitudes to Conflict

> The skilful management of conflicts is among the highest of human skills.
>
> (Hampshire 2000, p.35)

This chapter focuses on the perspectives on conflict of the contributors (rather than, as is more common, of the disputants), as the most central and pervasive of those recognised 'objectively difficult circumstances' – historical, substantive, institutional, contextual and individual circumstances – that typify the subject matter of mediation, whatever the field of practice (Kressel 1985, p.203). Comparing the intensity of conflict in different arenas may not be easy. There is a view that 'a particular bitterness characterises conflicts within relationships' and that:

> The deepest hatred grows out of broken love…to have to recognise that a deep love…was an error, a failure of intuition, so compromises us before ourselves, so splits the security and unity of our self-conception, that we unavoidably make the object of this intolerable feeling pay for it. We cover our secret awareness of our own responsibility for it by hatred which makes it easy for us to pass all responsibility on to the other. (Simmel 1908b, p.93)

Notwithstanding the strength of such conflict, it is necessary to recognise that the *consequences* of conflict across different fields may be of a significantly different order, not least in respect of the protraction, proportion and scale of violence and destruction attending intractable conflict in the international sphere.[1] Here the intermediary role is itself *defined* in terms of its conflict management function – 'Intermediary intervention, it turns out, is a method of conflict management distinguished by the intermediary's peculiar role, of being neither party to nor completely removed from the dispute' (Princen 1992, p.214).

This quote highlights two additional relevant points – first, that of the tension inherent in the intermediary role itself, 'peculiar' and fraught with a contradiction and ambiguity (as already noted) arising from the necessity to maintain a calm, disinterested, creative and rational presence in the midst of parties' conflict, stress and distress (Kressel 1985). Second, a slippage occurs in the use of terminology, not uncommon in the literature.

In the international field, the definition of 'conflict', for example, frequently covers a range of types, and attempts have been made to classify conflict according to various criteria such as severity, protraction and intractability. Therefore, definitions are recognised to be vague and their applications frequently inconsistent (see for example Bar-Tal 1998). A similar problem is associated with the distinction often drawn between 'conflicts' (consisting of interpersonal, structural and conflicts of interest, resolvable when basic differences of fact, value or power are removed) and 'disputes' (the specific, identifiable issues that divide people, including lawyers' representations of disputes as 'cases') (see for example, Felstiner, Abel and Sarat 1980–81; Roberts 1983; Caplan 1995; Roberts and Palmer 2005). While a few contributors did make definitional distinctions, the same slippage that occurs in the theoretical literature emerges in the contributors' accounts.

Variations in intermediary intervention inevitably reflect variations in the form, scale and focus of conflict as well as differences in responses to conflict and its meaning (arising, for example, from cultural values and beliefs). The attitudes to conflict of the contributors correspond with those broad distinctions identified in the social theory literature: there were those who, in line with the Durkheimian approach, perceive conflict to be pathological, a bad thing, distasteful, damaging, appalling in some circumstances. And there was another, majority view, that conflict is a normal phenomenon, universal, inevitable, necessary even, and often serving an important function – more in line therefore with the perspectives of social theorists such as Simmel who, observing that conflict is 'after all one of the most vivid interactions which furthermore, cannot possibly be carried out by one individual', writes at the beginning to his essay on conflict that 'there probably exists no social unit in which convergent and divergent currents among the members are not inseparably interwoven' and even if an absolutely harmonious group could be conceived in theory it 'is empirically unreal [and] it could show no real life process' (Simmel 1908b, pp.70, 72).

Some contributors expressed the view that conflict could be exciting and energising in certain circumstances, and could certainly generate opportunities for change and progress. Attitudes could not be associated with any one field of practice. Nor did particular attitudes to conflict appear to reflect any individual childhood experience. Views about how best to approach conflict personally or professionally were also varied.

For one contributor from Germany, childhood experience, the powerful influence of a father in particular, was formative in determining his approach to conflict.

Christoph Paul: The thing is I'm not afraid of conflict. I had a pretty strong father, a father who did not give me the chance to make too many experiments with this pattern with him. But he had a very, very creative way how to handle conflicts. He wasn't afraid of conflicts at all. So I saw how *he* did it and he was a very, very straight person. Whenever conflicts came up he immediately mentioned them. He had no fear at all. The only thing [was], he was 50 years older than me and he didn't want to see his little son participate in this way of handling conflicts. He had a wonderful way of handling conflicts.

He confronted it. He confronted it very directly. A couple of times I realised that when there were arguments, I met my father saying to people if you bring up this subject then I would like to discuss it directly from the very bottom. Start at the very bottom. No fear at all. He said I don't have to lose anything. I think it was also the experience of two world wars [in which] he participated as a soldier and so on. He said I have to lose nothing.

Conflict: dimensions and responses

Whatever their childhood experience of family conflict, both positive and negative, all the contributors became mediators. So early influences, while powerful, are so varied that they appear not to be determinative in any clearly discernable way. Nor is it possible to distinguish, in terms of background or upbringing, between the views of those who regard conflict as damaging and frightening and those who regard conflict in a more positive light. What unifies responses is the recognition that, with experience, conflict loses its fear and that one can learn from it and be better equipped to address conflict constructively.

Adam Curle: [Conflict is]a bad thing...terrible in some cases. And I mean I just feel that conflict is something to be avoided really – I don't mean getting away from it but resolving it, dissolving it, whatever is the right word, transforming it might be the word. It is damaging to all concerned.

Experience of conflict as a mediator, compared to that as a lawyer, enhanced the next contributor's capacity to deal with conflict.

Christoph Paul: To be honest, I wouldn't say I can handle all conflicts pretty well. Some conflicts frighten me. But the more I practise as a mediator, the more I can handle conflict and I see the chance that within conflict there is resource for a change or for a solution. My first years as a lawyer were filled up with conflicts. I was a criminal lawyer and I had conflicts to handle in court. The way of handling these conflicts didn't satisfy me at all. Because there were nearly no ways of looking at the chances that conflicts had. Because you had to handle the conflict either for your client, to win for a client or you lost. Whereas the more I do mediation the more I realise that conflict has something in it. Whenever I see a conflict now I say there must be something in it that creates this conflict and there must be more than what is to be seen at this very moment. So the more mediation I do, the more ability I have in myself to handle this conflict.

Understanding the impact of conflict on oneself, possibly as a consequence of childhood experience, can contribute to its effective professional management.

Tony Willis: I think it is an interesting question [what is your attitude to conflict?] because I can't give you a very good answer to this which suggests some sort of deeper turmoil in me than there should be. I think I am disqualified to answer really. I think a background which includes some personal experience of conflict, and possibly leading to a distaste for it, or a wish that it didn't happen affecting me personally – I think that is a component of *my* background. And that is probably why these answers came out fairly routinely and why I wanted to treat this as a joke question. No, [conflict doesn't frighten me]. I think this is the interesting thing. I think probably it frightened me as a kid in the way it frightens people in dysfunctional families. When you're doing it professionally you distance yourself. [It's] part of your independence, and it is I think part of one's professionalism that you understand it from your own background and the way you react to it, but you are able to deal with it between others, otherwise probably you'd go bananas, so I think it is about understanding.

A similar perspective reveals the interrelationship of the personal and the professional response to the management of conflict.

Marian Liebmann: I have always thought of myself as somebody that didn't really deal very well with conflict. Didn't enjoy it, felt I came off worse, got very frightened of it. So to be involved in the conflict field is a kind of personal thing of trying to get a few more skills to be able to cope with it better. I think to a certain extent I've achieved that. It doesn't mean to say that I love conflicts totally, but it means I'm not so frightened of it and I've got a few tools to think about it, either for myself or for other people. I use very many of the tools that I've learned for my own conflicts as well. So professionally I suppose I tend to think of conflicts as things that implicate, that *something needs looking at*.

The distinction between sources of conflict and the kind of resolution possibilities that are available is further explored by the next contributor, first distinguishing between his personal and professional attitudes to conflict.

Philip Naughton: I would say that in my personal life I will tend to seek reconciliation rather than encourage my side (i.e. me) to do better by confrontation. But I am likely to be very contrary if I feel strongly that I am right and a competing proposition is wrong. I am not a very brave person when faced with a risk of physical harm from an opponent (or a field of frisky bullocks) and there may be a link between my attitude to wars of words and my reaction to combat. But if I must stand up to a threat, I guess I will.

In my professional life I have enjoyed conflict. I stopped doing criminal cases many years ago but enjoyed the aggressive interplay with other counsel, the judge, witnesses. I still take great pleasure in demolishing expert evidence. But I will rarely raise my voice in the course of cross-examination. All done quietly. Not much practice as an advocate nowadays.

Is mediation the antidote for conflict or is it merely a more honourable way of resolving conflict than trial? One often sees competition pursued through the mediation process. I guess that all conflict is ultimately resolved in one way or another, but the task of the mediator is to assist parties in finding the most efficient path to that conclusion.

Conflict may be divided into that which is necessary and that which is avoidable. Necessary conflict arises where the parties have received differing legal advice or have been told different stories by witnesses and for one party – and possibly sometimes for both – when there are external factors, such as impecuniosity, which cause them to act in a manner which is apparently unreasonable. Resolution of such conflict may be achieved through compromise, exchanging part of a reward for a valuation of resolved risk, but this is a compromise and should be recognised as such.

On the other hand, some conflict is unnecessary, for example that based upon misunderstanding or bloody-mindedness. This should be capable of resolution without compromise and affords an opportunity of a true 'win–win'. Should the question be, 'Are you a fighter or a conciliator?'?

The view of conflict as universal and normal is shared by contributors working in a range of contexts: 'the broad context in which you work, in which people are at odds with each other for whatever reasons, emotional, or personal, or political, or ideological or whatever, [where] conflict is a naturally occurring behaviour, phenomenon, if you like' (Andrew Acland).

This approach to the 'normality' of conflict in all aspects of life is illustrated in the international mediation field.

Diana Francis: Not just intellectually, but experientially, I can say that I find conflict to be absolutely normal. I even think that life without conflict would be extraordinarily dull. I think hurting is something that I would always want to avoid, inter-personally and in larger groups, and I think that too much conflict and not enough stability makes other agendas impossible to pursue, and therefore human beings can't thrive if conflict is too disruptive as well as too hurtful. So I do see the need for stability and affirmation and respect.

I am saying that you actually need stability, so it's the question of which is the chicken and which is the egg, and it goes round and round. But I think societies need a degree of stability, so to have everything always up for argument makes continuous life very difficult. So as any parent of teenage children would know, that you go through these wearisome years where life is one long negotiation, and that seems to be what your relationship consists of. Well it's OK but it is a bit tiring and it's a big relief when it stops being like that. And I think there is some relevance of that to the social and political.

So I think it's both not having conflicts erupt too drastically and too violently, particularly not with violence, and also having a culture in which conflict can be regularly processed in non-destructive ways. That there are systems, there are assumptions, there are norms that allow for the destructive ongoing dealing with conflicts, as they arise. And that's also in order that injustices, perceived and actual, can be addressed. Particularly, for instance, groups are not excluded for who they are, or the weak constantly pushed to the margin.

The notion of 'normality' is extended in the context of labour relations where conflict is seen to be as 'inevitable' as the need for it to be resolved.

Roy Lewis: I would regard conflict as inevitable in the labour field. It is actually inevitable whether it's collective or individual. Conflict is inevitable. On the other hand in more situations than not, the resolution of the conflict is in all parties' interest rather than just fighting it to the death, either in straight economic terms, i.e. strikes and what have you, or alternatively in litigation which is consequently longer and expensive and it doesn't actually necessarily resolve any underlying issues. Although I would be the first to recognise (a) that conflict is inevitable; and (b) some disputes aren't even really amenable to anything other than fighting it all the way through, I think the majority of conflict situations can be resolved one way or another, broadly speaking, to the greater satisfaction of the parties.

The inevitability of conflict as an aspect of life is similarly explored in the context of family disputes. Here the chief casualties of conflict are often the children.

Lorraine Schaffer: Conflict is absolutely inevitable as a part of life really. And I think one of the things that happens when you are teaching about conflict is that it is seen as a negative for the most part. When you ask people to do word associations or brainstorms about conflict mostly you pick up the negatives. But in fact I think conflict has a lot of positive attributes and I think life would be very boring if we didn't have conflict. And actually people prove that because what they are most interested in, when you're in any group situation of people, is whether there is some level of conflict. If people just agree with each other and were nice to each other all the time, I think it would be quite a boring world really. So I think it is inevitable. It's not about trying to get rid of conflict, trying to resolve it in a way. But I think the question is helping people manage it so that it doesn't become destructive and it doesn't destroy relationships, and particularly with parents. I think the most important thing with parents in family mediation, is that if they have children, particularly young children, it's very important that they find a way to deal with the conflicts so children don't suffer. So I think that's probably my motivation really in wanting to work with families in this way. And I think being a parent, you also do appreciate what a hard job it is. So that gives you another perspective.

I think you have to be calm as a mediator – just going back to the other qualities. You have not to be frightened of conflict and you have to believe that people can actually find a way to deal with it. And I think sometimes it's the timing that's wrong, but I don't believe people ever choose to want to stay in conflict with each other. The sad thing is that sometimes they do. And, just as an aside, we do occasionally get referrals or queries about, not divorce or separation, but other family disputes, adult siblings, we've had a few cases here. I've spoken to people on the 'phone even if it's never come here. And it's just quite amazing the level of pain that can be caused even with adults.

So I think conflict within families, as within communities or anywhere else, hearing a lot about neighbour disputes, makes you think that's pretty serious too. To have to live next door, or above or near somebody that you are in conflict with. So that's the issue really. It is helping people manage it so it doesn't destroy them.

A different context for exploring the dimensions of conflict (in comparison, for example, to the commercial, family, community and labour fields represented above) is that of the international field. Here the implications of notions of 'unproblematic', even 'desirable', conflict are explored.

Mark Hoffman: Part of the problem is actually conceptual language in the field itself and, in a sense, the focus on the idea of conflict resolution is part of what you are trying to do is actually not get rid of conflict itself. Most people start from the point of view that conflicts are actually desirable in terms of differences within societies. And you are not trying to produce a grey, homogenised lamb sausage – everybody the same as everyone else. And so it's actually then focusing on the modalities that people will turn to when there are differences within a society, and particularly when the society fails to be able to put in place or draw on mechanisms for constructively managing conflicts. And channelling those differences in a way that is productive for the society in terms of producing honest debate about political goods and political futures.

So the real interest is the idea that people turning to violence, using political violence as a means of trying to get what they think they want and need, is problematic. So to that extent, in terms of an attitude towards conflict, conflict itself is unproblematic. John Burton had this great line: conflict is like sex; it is something that has to be carried out by consenting people and it is something that they have to feel good about. So the problem is the pathology of violence rather than the conflict.

So in terms of the attitude towards violence, the interesting thing is that you can then, looking at particular societies in conflict, you can actually understand why people would find themselves either compelled to, or would need to, make *recourse* to acts of political violence in order to pursue particular kinds of interests they have. Or use it almost as a way of communicating the grievances they have within a particular kind of society.

In certain circumstances it is necessary to engage in conflict in order to achieve what is valued as a principled outcome.

David Shapiro: There are certain cases which involve important principles in which I am very pro-conflict. The first 15 years I was practising law, I was very much involved in issues, in civil liberties issues. Those cases couldn't be settled, I wasn't interested in settling those cases. I was out to kill the guy [without being killed]. And I did. I did that for 15 years. In effect, given a certain kind of case, I am very pro-conflict.

No, [conflict does not scare me]. The older I got and I moved away from principled issues and basically, while still principled issues, they were really money-driven; I early came to the notion that every case has hair on it. Every case. Every case has got a problem with it. There is no a perfect case anywhere. There is always going to be a problem. And essentially what one tries to do is look if I can get a really good settlement for my client. Why start running risks I don't have to run? You try to get the best settlement you can even though you are very prepared that they didn't come up with what you thought was a reasonable approach. Again you didn't go into this nonsense about positional bargaining. You said, this is what the case is worth, this is what I want... and they were arguing up and down. It took them six months. OK. And I said forget it. We're going to trial. That's enough. And you're getting a steal. You're getting a steal.[2]

It is necessary to recognise that positive professional and personal attitudes to conflict can be viewed 'as an essential stage to progress and change, which of course can be destructive as well as constructive' (Yvonne Craig) or as a principled strategy. Furthermore, these attitudes do change as a result of experience, disillusion, or the passage of time.

Yvonne Craig: In my work I don't [find conflict difficult or shy away from it]. In my personal life I have noticed the change whereas in the past when I was younger I found it quite exciting and stimulating, now at 80 [years old] if something goes wrong in the house – I've just been told that one of my gas fires is unsafe – the conflict involved in that situation makes me panic. Because I don't want to have the whole of my fireplace out. I think that is age. The conflict that we are having with the landlord. I might require a mediator to deal with them. [Conflict] which is contingent upon my personal comfort and peacefulness [doesn't excite me any more]. I'm being a little frivolous here.

Dealing with conflict

According to Gulliver (1979), mediation serves a negotiation process and the role of the mediator can only be understood within an understanding of that process. This encompasses a necessary, relatively early phase – the phase of 'exploring the field' – when the emphasis is likely to be on differences between the parties rather than on their common interests. The messages passing between the parties are intended not to influence or shift the other, but to explore the dimensions of the field within which further negotiations are to occur. This is when the parties have to have the opportunity to experience what Douglas refers to as the 'exhaustion of their demands', warning that premature movement robs them of this experience: 'the exhausting of topics offers one of the most useful criteria for measuring the timeliness of movement.' At this stage initial maximal claims and demands are likely to be set and extreme assertions expressed. 'There are vehement demands and counter-demands, arguments and counter-arguments' (Douglas 1962, pp.14, 42). This is recognised to be the stage of greatest hostility between the parties and of greatest distance, a distance that is necessary if subsequent movement is to be apparent.

One understanding of how the mediator ideally goes about managing the conflict is summed up as:

> the attempt at limiting all complaints and requests to their objective contents. Philosophically speaking, the conflict is reduced to the objective spirit of each partial standpoint, so that the personalities involved appear as the mere vehicles of objective conditions. In the case of conflict, the personal form in which objective contents become subjectively alive must pay for its warmth, color, and depth of feeling with the sharpness of the antagonism that it engenders. The diminution of this personal tone is the condition under which the understanding and reconciliation of the adversaries can be attained, particularly because it is only under this condition that each of the two parties actually realizes what the other *must* insist upon. (Simmel 1908a, p.148).

In practice, how mediators respond to the conflict arising in mediation varies, depending on their theoretical orientation, practice model and individual style. Some mediators, for example, disallow the overt expression of conflict between the parties, particularly if it is focused on the past (for example, this is an explicit tenet of the approach of Dr John Haynes (1993) whose view is that the past is where the problem is while the future is where the solution lies); some consider helpful the limited expression of powerful negative feelings, termed by some, 'ventilation', and others regard the opportunity to express anger and fault arising from the past, as a positive source of energy leading to clarity and strength (for example, Grillo 1991).

A. General approaches to dealing with conflict

Conflict is viewed as an opportunity for personal development and social change

Yvonne Craig: It is the work of a mediator to assist people in themselves seeing conflict as an opportunity for personal growth and for social change that is going to be beneficial and enjoyable. Having said that, of course, one sees that in any situation in which one mediates and indeed in the world, unresolved conflict and the stages leading up to conflict can be associated with pain, hatred and suffering.

Constructive management is the key

Tony Whatling: I do think conflict is actually quite essential in practically everything we do. The key clearly is whether it is constructively managed. When I am teaching social work management skills and management training, a lot of the work I do is about managing change and conflict constructively. So there's a lot of cross-over between the learning I have gained in mediation and in helping people manage conflict in organisations. So I think [conflict] is inevitable. It's a question of how you can get people to do it more constructively, take control of it rather, don't let it control them. So I'm much more comfortable with it now than I grew up to be.

Conflict as a positive means of making personal and professional links

Costanza Marzotto: The conflict is a basic instrument to build ties, not only in the family context, but also in the professional and teaching context. But it is also true that people are afraid to fight! When I meet people who try to avoid the conflict or use the conflict to contaminate all the relation, I try to fix the limits of the controversial. I have learnt in my personal and professional experience to remain in the middle of the conflict and with patience I have found a possible solution. For me the conflict is a positive occasion to regenerate/to revive the relations in the family context or in the community situation.

Learning not to show the effects of conflict – maintaining 'unflappability'

Andrew Acland: What it suggests is that however churned up [by the conflict] you are inside you don't show it. Certainly this was a hard lesson. I used to be flappable. Certainly I can remember in my very first experiences finding the whole thing extremely difficult. Personally not to get emotionally involved in it, but also not to show it – I found that very hard. And there was very much learning I had to do. I think if you don't have any reaction to conflict at all then you are probably not sufficiently sensitive to what it does to other people actually.

Recognising when the situation of conflict makes mediation unsuitable

Recognition of whether a situation is mediable or not involves acknowledging that some conflict may not be amenable to conciliatory approaches whatever the area of dispute, industrial, family or international. As has been noted already above:

> **Marian Liebmann:** ...it depends what the conflict is about, and you know whether you think it's mediable or not. *Some things are, some things aren't.* One of the most intractable types of conflict is where one or probably both sides says, well that can never be because in 1389 XYZ took place. There are historical things. You get this in Northern Ireland, you get this in Israel and Palestine, and you get this in Serbia and Kosovo. And there is no way out, I haven't found a way out of those situations really.

Practice models vary in the extent to which structure is deployed to address conflict. Shuttle mediation separates the parties physically in separate places and the mediator moves between them. Structural and procedural features should exclude unsuitable cases and create safeguards to ensure a safe and calm forum for negotiation (for example, pre-mediation screening; the use of the caucus; separate time within a joint session, etc.) (see Roberts 2005).

B. Specific approaches to dealing with conflict

Two specific practice approaches for addressing conflict were highlighted by the contributors. The first approach, in the case of family conflict, is consistent with the contributor's view that the underlying reasons for conflict, including the purpose which it appears to be serving, need to be understood if mediation is to make progress. This approach explicitly highlights a controversial topic in the field relating to the extent to which it is appropriate for mediators to delve into the past (beyond, that is, that which is relevant for a proper understanding of the dispute). Some would argue that, while it is necessary to acknowledge past grievances, there is nothing about the past that can be negotiated – neither facts, values nor perspectives.

> **Christoph Paul:** For example if I have a couple in front of me and I realise that they are acting very aggressively, I see the conflict – either they show it or I feel that there is a conflict. I want to know it; I want to get into it. I don't waive the conflict. I really want to know it. I want to name it and I want to have it and I

want to have it in the room and I want to see how I can use the conflict, and can use what is beyond this conflict for them to help *them* to find a solution.

It takes me back into the past a little. Of course there is this way of not looking back and only looking to the future, and say we don't want to know what caused this problem. Of course I am not going to help people to solve all their problems and all the conflicts they have. But if there is a conflict I think it is necessary to look a little bit beyond it, to understand what created this conflict and what created this not only because of *their* situation, of the two [of them], but as well a little bit of what created this conflict within this person, within his personal history. And I think if I want to understand this person and help them find a solution, I have to understand quite a bit about his past.

Mostly I can't [do this in mediation]. I am not a trained therapist. And of course I would not dare to go too deep. But mostly I speak to them [about] what my hypotheses are and what I see then are [what] mostly people show to me. I react to their behaviour, to the way they move, how they sit, their voices, and this gives me a chance to look a little bit back. They give me something so it's not as if I'm asking beyond something that is not in room. I only think what is in front of me and in the room. What people show me.

The second specific practice approach for addressing conflict in practice relates to the industrial relations field. Here the typical structural and procedural approaches devised for managing conflict in the sessions are outlined. It is pertinent to note too that even where representatives, rather than the individual parties themselves, are engaged in the negotiations, the expression of powerful emotions in the process can play as much a part in the exchanges as in any family dispute.[3]

Roy Lewis: If you are doing a mediation most of it takes place with the parties in separate rooms so that solves that problem. Side rooms, caucusing, whatever you want to call it. [You are not putting them in the same room] because that's likely to make things worse. And that would be true again both of the collective and the individual sides. The bulk of the mediation activity would be with the parties being separate from each other, in separate rooms, and the mediators shuttling backwards and forwards between the two.

Again that involves certain things that are both ethical and may be bound by the terms of reference. The one thing you must not do is disclose information that one party doesn't want disclose to the other. But on the other hand, precisely how you put a point yourself to one of the parties, that doesn't get outside of that room…there can be a great deal of conflict, that would be apparent, especially I think, in individual employment disputes. With the collective disputes you can just have professionals on both sides who are viewing it professionally. But even then if it's reached the point of a third party intervention, the chances are emotions are running high. Again, faced with a choice between an arbitration and a mediation, I must say an arbitration is a lot easier, however difficult the actual technical problems you are dealing with, because you are not dealing with people's emotions, the people who are upset about something, feeling very strongly about something.

Summation

Whether conflict is regarded as a negative and inherently damaging phenomenon, or as a normal, even positive opportunity for change, there is consensus both that the 'conflict-ridden condition' is endemic in the context of mediation work and that the ability to successfully manage conflict is a vital skill required by the mediator in the pursuance of a difficult task (Douglas 1957, p.70). This requires a unique combination of qualities, knowledge and skills.

Notes

1. Intractable conflict, in its extreme form, is characterised by four main features – that it is protracted; that the goals giving rise to the intractable conflict are perceived as irreconcilable; that intractable conflicts are violent resulting in wars and terrorist attacks causing human devastation; and that the parties engaged in the conflict have vested interests – military, economic, and psychological – in the continuation of the conflict. It is possible, however, that those societal beliefs that perpetuate intractable conflict can be modified positively by a variety of means including the opening up of new perspectives and alternatives to conflict, for example, by involving a mediator and by the use of problem-solving workshops. In this way a the transition can be effected from intractable to tractable conflict (see, for example, the Middle East peace agreements of 1979 (Israeli–Egyptian) and of 1994 (Israeli–Jordanian) (Bar Tal 1998).
2. When asked about his personal attitude to conflict, this contributor replied, 'You'll have to ask my ex-wives'!
3. Because the parties mostly do not know each other in victim–offender mediation, there is, curiously, much less overtly expressed conflict in comparison with other mediation fields.

Mediation

5

The Nature and Purpose of Mediation

> ...mediation still represents an elusive, fugitive label, presently resorted to all too easily and with little precision in the context of contemporary transformations in the management of disputing.
>
> (Roberts and Palmer 2005, p.153)

This picture of manifold and confusing development, associated with what Roberts and Palmer describe as the West's re-discovery and institutionalisation of mediation in the latter part of the 20th century, may be contrasted with the greater clarity of an earlier period when leading theorists of the past century were agreed on the defining characteristics of mediation, observable across cultures and across times. Mediation has been distinguished clearly from other interventions, in particular from that other primary form of third party decision-making, namely, adjudication (see for example, Simmel 1908a; Fuller 1971[1]; Gulliver 1979; and for a comprehensive analysis of developments, Roberts and Palmer 2005).

The mediator is distinguished as a disinterested, non-aligned third person,[2] facilitating communication exchanges between the parties that lead towards their own consensual joint decision-making. The mediator has neither a stake in nor any authority to impose an outcome on those parties. The non-determinative nature of the mediator's authority and a non-partisan alignment within the parties' negotiations are recognised to be the two core characteristics of a mediator's role and function. The difference between mediation and other forms of decision-making has been summed up in this way: mediation 'involves helping people to decide for themselves'; arbitration (and adjudication), on the other hand, 'involves helping people by deciding for them' (Meyer 1960, p.164).

Beyond this core and perhaps simplistic differentiation, consensus about what constitutes the purpose (or purposes) of mediation cannot be assumed. Complexity emerges in the light, not only of the rapid proliferation of mediation training bodies and practitioners, adopting a multiplicity of approaches, models and styles of practice (all labelled as mediation), but also of the growing ambition of practitioners in making expansive claims as to what mediation can or should achieve. This is exemplified in one debate that enlivens the field, most recently and notably, that generated in North America in relation to the fundamental distinction postulated between the so-called 'problem-solving' and 'transformative' purposes of mediation (for example, Bush and Folger 1994, 2005; Gaynier 2005).

If ultimately what is at stake is the protection both of the public as well as the integrity of the mediation process, expectations of mediators relating to the purpose of their intervention must obviously be consonant with those of their clients. Furthermore, there needs to be conceptual congruence on the fundamental issue of the purpose of mediation, not only between mediators and the parties, but also with other professionals, and funding bodies (for example government agencies providing legal aid for mediation). Congruence of purpose is bound up crucially too with expectations as to what does or does not constitute success or failure of the process and with officially sanctioned ethical and professional codes of practice and approved standards of training, practice and evaluation.

In the light of the current complexities outlined above, the extent of the congruity amongst the contributors in relation to their understandings as to the nature of the purpose of their task is noteworthy, particularly as there has been little, if any, direct or indirect exchange, formal or informal, across the diverse fields, developing largely in isolation of one another. Three aspects of this subject will be explored – the perspectives of the contributors on the purpose(s) of mediation, on the nature of mediation as an autonomous intervention, and on whether or not there are any qualitative advantages of mediation over other forms of dispute resolution.

The purpose of mediation

Perspectives converge not in any view about *the* purpose of mediation, that is, that one purpose fits all mediation situations, but in the view that there is a spectrum of possible purposes ranging from the most idealistic to the most pragmatic depending, predominantly, on the particular *context* of practice. Overall, what unites practitioners across fields is the common view that mediation provides *an opportunity* for *the parties* to achieve what *they* want to achieve, whether it be the settlement of a dispute or some less specific purpose such as an improvement in personal communication. It is also the common view that the achievement of more that one objective creates 'added value' and therefore elevates the success of the outcome accordingly. There is consistency too in the view that it is *the parties'*, rather than the mediator's, expectations that are what matters.

The idealistic purpose – moral, political and social

It is perhaps paradoxical, though not surprising, that those who highlight a larger purpose to their mediation task have worked in the most difficult of circumstances, the realm of international conflict. This is an arena where the work of intermediaries is acknowledged to be extremely complex, slow and painstaking, 'with few breakthroughs or outright success' and where 'much of the work is, by its very nature, quiet and behind the scenes' (Princen 1992, p.4). Before negotiations even start, much has to be done to ensure that expectations of the disputing parties over the mediation intervention itself (its norms and procedures) converge. A complexity of a different order, one specific to international disputes, lies in the connection that has been drawn in the literature between the conception of the nature of the mediatory role and the purpose of the task. In this context what is significant about the two kinds of intermediary roles is their differing impact on the disputants and their interaction, the 'neutral mediator' achieving the purpose of enhancing direct interaction while the 'principal mediator' is better perhaps at securing agreements (Princen 1992).

This view appears to be confirmed by all the contributors working in the field of international conflict as 'neutral mediators'. The purpose of mediation is thus described by the most experienced and longest serving.

> **Adam Curle:** Well, [the purpose of mediation is] primarily achieving a sort of degree of – I can't think of the right word now – but a degree of non-agitation, a calming down, which would bring about a gradual resumption of good relationships, a gradual cessation of suspicion, sheer hatred, gradually these things dying down. A very good example, of course, is the Marshall Plan in Europe.

Another contributor, drawing directly on that heritage, expands that ideal in more precise directions, describing the combination of purposes that could be involved, practical and transforming, and the parties' ultimate responsibility for a solution.

> **Mark Hoffman:** The long-term aim is to contribute to societies in conflict situations to resolve successfully that conflict to be able to bring about constructive management of it. That may be helping to foster communication between the parties and communications within the parties, in their capacity for innovative and critical thinking. It may actually be developing certain sets of skills basically involving a kind of social capital within those groups in society who may not have the skills to engage in the negotiation and the mediation process.
>
> I think the lodestar through all that, is conflict resolution and transformation. I use those [as] terms of art…but from our point of view, and the principle is in a sense derived from people like Burton and Curle, the solution has to lie with the parties themselves. It is not something that can be imposed from outside and so rather than bring them the solution and how to get them to it…it is drawing

out of them what would be an acceptable solution between the various parties involved in the conflict that would make it work. Burton's view is [that you] need to be an expert in process rather than be an expert about the particular conflict, and what's at stake and appropriate solutions, [that it is] actually undesirable to have somebody in the team with that expertise about the particular conflict situation. Burton's argument was the less you knew about the conflict in terms of detail, the better you might be because then you could bring in examples of other kinds of conflict and be more process oriented. I have doubts about whether that's sensible.

Another account illustrates the scope of purpose and the complexity arising from the separate yet linked, multi-layered levels of interaction involved.

Diana Francis: I think it [the purpose of mediation] involves all those levels [settlement, problem-solving, transforming relations, etc.]. At the level that I am usually working, which means middle and grassroots levels, it would be very much about changing perceptions. So building more constructive relationships, deconstructing enemy images, finding common ground, improving understanding. And then also, with luck, finding common agendas and even the possibilities for working together, or at least in the knowledge of each other. And the words 'peace constituency' come to mind. So that in broader terms you become part of the body of people who are encouraging their political decision-makers in the direction of peace.

Sometimes you have, I think, to be a bit of a sort of self-deceiving idealist to think any of this makes any difference. I think what I do think is that 'reality' is not just what gets done at the official level in making history. Reality is also people's lives, wherever they are lived. It's all relative and it's all transient. So as Adam [Curle] would have told you, the people in Osijek (Croatia)[3] failed to stop a war, but actually kept alive a community of decency, respect. Even if they then all had been killed, the reality of what happened is different from the reality of what would have happened if they hadn't been there. It's a different reality with those people in or out. And given that most violent conflicts give way to some kind of, however an imperfect, peace eventually, for whatever reason, it matters that some people keep certain values alive, behave in certain ways, save some lives, having something to hand on to other people who want to make life better for themselves and others.

A final quote illustrates the explicit moral idealism influencing this contributor, incorporated in the combination of purposes ascribed to mediation, one social, the other individual and personal. This depiction of litigation and adjudication as conflict resolution methods coincides with that of Simmel, who, a century ago, described legal conflict as 'the most merciless type of contestation because it lies wholly outside the subjective contrast between charity and cruelty' (Simmel 1908b, p.85).

> **Andrew Acland:** I'll give you my high-minded spiel on this. It's very simple. Since we crawled out of the primal swamp however many million years ago, we have only had established a reasonably settled form of civilisation at all for the last thousand years at best, and arguably for much less than this, and in some places there is still a way to go. But even in the most 'advanced' societies, frankly our conflict resolution methods are still Stone Age. The courts are effectively a more sophisticated version of Stone Age man with the club. They are adversarial; they are basically about who has the power and the money and can win the fight. This is too primitive. The judicial system is simply a more sophisticated version of trial by combat. And I just don't think that it's good enough to resolve the complexities of modern life. I think we need something which is less costly. I think it's a very blunt instrument. One of the things I would like to say to any commercial mediator or matrimonial mediator, that every time you help people to resolve a dispute by non-adversarial means, you are actually advancing the cause of civilisation, because you are teaching people how to resolve conflict without belting each other round the head. That is the moral cause.

The shared goal for party control

The emphasis on the opportunity that mediation provides for individuals to sort out their own affairs is shared by all the contributors whatever their field of practice. This purpose may be expressed in a variety of ways.

> **Andrew Acland:** The main purpose of mediation, as I see it, is to help people take responsibility for resolving situations in which they find themselves. I don't think it is the responsibility of the mediator to get a solution. You can say, in a form of shorthand, what a mediator is paid for is to get a settlement. But that is a very reductionist, somehow, approach to it. I think what a mediator should aim to do is to give the parties the best possible *chance* of finding a mutually acceptable solution. As soon as you start beating yourself up about your responsibility for getting a settlement, you are probably looking at the wrong things.

In remarkably similar language, a commercial mediator makes the same point.

> **Tony Willis:** I can give it [the purpose of mediation] to you in a short form. It is to give people the maximum possible chance of doing what *they* want to do. If you ask what's the product that we're selling? What's on the tin? It is, for most of the cases I do, and most of the lawyers who come to you, it is to settle. That's what they come to you for…the lawyers who are the gatekeepers. They come to you because they want to go through the process and nearly all of them, there are rare exceptions, but most of them, because they recognise that it is in their clients' interest to give them the maximum possible chance of trying to crack something themselves. And that's what I'm there for. Some people, I think foolishly, say that they're *only* here to achieve a settlement. I recognise, and have done for a *very* long time, that's not what I'm *only* there for – and that there are cases that are not

> suited to mediation, and on the other hand, it's a very good thing for them to have tried...and you've just given them a chance. You've given them, most times, a structured, or if you like, a properly and constructively, structured way of trying to seek out a solution. In the end the decision is down to them. You're not there to guarantee anything. You're there to do the absolutely, to do the most professional job you do and to do the best you can – to give them the best chance of doing what they really, really want to do...what they really, really want to do.

In the field of community mediation a similar view prevails.

> **Marian Liebmann:** I think it [the purpose of mediation] can be all those things, but I think it should be up to the parties concerned what they want out of it. This is where I part company with the transformative mediation advocates. It may be I have got it wrong, but they seem to be saying, we have decided that what people most need is to have their relationships transformed and then everything else will be easy. While the second half of that might be true, I don't think I've got a right to say to somebody, 'You need your relationships transformed.' And if somebody says, 'What we want is to resolve this particular dispute, we don't want to be friends with them, we just want to get this sorted out,' that's fine. Because I think you can do all those things.
>   And sometimes people set out with the one aim and achieve the other. Very often they say, 'I'm never going to talk to them, I'm too far gone to be friends, but we do need to sort out this particular issue for us to carry on living side by side.' And they end up helping each other and going out of the room and talking for 20 minutes on the doorstep. And it's quite obvious that something in their relationship has shifted.
>   I went on a couple of days training in the transformative mediation model and I thought some of the questions were good, some of their questioning techniques, but those are things I would want to use in ordinary mediations. It's the standard question: 'Tell me, things sound really bad now but – was there a time when you and your neighbour got on really well?' You would ask that anyway. I can see the point of transformative mediation in the US, where a lot of mediation has got coerced into this settlement-driven thing.
>   If people provide the money they want outcomes, and so people feel pressured to get people to agree. And I don't think most British mediation services have got to that stage. The general arrangements are usually that people will report back to authorities like housing departments. 'Yes, they came to an agreement, though we can't tell you what it is. They came to an agreement and that particular conflict is sorted.' Or, 'No, they didn't come to an agreement so it's back in your patch and the housing department has to do whatever you do.'

The situation involving the elderly living in sheltered housing illustrates how the institutional framework can affect every aspect of a person's life, both in relation to the cause of dispute, the effect of conflict, and the likely impact of mediation. Circumstances may circumscribe the chances for reaching more than a limited concrete solution though, even so, higher hopes may be realised such as an improved relationship.

Yvonne Craig: [In respect of success of mediation], well, in concrete terms in my work for Age Concern, what Age Concern like to see, what they call a success, is a nice written agreement whereby one party says they will do this, the other party says they will do the other and both agree. And what happens is that, again in the process of mediation if such an agreement is forthcoming, we write it out there in their presence in *their* words. We itemise it, 1, 2, 3, using names, Mrs So and So, we try to do it for each person who makes an offer in terms, or in their own words. We read this agreement out to them. Anything you'd like to change? Anything we've got wrong? Anything we didn't hear correctly? Sometimes they don't like this or that.

Then we ask them, once they are satisfied that that is what they want, that is what they have agreed, we invite them to sign it. We witness the signature as independent mediators. That is taken back to the Age Concern office, it is printed out beautifully and each party is sent a copy. If it is between two residents, they know that we do not send a copy to management. It is all confidential and they know it. If they want to show management [it is up to them]. That's the process. If that is a genuine agreement, I am pleased; the parties are pleased; my co-mediator is pleased. So we are pleased with that and it's a bonus. We are double pleased if we feel that, apart from the agreements for situational changes – those are the easiest ones and those are the most successful – if that situation agreement is also the product of a relationship enhancement, that may not be written into the agreement. But then of course my co-mediator and I, we have a giggle coming back. Wasn't it wonderful. That's the real pleasure. When we feel that people are going to be able to talk together in future when they haven't before. But we don't have any long-term expectation of peace and resolution.

Because of this, some of these questions [remain] of mental ill health and decrepitude, and living in boxes next to one another, and sheltered housing is always built in poor land miles away from transport. Because it's cheaper than land near railways. Not close to transport. No exterior life. They have to live in these boxes miles from any family, if they've got family. So I have no messianic belief that the harmony that we hope we have established in that particular instance is going to be with that person or those people for the rest of their lives in that sheltered housing.

An improved relationship is one hoped for too in the family context.

Tony Whatling: …if a couple transform the crisis that they have come in with into some reformatting of their relationship and their lives as people and they are happy, even though they don't necessarily reach settlements, that's a good piece of work.

The mediators and the parties are not the only ones whose expectations as to purpose and notions of success are of significance. These expectations have implications inevitably for funding bodies of mediation, for example, in the government provision of publicly funded family mediation through legal aid administered by the Legal Services Commission (LSC). Mediation is no different from other professional activities in having to meet the demands of the 'new accountability' that have characterised the government trend towards quality assurance over the last decade represented, in particular, in the abstract system of oversight and control of the audit with its recognised financial and quantifiable limits (O'Neill 2002).

The audit combines with pressure to accept an externally introduced notion of 'success' defined in terms only of cost-effectiveness, i.e. measurable, quantifiable outcomes that reflect government priorities, such as reducing legal aid expenditure particularly on family disputes. The current LSC definition of a successful mediation is one where the clients who participate in mediation do not subsequently apply for legal representation and there is, therefore, diversion from contested legal proceedings. This approach cannot take into account more elusive, though no less important, indices of success that represent the unique 'process' advantages of mediation such as improved understanding and the reduction of conflict. These dilemmas of external funding and regulation are not confined to the arena of government funding of family disputes, as the same problem, of *demonstrating* mediation outcomes, particularly to donor funders, taxes those working in the context of international mediation.

Mark Hoffman: And because you're often working at the level of relationships, ideas, concepts, perceptions, it's actually very difficult to measure this. I remember after one of the first workshops we did in Moldova. We went back and we had a communication from the then Head of OSC (Organisation for Security and Co-operation in Europe) saying, 'I don't know what you did with these guys but you completely rearranged their mental furniture. They are now talking with each other in a different way and are using a different kind of language.' But you can't measure that.

The aspiration for a negotiated settlement

A pragmatic purpose, unsurprisingly, predominates as the central but by no means exclusive focus of the task, particularly in the majority of commercial mediations. That is not to say that larger aspirations may not occasionally be fulfilled. The perspectives of two commercial mediators testify to this larger hope highlighting, at the same time, the kind of practical constraints associated with the context and content of commercial mediation practice.

Philip Naughton: I think it very important to recognise that the principal function of mediation is simply to improve the prospects of succeeding and resolving a dispute through settlement negotiation. And in very few cases, I'm afraid, is one significantly adding value in the aspects which are so loved by those who eulogise about mediation as a process. It's pretty down to earth.

One thing which is noteworthy is that nowhere is it mentioned that in most commercial cases, probably in the majority of commercial cases, insurers are involved. And insurers are only interested in one thing – which is How Much? There may be different aspects…but essentially it is How Much? And I allow, I immediately allow for the position that it is different in family mediation; it is different in employment mediation; it is different in many public law fields and in community mediation. Absolutely. In commercial mediation it is always strived for – how can we add value in this case? How can we make this palatable? But it is not often that one achieves it. It certainly does happen – it happened in the case I did last week. I think there's the opportunity that you get in mediation rather than the function of mediation.

Greater personal satisfaction comes with the 'added value' outcome.

David Shapiro: Let's face it. Every mediator will tell you that if I can create a win/win out of this, no matter what they pay me, OK, somebody's paying me extra. That's the reward. The answer to that question [can there be a more elevated purpose such as better understanding] is that it depends on what kind of mediator you are. If you are a family mediator the answer is yes. If you are a commercial mediator the answer is probably no.

While the settlement of the dispute is an important objective, another, as important, is to avoid the parties finding themselves worse off at the end than at the start of mediation.

Roy Lewis: [The purpose of mediation] depends on the terms of reference. But the typical one is to try and encourage the parties to settle a dispute in terms that they agree but with the mediator's assistance. Regarding improving relationships, that's rather ambitious. But of course in the collective labour relations field that is actually sometimes the explicit purpose of the exercise. What you don't want to do at any time, I think, as a mediator, or indeed as an arbitrator, is make matters worse if you can possibly avoid it. That must be very true in the family field. Whatever you do you don't want to make it even worse.

It is noteworthy that those mediating in the family field, in Europe and in Britain, display a similar caution, a modest approach even, both in their views about the purpose of mediation and in defining what constitutes success and failure. The parties' improved capacity to negotiate in the future without the assistance of a third person is certainly one recognised index of success.[4] A German perspective of a mediator, working in inheritance as well as the divorce and separation aspects of family disputes, identifies another view about the meaning of failure.

Christoph Paul: I think it is a very idealistic view saying that you transform relationships, that you change, or you give them the idea how to live, their lives generally. For me it is sufficient if I say I settle the dispute. Finally, if the result is that the experience of the mediation gives them the idea how they might settle disputes themselves, without me, I think that would be a great success. Sometimes I say it – 'You are so good why don't you continue on your own.' But there is one thing in German mediation, we don't have any tradition of contacting the people after the end of the mediation. There is also no [such] tradition in our work as a lawyer. If the dispute is settled, no matter how, by the court or if it is settled in mediation, you say bye-bye and that's it. And I think it's a pity. I think for the people it would be helpful to be somehow reminded of the experience they [had] during mediation. It [the absence of feedback] is [a matter of] time and organisation. I think it's a lack of quality. You asked about transforming relationships. It would be wonderful but probably too ambitious. A successful mediation is when at the very end the clients say, 'You helped us in settling our dispute. You helped us.' But you must be sure it's *their* work. It's not the work of the mediator. Failure is just the other way round. If they say *you* did a good job.

It is noteworthy that, while emphasis may be placed on fulfilling the expectations, not primarily of the mediator, but those of the parties, those expectations must fall within the stated remit of the *mediation* task. In the family mediation field the mediator has a particular responsibility to ensure that different objectives are not confused and that professional boundaries are maintained.

Lorraine Schaffer: Nearly all of those [purposes] of mediation [apply]. I don't subscribe to having one model or way of working. So I certainly don't think we are settlement seeking only, nor are we there to transform relationships. I think mediation is about, as it is defined, *assisting* people to find a way forward and also a practical role, which I think therapy and some things always are not. And I think that's an advantage of mediation. People want to come out with a plan of how they are going to see their children, they want to make decisions about how they are going to split their finances, whatever the issues are. If they are in a neighbour dispute, they want a way they are going to deal with noise problems, whatever it is. So I think there is a practical side which is very useful.

And I think we are really there to facilitate people trying to find an answer to their difficulties. So if communication is something that is important to them and they are of the mind, the kind of people that want to talk about relationships, that's fine. And I think as mediators we can help them with that. If they are not interested in that and they want just a solution then that's what we are there to do. What people want probably what we don't always do, I think if you are a transformative mediator only, and you are quite clear that is your approach, then I think you should say to clients this is how I see my role. I think we introduce

> mediation in order to assist them to make arrangements that are in the children's interests, all of those things. Maybe that isn't enough.

There is convergence of contributors' perspectives in the recognition that the context of practice – substantive, institutional and circumstantial – can have a significant impact on the weight the parties themselves might attach to their expectations of mediation, its purpose and outcome. Perhaps the following quote from a mediator, who has worked in several areas of practice, exemplifies this most vividly in relation to the context of elder mediation that she has pioneered.

> **Yvonne Craig:** There again I don't have an ideological view about this [the purpose of mediation]. My view is responsive to whatever is needed. It comes and sometimes it is, if you like, a high ideological thing. Sometimes it is just a very concrete situation that can be improved. Sometimes a relationship can be transformed as we know when two people suddenly realise [for the first time that] they are making somebody miserable. And very occasionally you can get this flowering. People hug where they only swore at each other before. I do not have any messianic views about personalities being transformed, particularly ageing people who are very formed. One interesting thing about working with older people and this question of empowerment is that – it is well known in other spheres but it is particularly important in ageing conflicts – when you are angry the hormone of adrenalin is strong. And older people who are on the whole losing their hormonal essences, being angry is a flash of adrenalin. It makes them feel great. It makes them feel once again on top of the world. Being angry is quite therapeutic for older people. And of course we legitimise anger. We just say, well, it is *how* we express our anger, are we hurting somebody? The ageing thing is important because we are all ageing. It's one thing that comes to all of us.

Overall, contributors are agreed that a core purpose of mediation is the opportunity it affords the parties to attempt a more consensual approach to sorting matters than would otherwise be available. The practical, concrete settlement of a dispute is not perceived to be the only purpose of mediation, important though this may be. As important is the objective of improving communication between parties in conflict. In addition, another purpose, in the longer term, is to achieve an improved capacity in the parties to negotiate together in the future. In the international sphere, the equivalent purpose is the acquisition of 'social skills' by groups or societies in conflict. A minority of mediators ascribe a higher purpose to mediation, affirming its potential to enable human beings to manage their conflicts in more constructive and more civilised ways.

Mediation as a discrete and autonomous form of intervention

Two themes emerge in answer to the question about perceptions of mediation as a discrete and autonomous activity. The first expresses the common view that mediation is founded in ancient human negotiation processes where a non-aligned third person might intervene – out of goodwill, social altruism or with a personal interest in peace making – in the affairs of others, whether as a stranger, neighbour, friend or as a member of the family or community. All, in hoping to achieve the restoration of 'normality' and good relations, could be said to have an interest at stake in the matter. In very simple terms, mediation is about getting people to talk to one another again. Talking is, after all, an everyday process and one of the most important means of avoiding trouble (Roberts 1979; Roberts and Palmer 2005). Mediation may be used as a tool in an array of different approaches and methods to enhance communication and resolve disputes. The consensus view is that while negotiation, mediation and conflict resolution skills may be deployed as part of a variety of interventions and in a variety of settings, the essentials required of mediation including an impartial presence of the mediator, and the confidentiality, make it a discrete intervention, distinct in fundamental ways from other interventions, however similar.

The second theme focuses on the risks that arise from a lack of clarity, in the public mind especially, about what intervention is being offered – particularly where this is a consequence of a combination, blurring or dilution of roles and functions. Dangers are compounded by increasing confusion associated with the development of a complex variety of dispute resolution and conflict management approaches, especially the motley of hybrid interventions occurring in the precinct of the courts, proffered by court officials carrying other, often incompatible, functions (for example, mediatory and assessment/report-writing functions of Court Reporting Officers operating in respect of family disputes).

Mediation and a 'suite of similar processes'

The relationship of mediation to other interventions has been a vexed topic of great interest to practitioners and to scholars. Controversy has arisen too as the more established profession involved in dispute resolution, the legal profession, has suddenly abandoned the exclusive partisan, advisory and representative role that it traditionally monopolised, laying claim to being the best equipped to offer the role of professional neutral. It is not fortuitous that this new appreciation of the virtues of non-partisan intervention coincides with the arrival of the new 'neighbour' and the threat that this is perceived to represent in encroaching on traditional turf (Roberts 2002; Roberts and Palmer 2005, p.157). While clarity is undisputed in respect of the *analytic* lines that have been drawn between the role of the mediator, the partisan, the adviser, and the arbitrator, it is recognised that there may well occur a merging of these roles where the impartial, facilitatory, advisory, directive and evaluative aspects shade into one another in practice. There are also other ways of intervening that may, at first sight, appear less than analytically distinct from mediation, particularly in relation to general management of conflict skills applied in different environments. Ultimately it is the purpose of the activity that determines that nature of the intervention. Some of these distinctions of role are disentangled in the context of practice in the environmental and organisational mediation field.

Andrew Acland: I see it [mediation] as a set of skills which can be used in a vast array of settings, from the very formal, as in mediation, to a way of dealing with the kids. So it is a set of skills which are useful. And I think it is management skill which is useful in most organisations. But then I can see also a place for a formal mediation in a very formal structure setting to deal with specific issues. This is [a] really interesting [question]. I think there is a kind of suite of similar processes. Mediation, and what I would call facilitation, which happens in contexts where there is possibly a lower level of conflict and the facilitator's job is to make a group simply be more productive than they would be without a third party there. For me mediation tends to be more directly conflict related. Though in fact I think that the roles are very, very, very similar. In fact, sometimes I think you switch from one to the other, almost moment to moment.

I am slightly worried by the concept of advisory mediation – or evaluative mediation – I'm slightly bothered by that because to me that is putting the third party into a quasi-judicial role. But it is giving them some authority over the content. I do think the separation of process and content is terribly important. And I'm quite sure that there is plenty of evaluative mediation. I'm sure it's very effective. After all, as somebody said to me once many years ago, what people want a third party to do ultimately, is to tell them what to do. But I think the third party should tell them what to do in terms of *how* to do it, not in terms of their content. Because you begin to dilute the principle that that is *their responsibility*. I think one of the things that mediation should always do is to take the responsibility away from the third party and put it back onto the parties themselves.

Let me stick my neck out here. I think going to the courts to adjudicate a commercial dispute is a way of ducking responsibility for the issues which you have created. Now I'm sure there are very good practical and pragmatic reasons for doing it. But on the whole people benefit from taking responsibility for sorting out their own problems and not giving them to somebody else to deal with.

I think the other thing for me is that once you have taken a position as a third party on a content issue then it is much harder for the parties to see you as impartial. I mean it must destroy your impartiality. There's certainly a risk of doing that. Very occasionally, again, I use the example of last week because it's fresh in my mind. There was one organisational point that they were struggling with. So I

> stopped the meeting and I said, 'OK, I am going to step out of role as your mediator/facilitator and I'm going to put on a hat as an organisational consultant.' I did it very explicitly and I said, 'If I was you this is what I would do,' and then I formally stepped back into the role. So to make an absolute separation between it. Because I felt that actually that would help them. But that is not blurring the roles.
>
> And I guess as an evaluative mediator you can do it. But I do think that you are doing that evaluation as the third party. I suppose you could step out of the mediation role and say, 'If I was an evaluator this is the value I would put on this case,' or something. I suppose you could do that, but I suspect that is slightly different – as soon as you put numbers on things, people immediately, their ears prick up in a way they don't if you're just telling them how to organise something.

In the context of international conflict it is clear that creative flexibility of response, rather than any rigid adherence to one fixed role, may be necessary if the momentum for making progress appropriately is to be maintained. Mediation may be but one of a suite of processes to be pursued in the light of changing circumstances. That does not mean that there need be any lack of clarity about what role is being deployed.

> **Diana Francis:** I think it's an interesting one [this question of the autonomy of mediation]. I think, in terms of my own approach, it is part of my philosophy of conflict transformation that you do not think of mediation as the be all and end all. It's not always the most useful thing to do. For instance, in the case of the Serb/Albanian dialogue over Kosovo, I mean political events shifted the whole thing into a quite other space and it reconstellated, if you like, in a very different way, with people working in their own individual contexts to address the *new* situation, which had been brought about not by them but by the military intervention. So if I said, 'Oh well, I don't mix things,' then I would have had nothing more to do with people…[but] actually I work with people in new ways and in the new context.
>
> And also if you did terribly well with your mediation, you went on to joint action plans. And if I was facilitating that bit, then it would be strategy and empowerment and a whole other bundle of things. So this is why I think I am tempted to say, 'Do you mean when I'm facilitating mediatory processes?' Because for me it is about I'm a facilitator supporting people who want to do things. And if at the moment that's having a dialogue which they couldn't otherwise have, then I'll do that. And if now, at this moment, they want to strategise together or separately then I'll do that. So it's a bit more of a fluid role really.
>
> It's not that I don't want to know what I'm doing and be clear about it, but because the storyline can be quite a complex and wandery one. Plus, it could be that, for instance, people who were part of a dialogue workshop were at the same time human rights activists in a much more partisan manner in another part of their lives. So they might have more lives than this one, in relation to the bigger

> conflict. And I think what is making this different is we are talking conflicts that are happening both at the level of the participants, but have a life of their own beyond those participants. And therefore the whole thing is going to be influenced in more complicated ways by external factors.

The degree and kind of complicated 'conflict situation dynamic' of the international sphere appears not to be replicated in other areas of conflict or dispute however intense or complex these may be. In respect of commercial mediation, lawyers, unsurprisingly, monopolise the practice with a very few notable exceptions. Therefore commercial mediators, as they are predominantly also practising lawyers, can routinely act in a multiplicity of adjacent roles – as advocates, representatives, negotiators, arbitrators, adjudicators and mediators. This could lend support, in theory, to an approach in commercial mediation that similarly welcomes the kind of creative fluidity of intervention possible, even desirable, in the international arena, though in less dramatic or life-threatening circumstances. One commercial mediator was of the view that lawyers can and do successfully play different roles within mediation because they have acquired the necessary expertise, negotiation knowledge and skills, in their legal capacity. He describes, for example, the way lawyers can be effective players in mediation as parties' representatives.

> **David Shapiro:** If a lawyer has the negotiating skills to be effective in a mediation, that's invaluable. That generally is softly, softly. It's well, let's take a look at the case, let's take a look at the issues. The mediator has raised this, he failed to raise another point which I think is helpful. He is in there buttressing the mediation process. That is the best. So to that extent mediation is not a discrete professional activity. The lawyer or representative who is able to use the mediation process to aid and assist the mediator, or pick the mediator up if he's fallen down, is a person who is invaluable to the process and so to that extent that is not discrete.

While clear differences of approach to mediating are identified, for example, in terms of how much case preparation is or is not necessary, commercial mediators place differing emphasis on the need for the role of the mediator to be distinct and autonomous.

> **Philip Naughton:** I think it [the issue of autonomy of practice] depends on what aspect you're looking at. Mediation is part of the dispute resolution toolbox – your word – which a lawyer should be able to use. So in the right case it becomes appropriate or would be appropriate to resolve the case by mediation – in other cases it may be important to press on at least for the while for obvious tactical reasons. The lawyer with the conduct of the case on behalf of the party, will have to think through or address the question of whether he should or she should mediate at this stage, adjudicate at this stage, sit around a table with the

other side, or just press on as far as he is as an actor in this field. I guess I tend to be, it's inevitable that I tend to be retained as a mediator or as an arbitrator or as an advocate and so my role in the particular case is determined, my actual role is determined by the manner in which I am appointed. Yes, [as a mediator] you take your lawyer's hat off – but you keep your passport!

Acknowledgment of the variety of roles that lawyers can play in processes of dispute resolution, particularly in relation to commercial issues, is not incompatible with an approach that places importance on distinguishing these different capacities unequivocally.

Tony Willis: I think if you are a professional mediator you have to take your lawyer hat off. It's an immense help, what the experience you have [is], what the understanding you have [is], all your implicit assumptions that come with having been doing a particular discipline for a long time, most of which you can't identify – are all there. It's part of why I knock on the door and come in and know that it works. Because instinctively something at the back of my brain tells me that's the right way to proceed. It [mediation] is, it should be, and it is increasingly a separate discipline. But it is so bound up in *my* field [heavy commercialism] with activities of [legal] professionals, that's a view that probably wouldn't be recognised by everybody. And I don't quite know where that will come out.

Maintaining the distinctness of the mediator task as an imperative of practice is not necessarily incompatible with deploying mediatory tools in the service of another professional role. That is the experience of the following mediator, working in Germany in commercial and family matters.

Christoph Paul: Actually I think it [mediation] is more autonomous. Not because of any theoretical aspects. There are so many mediation tools in the work of a lawyer that are helpful. And so many tools of a lawyer in the work of a mediator that are helpful. So I wouldn't say it's that. It is from the practice, from the aspect *as a practitioner*. When I do my ordinary work as a lawyer, I have to do one case after another. It all fits in here. Whereas when I then switch over to mediation it is something different. It is something different requested of myself. I would say the work as a lawyer is very fast work, you are always telling people what to do. And I think the mediator is not the one who is telling people what to do. The mediator is the one who is asking people what might be helpful for them.

There is a German proverb: '*Der Anwalt lenkt durch Sagen: der Mediator lenkt durch Fragen*' ['The lawyer guides by saying: the mediator guides by asking']. So [as] I see it, from the viewpoint of a practitioner, it is a challenge. It is a transition. As I was saying at the beginning, if I could live from mediation I would change my office, I would change everything, I would go to a round table not a square table. I would like two rooms.

The autonomy of the mediator role in relation to other interventions is asserted too in the family field in Britain. In Europe and Britain one main object of mediator training is to learn the disassociation of assumptions and practices of an existing profession in order to make the core transformation to the new role of mediator. This is in line with prevailing European and British codes of practice and standards of professional practice.[5] The requirement for the clarification and maintenance of professional boundaries is of particular importance in the context of family disputes where, because of the personal vulnerability normally associated with the breakdown of relationships, some parties may need other sources of assistance, such as therapy or counselling.

> **Lorraine Schaffer:** I think mediation is autonomous and I think if you are being contracted as a mediator then that has its own professional standards and process, training all the rest of it. I do, of course, think people use mediatory skills and that having a knowledge about understanding conflict and how conflict arises and ways of managing conflict are very essential for anybody if they are working with people. I've certainly had cases where we start to get quite into the relationship. And I've stopped or they've stopped and said we seem to be moving into the realm of therapy and counselling. So I think there is very clear delineation between mediation and those things. We do stop and say, if these are the kind of things you want to go into in depth, it might be helpful if you go and see a therapist or a counsellor because in mediation it is not our role to do that.

The need for 'professional discernment' in recognising and maintaining professional boundaries is confirmed in yet another arena of mediation practice where the parties may well be vulnerable for reasons other than the break-down of personal relationships.

> **Yvonne Craig:** I think that it is essential today that social workers, doctors, schoolteachers, others in caring situations where they have responsibilities for people, should understand communication skills. Should be able to listen and should in their work be able to deal with minor conflicts, minor disputes, minor problems. And therefore I am in favour of – as I have done, I have trained nurses, I have trained social workers – I am in favour of training multi-disciplinary workers in communication skills that will help them to prevent unnecessary conflict and to deal with it.
>
> However, part of that training is about saying there are some disputes which are complicated, there are some disputes in which professional mediators are best employed. And therefore I try to raise in multi-disciplinary workers the need for them to have communication skills and also the awareness of when they need to step back and when they need to refer. I am very conscious of the fact that some people, particularly the poor, the ill-educated, suffer from having a multitude of professional workers on their doorstep. Some exploit that by telling their stories to four or five different people in order to get re-housing, in order to get more

> benefits, in order to get rid of the neighbour next door. But I do think that there is a good case for multi-disciplinary teamwork in some of the ways that I have suggested.
>
> Social workers and teachers, they were dealing with if I can use that horrible word 'low-level conflict' – and I hope I made it clear that those people should be specifically made aware that they needed to refer on to professionally trained mediators in very difficult cases. It's a question of *professional discernment*. I do see social work, advocacy, counselling and mediation as separate professions. What I see them as is working in teamwork, in multi-disciplinary co-operation. And not in nasty rivalry…

Another example from the practice of community mediation examines similar concerns, compounded where the mediator has co-existing qualifications in relevant adjacent fields.

> **Marian Liebmann:** You could be a therapist and a mediator but not at the same time. You could be a therapist that has a good grasp of mediation skills and uses those with good effect in therapy, which I quite often do, but I am not mediating at the same time. And I couldn't mediate if they had a problem. I wouldn't be the right person to mediate. So I thought your question also meant something different in the sense that there are a lot of lawyers who think, ah, mediation, here's another skill to add to our bow. I don't see anything wrong with that. I think it sits very well with a whole lot of other professional skills. But I don't think you can be doing the two different kinds of work, in the same case and at the same time. I think there probably is a place for somebody who is a mediator and can mediate in lots of different circumstances. And I think circumstances vary to the degree in which you need extra knowledge. So in some commercial mediations, or some workplace mediations, you might need some particular knowledge of the context.

The hazards of a lack of clarity of role, of blurring, of combining or of confusing interventions are acute, particularly where the assumptions, objectives and methods of different practices are potentially incompatible, where the parties are vulnerable, where the arena of practice, the coercive context of the court, makes it impossible for the fundamental principles of mediation, voluntariness of participation, impartiality and confidentiality, to be seen to operate. These concerns are well documented in the mediation literature (see for example, Haynes 1992; Roberts 1992a, 1997, 2006).

A better way?

The advantages of mediation are frequently cited in support of the claim that mediation can and does provide a qualitatively better way of sorting out people's quarrels than other, adversarial, dispute resolution processes, such as litigation or adjudication. The consensual decisions in mediation are made by those who have to live with them rather than by some third person, however wise and well-meaning. Retaining control over one's own decision-making can assist in the recovery of dignity and self-respect. Voluntarily fashioned agreements rather than imposed solutions are more likely to be adhered to because they are more likely to meet the needs and circumstances of the parties.

The procedural flexibility of the process allows issues to be addressed that may not be legally relevant but are important to the parties (ethical and psychological concerns, for example). The process of mediation, essentially forward-looking, can lead to enhanced communication and understanding and therefore to the reduction of conflict, benefiting not only the parties themselves but third persons directly affected by the outcome, children especially. The process benefits include the potential for an improved capacity in the parties to negotiate directly together in the future without recourse to intermediaries. More practically, evidence indicates that disputes are resolved more quickly in mediation than by adversarial means, and that costs, including legal costs, are more predictable and lower in the main, compared to lawyering or adjudication (Glasser 1994; Walker, McCarthy and Timms 1994; McCarthy and Walker 1996; Emery 2001).

Contributors' reflections on this question revealed its complexity and the further questions that needed to be addressed. Who is to decide if mediation is 'a better way'? Who does the work? Who are the beneficiaries of the process? Under what circumstances is the judgment to be made? What are the requirements necessary for mediation to be a better process?

Why mediation can be a better way

There was a virtually unanimous expression of the view that it is for those experiencing mediation, *the parties*, rather than the mediator, to decide whether or not the mediation process has essential benefits.

A small cluster of responses highlights the unique ways in which mediation has the potential to provide unequivocal benefits, unavailable in other processes. These reflected the range of fields. One perspective founded in the experience of the international field cited the qualitative advantages of mediation.

> **Mark Hoffman:** I *do* think that it [mediation] is a qualitatively better way of trying to deal with managing differences in society. That, in a sense, in terms of both building skills and social capital and so on, part of what the process is trying to do is to help societies draw on their own social capital in a way that allows them to manage difference without the recourse to acts of political violence...so in a sense building into society some institutional standard conflict resolution mechanisms. So yes, I deeply believe it is a qualitatively better way than the recourse to violence and other forms of [coercive] power.

Family mediators (one British and one German) and a community mediator describe their experience of how mediation in their experience can achieve qualitatively better outcomes, for example, in providing a 'learning experience and engag[ing] people to accept responsibility for what has happened and what can happen' (Tony Whatling).

Research backs the view that the beneficial experience of mediation lies in the opportunity it provides the parties, as negotiators, by participating in a dynamic process of exploration and learning, to personally experience the 'search process' (Stenelo 1972, p.192).

Christoph Paul: I think it [mediation] is a qualitatively better way. I'm pretty sure and I think there are also researches on that. That settlements that have been made in mediation hold more strongly than settlements that are made on the good advice of the best lawyer in the country. I think it has another quality. I have so many clients who have the experience of very difficult litigation in court and then finally they come to settlement, or if they come to settlement within the process of mediation, that is something very, very different. And of course mediation has the chance that better relationships are formed. And even the best settlement in court hasn't that. So I think it's different.

The community field yields a similar experience, again perceived from the parties' perspective.

Marian Liebmann: I think it [mediation] has a lot to offer in helping people to gain understanding of each other that they couldn't do any other way. I think it's also the only way that certain things would get sorted out but I think it has a much broader use really, building understanding.

Another perspective argues for mediation to be judged not as a method in itself but to the extent that it serves in the attainment of certain values.

Diana Francis: Well, I think negotiated, respectfully agreed and inclusively agreed settlements are the goal for, certainly, disputes and, wherever possible, wider conflicts. And that is a values question to me, because inclusiveness and respect and meeting the needs of all are matters of value. So to me that would be a goal. They may not be possible in a particular moment. *Mediation* is not a value in itself. It's at the service of those other values. And if people can manage to settle their disputes constructively, peaceably, respectfully, without the help of a mediator, hallelujah! And the chief work has to be done by the parties to the conflict.

In a labour relations context, the advantage of mediation, again from a party perspective, is that wider issues can be addressed than those that are legally relevant.

> **Roy Lewis:** I think the answer is that it depends. By and large I think qualitatively it [mediation] is a better way. What are the alternatives? No, I wouldn't put mediation in a hierarchy like that. Ultimately the parties have to get on with each other or not as the case may be. If they can resolve something themselves that's fine. If they can resolve something with third-party assistance that's fine. If they can resolve something, having been given an award by an arbitrator or a court, that's also fine. But the difficulty is that certainly if it comes to the court handed-down decision, though it might apparently suit the party that wins, because they might win 100 per cent, it isn't necessarily a way of resolving any underlying issue.
>
> So there can be situations where qualitatively an agreement could be better than at least a court decision. It's not so much [because of the process benefits]; it's more the end product. Because they can produce something that actually addresses some problem as opposed to simply processing a legal right. And if you process a legal right, well, you might win and that's it, fine; or lose, which may not be fine, but it doesn't necessarily address anything else other than whether a court is prepared to uphold that right. So you might still be left with much the same problem that you had before. Or it could be worse.

The limits of an adjudicated outcome of a legal dispute form part of the balancing of benefits as the following example from commercial mediation illustrates.

> **David Shapiro:** I think basically in the non-principle cases a mediated result is eminently more satisfactory than a litigated result. It's cheaper. It's quicker. It could very well be because the law may not be able to give you the remedy that you really want. And a negotiated remedy which in effect turns out to be everybody wins, nobody loses, may be a hell of a lot better than anything a court can give you. For example, in a libel case, the most a court can do is award you damages. In mediation, you can get a retraction basically, or 'nice words' about you. That, for many people, is a much more satisfactory outcome than getting £50,000 from some jury.

While early writings expressed feminist fears about the detrimental effects for women of mediation, unsubstantiated by empirical research, the prevailing view is that, as a process, mediation is not inherently good or bad, for women or for men, and that what is decisive is the skill and competence of the mediator (Menkel-Meadow 1985; Roberts 1996). Contributors' perspectives confirm this finding, endorsing an approach to mediation of healthy scepticism rather than overzealous promotion. In these examples, two powerful determinants are both identified as significant if there is to be any qualitative judging of the mediation process – first, the commitment and good faith of the parties *and*, in commercial mediations, their referring lawyers – and second, the institutional framework within which mediation provides an alternative.

> **Philip Naughton:** 'It [mediation] is not a better way; it is a different way. I get very concerned about the enthusiasm with which mediation is elevated to a sort of altar-like position[6]. It is a way of improving prospects of settling a case, for instance, and if you can settle a case, you should settle a case. Settling a case will always be cheaper, will normally be cheaper than fighting... There is an almost messianic fervour that one finds [a cause for concern]. Having said that, look what's happened today. There's a case for a claim for hundreds of millions which was listed to take eight months, where the parties probably would not have been able to settle without a mediator. It's a very good tool. It is a very efficient tool but 80 per cent of mediations, commercial mediations – I wouldn't say it is as high as that but they say 80 per cent settle – but 20 per cent don't, and they cost a lot of money. Mediation is not cheap in commercial cases.

The literature has long highlighted the fact that all private ordering, bilateral party negotiation, lawyer negotiations and mediation occurs, not in any vacuum but, on the contrary, within the famous 'shadow of the law', those public norms, values and legal rulings that constitute the 'defining context' within which informal negotiations are fashioned (Hamnett 1977, p.5; Mnookin and Kornhauser 1979, p.950). Research also reveals that, in practice, so far as lawyer negotiations are concerned, many cases settle for reasons that have nothing to do with moral or legal standards (Menkel-Meadow 1993).

In the context of commercial mediation practice, there is recognition of the necessity for an effective adjudicative framework, providing both the incentive for mediation *and* for third-party determination, should mediation fail.

> **Tony Willis:** I don't think I'd ever say that it [mediation] is just intrinsically better because that implies that it is a genuine alternative. It just isn't an alternative. Mediation wouldn't work, I don't think, except in rare exceptions, in a society where there is not an effective adversarial court system to sort things out. Because why the hell should people settle if there is not a judge across the road who is going to decide what is going to be the result, if necessary. Which is why there is a whole industry out there bringing mediation to countries where the judicial system doesn't work as if it's a panacea. It is a complete mistake. It won't work in societies where there is no efficient court system because *you need the range*.
>
> So I would never say mediation is intrinsically better as an alternative. I think it's intrinsically better when it works and leads to an agreement. But it is for the people in question who've reached the agreement to say whether it is intrinsically better at the outcome. There may be equivalent degrees of pain and suffering and that's right too... If they do a deal which is to be most effective... it's because they have got what they wanted and have got it by a process which is to them fair and explicable and with which they've engaged properly. In cases that don't settle on the day or shortly afterwards, again they [should] feel that they have engaged in a fair, productive, properly managed and explicitly sensible

> process. As you can see then, what's satisfactory, what's prudent, works for them and also what doesn't. That's what I was saying to you about giving them the chance. And that's what's on the tin, giving them the chance. The opportunity.

This emphasis on the parties' own experience, their meanings, their sense of fairness of the process, is one that recurs throughout these discussions. The parties' *responsibility* too is the other side of the coin of satisfaction: responsibility for making the most of the opportunity that mediation can offer. A mediator experienced in several fields of mediation practice adds extra freight to the common practice view that mediation requires the parties' motivation and good faith as participators. Mediators require a corresponding *discernment* to identify when this is lacking. This quality so described also recurs as part of the mediator's job to establish, wherever possible, prior to engagement, the suitability of the parties for the process.

> **Andrew Acland:** People do need to have the motivation. They have to want to actually improve the situation they are in and they have to be people who are minded to do it really. So one of the first questions I always ask people when they want me to do something is, What are the motivations? Why would people want to do this?
>
> The other thing, though, I would be wary of, and this partly goes right back to my very, very early experiences [in international mediation], I think there are situations in which you do not have people of goodwill. You have people whose nature and motivation is essentially destructive, in which mediation is not a good idea because it exposes other people to manipulation and dishonesty and all the rest of it. I think I remember writing in that first book, that mediators need a healthy sense of evil, the word psychologists hate but I've always defended on the grounds that there are certain people for whom ordinary ethics or morality or whatever, simply have no meaning – people who are sociopaths. And a sociopath in a mediation makes the other people very, very vulnerable. It is about them coming in good faith.
>
> And it's also about the *mediator* having some ability of *discernment* of what is really going on. I think discernment is a very important skill. I'm not sure whether it's a quality or a skill really. But that's a good theological word you see. I would hope I would discern it before it got as far as the mediation and would simply decline to work in that situation. I think that there has to be some minimum of goodwill and willingness to talk. If somebody goes into it with the intention of manipulating the situation to their advantage, I find I would rather, in that situation, they went to the court and hopefully got trounced. Because that is the way they are probably going to learn.
>
> Mediation has to be, is always, a learning process. If people are not willing to learn from it then I think it's doubtful about how valuable it is. It might deal with the immediate settlement but it does not actually fulfil what for me is the wider purpose, which is actually teaching people how to deal with conflict. It is not as

though they shouldn't go to mediation. But sometimes some people may learn more about conflict by losing badly than they will by reaching an amicable settlement.

Summation

Out of their extensive and wide-ranging experience, a consensus emerges amongst the contributors as to the nature and purpose of mediation. Convergence of views cohere around several central themes summed up below:

- The primary attention and worth afforded to *the parties* to mediation, their universe of meanings, their expectations and their definitions of success.

- The independence yet alliance of possible purposes of mediation, idealistic, pragmatic and relational, that co-exist as possibilities for the process.

- The importance attached to the objectives of the practitioners coinciding with those of the parties notwithstanding differences of emphasis that may be placed on meeting the specific requirements of the individual situation.

- The conspicuous absence of a language of duality that appears to drive a wedge amongst practitioners and theorists alike – as in the USA in relation to the problem-solving/transformative approach divide.

- While mediation exists as an autonomous and discrete form of professional practice requiring training, accreditation and continuing education, conciliatory tools can be deployed in the service of other professional purposes as long as there is clarity and an avoidance of role-blurring. The combination of incompatible roles creates risks of conflicts of interest and confusion, damaging to the core principles of mediation, impartiality and confidentiality in particular.

- Mediation as a process can, but may not necessarily, be a better way of resolving quarrels. What is undisputed is the view that mediation can provide an opportunity, in suitable circumstances, at least for negotiation to be attempted. Factors of relevance for achieving a fair and effective process include the expertise of the mediator; a conducive institutional framework that contains the full range of genuine dispute resolution alternatives, of which adjudication is central; and the good faith and commitment of participants including legal representatives.

These reflections cast doubt on the accuracy of the picture of the imprecise and 'fugitive' nature of mediation (as quoted at the head of this chapter). On the contrary, a clear, consistent and coherent view, based on practice experience across fields, emerges about the nature and purpose of mediation.

Notes

1. ...the primary function of the mediator...is not to propose rules to the parties and to secure their acceptance of them, but to induce the mutual trust and understanding that will enable the parties to work out their own rules. The creation of rules is a process that cannot itself be rule-bound; it must be guided by a sense of shared responsibility and a realization that the adversary aspects of the operation are part of a larger collaborative undertaking. (Fuller 1971, p.326)
2. '...impartiality consists in equal distance or equal closeness' (Simmel 1908a, p.152).
3. The Centre for Peace, Nonviolence and Human Rights was founded in 1992 in Osijek in Croatia by local peace activists with the central goal to 'both stimulate and preserve the values on which harmony can eventually be restored'. It offers a model of dealing with modern sources of violence through peace-making that focuses on restoring and preserving a sense of relatedness among people.
4. See the consumer study of family mediation where findings reveal that mediation did leave parents in a better position to manage *future* negotiations themselves (Davis and Roberts 1988).
5. The Council of Europe's Recommendation R (98)1 (1998) of the Committee of Ministers to Member States on Family Mediation makes clear that mediation should be conducted according to certain principles which mark it out from other interventions or dispute resolution mechanisms (S.37). Principle IV, 56 begins: 'This principle reaffirms the belief that mediation should be an entirely autonomous process.' The Code of Practice of the UK College of Family Mediators, S.4.4.4 stipulates: 'Mediators must distinguish their roles as mediators from any other professional role in which they may act and must make sure they make this clear to the parties.'
6. See Naughton, P. (2003) 'Mediators are Magicians: A Modern Myth.' A talk given to the Society of Construction Law, London.

6
The Principles of Mediation

> It strikes me that if you have some kind of grading scale for your institutions, like courts, schools, and hospitals, as to which gave the participants the most adult setting, it might be interesting to see how different institutions rank. Are you told what to do or asked what you want to do? Are you made to wait or is your time valued? Are you allowed to know what is going on or are you kept in the dark? Are you powerful or powerless? Are decisions made for you or do you get to make the decisions? Are you treated as a human being or are those qualities not considered? One of the things that strikes me in mediation is that it comes out much higher on that scale than many of our institutions and I think that is why it works.
>
> (Davis 1984, p.54)

It is significant that the task of mediation is itself *defined* in terms of its core principles – both ethical and professional. These are the impartiality of the mediator; the voluntariness of the process (because the mediator has no power to compel participation or impose an outcome); the confidentiality of the relationship between the mediator and the parties; and the procedural flexibility available to the mediator (McCrory 1981, p.56). McCrory goes so far as to say that if any of what he describes as the four 'fundamental and universal characteristics' of mediation are altered or if one or more is absent, then the process cannot be characterised legitimately as mediation. These core principles of mediation in defining the practice itself, going beyond the endeavour, valuable enough, of acting properly and ethically. These essential principles inform the panoply of safeguards – procedural, structural and professional – that are designed to ensure the realisation of a safe and fair process and outcome.

The views of the contributors on the question of what principles inform their practice of mediation yielded a remarkable consistency across fields of practice. The order in which they appear below does not reflect any hierarchy of the contributors – on the contrary, their interrelatedness is their conspicuous feature.

Respect

A core aspiration of mediation manifests in the responsibility of the mediator to treat each person with respect, in particular with respect for that person's own meanings and for his or her capacity to decide and make choices, through the exercise of critical reflection and the awareness of alternatives.[1] The contributors reveal how the principle of respect interlocks not only with other principles of mediation – impartiality, the autonomy of the parties – but also with other central aspects of practice, such as the quality of outcome, its fairness or justness. In its application to the international arena, the principle of respect is considered in this way:

> **Diana Francis:** ...I suppose respect is absolutely fundamental. And then perhaps the most feminine version of that would be care. So that respect is not just what I won't do to you, but implies a level of care and tenderness, actually. I don't know whether this is relevant here. There's a John Paul Lederach exercise which I use quite a bit in workshops, because it does seem to be a very useful way of having a conversation. There is a verse in the book of Psalms [Psalm 85 verse 10] which says mercy and truth have kissed, justice and peace have shaken hands together. I think that's the wording. So you ask people to opt for one of these values and make a case for why that value is of the greatest importance in dealing with conflict. Peace and justice are often seen as counterparts of each other, particularly, 'there is no peace without justice'. Well, I think, actually, in the name of stability and the name of what we can actually achieve, very often we are making some kind of a trade-off between those two. But also it is curious that it is very hard to get people to stick up for mercy. And more and more I think without mercy we're stuffed. Because we do make a mess of things and it will never be as good as we need it to be. And at some level compassion, mercy sounds rather condescending, but compassion – I just think it's fundamental. And that is why, although respect, I think, is a kind of nice, clear value, I want it to have compassion, care and also energy in it as well.

Respect serves a social as well as a personal purpose in the field of family disputes (in the Italian context, in the next case):

> **Costanza Marzotto:** For me family mediation is a social answer to a community demand. It is a process where negotiation is only a fragment and pre-mediation...has a fundamental role. In my practice and during the training courses I try to explain that family mediation is *an opportunity to recognise the Other as subject, to legitimise the Other as parent*. It is fundamental to offer an occasion to explore [a] family's history and to acknowledge the needs...of the couple. The family mediation process is founded on a constructive conception of conflict; it gives to this process the task of caring for the transmission of the family core beyond the tearing apart of the couple: we can summarise that this trajectory is

like a 'rite of transition', not only an adjustment to the new event! [Emphasis added.]

The importance of respect is that it needs to be *demonstrated* in practice – and experienced by the clients. It is difficult to achieve the orchestration of 'the experience of respect' (Sennett 2003, p.149): '[respect] can, I suppose, be tied up with the discernment to know what can be tolerated and what requires an intervention in the first place' (Yvonne Craig).

Another contributor working in community and workplace mediation avers to the many factors that put that aspiration for respect to the test.

Carl Reynolds: So when I am working with people I am conscious of the fact that am I being influenced by my response to class? Am I being influenced by my response to gender? By my response to sexuality? By my response to race or whatever… So I suppose I also have an orientation of respecting equality, but at the same time trying to understand that equality isn't that everybody is able to pick up an apple, it's that some people might need a tool to pick up the apple.

Various means of demonstrating respect are described – a non-judgmental stance in respect of *both* parties in the context of family mediation.

Tony Whatling: But I think too some more basic [principle] around non-judgmentality, which I find is often not understood in terms of the social work context. You don't write people off because of their behaviour. You can judge their behaviour, but you don't say this is a bad person. They may be late or they may be not doing certain things or doing what they shouldn't be doing but you don't write them off. [So] I think respect, respect for the people you are working with and the demonstration of that is crucial to what happens once you sit down in a room together. And I think that needs to be genuine.

Perhaps as a result of the social work background, and the sort of personality I am, I am very disinclined to make judgments about people, but to work with them in the here and now and treat them with respect. Empathy is a crucial principle I think, trying to put yourself in the shoes of the other person. Not judging their behaviour, but recognising that behaviour is often a symptom of something much deeper. So, for example, when mediators respond to an angry person because of their problem with anger, they completely miss the point that the angry client may be frightened. And they happen to be manifesting that fear with angry or aggressive behaviour which may not be as comfortable for me as the one who is dealing with their fear or sadness or tears. Just trying to not be too quickly responding to what I call the symptoms rather than the person. Even-handedness. Clearly desperately important. Desperately important. I think the demonstration of those principles, you've got those principles down on paper, but they don't mean anything until the client experiences them.

The next quote illustrates the way in which patience is seen to advance the objective of realising in practice the principle of respect – for individuals, *their* meanings and perceptions – however much or precisely because these differ from those of the mediator.

> **Tony Willis:** I'm sorry, there's absolutely no doubt that if you're a sentient being, then you carry with you some principles. In the mediation context, I have tried to isolate some of these, and I found it generally unsatisfactory because I feel like a chemist who knew there were a series of component parts of a compound and in only isolating one or two of them, I've missed the 50 that were in there. But one of them was respect for individuals and respect for *their* issues and *their* matters and *their* way of expressing them and dealing with them. So I found myself saying that one of the things that, I think, in the mediation context, is described as patience, is the ability to listen to someone who is perhaps expressing a view with which I wouldn't agree or a view which I think is lamentably wrong, or a view which is foolish, or a view which is counterproductive, or stupid, and all these things – but respecting the fact that that's the way they are, and that's the way they feel about it, and that's the way they damn well want to get it on the table. So respect for individuals and respect for the way they want to do things is probably quite high up my list. But I have difficulty in expressing this and I don't know whether it is one the *big* principles that motivates me or just one of the little indicators.

It is interesting that in a single German term, 'Balanzierte Wertschätzung', several principles central to the practice of mediation are brought together – the principles of respect; of impartiality or even-handedness; and of a fair, 'balanced' outcome.

> **Christoph Paul:** There is one thing, you call it impartiality. There is one principle in Germany, we call 'Balanzierte Wertschätzung' which is a kind of balanced respect. I think this is one of my major principles at work, that I try to create myself towards these people – respect, a balanced respect, and help *them* as well to find their respect towards each other and go to some kind of balance again. I think this is one of the basics. The more mediation I do the more I like it. And the more I have the feeling that…for example, I just had a telephone call yesterday from a man, a West German, who is married to an Israeli. They have a two-year-old daughter, who is now with the mother and the mother wants to go back to Israel. So it is really a situation that is horrifying for him, losing his daughter… The more I do mediation the more I have the feeling I want to bring respect to them and to see how I can help them bring their situation in balance.

Impartiality

Maintaining an intermediate position between the disputants is considered to be one of the most essential of the attributes of the good mediator who must always be above suspicion of showing any bias for or against one or other party. This 'non-partisanship' required of mediation can manifest, according to Simmel, either when the mediator

> stands above contrasting interests and opinions and is actually not concerned with them, or if he is equally concerned with both... The idea is that the non-partisan is not attached by personal interest to the objective aspects of either party position. Rather, both come to be weighed by him as by a pure, impersonal intellect; without touching the subjective sphere. But the mediator must be subjectively interested in the persons or groups themselves who exemplify the contents of the quarrel which for the moment are guided more by will and feeling. (Simmel 1908a p.149)

The difficulty of achieving this complicated stance is clear, as is the recognition that impartiality is essential to the achievement of the trust that the parties must have in the mediator if that intervention is to be effective. This depends on skill and knowledge as well as on the personal integrity and commitment of the mediator. Impartiality constitutes therefore a fundamental principle of practice as well as an essential attribute, duty and skill. The credibility of the mediator depends not only upon being impartial, but on being perceived to be so.

> **Roy Lewis:** You have to have that credibility. You can't, certainly in the labour field, you can't be taken seriously if they think, as a general proposition, you are going to favour one side or the other. There's no question about that.

In exploring the contributors' perceptions of this principle, its more complex implications and applications emerge. First, impartiality is distinguished from neutrality. This is not merely a terminological distinction. Assertions of neutrality by the mediator bring their own problems. The first is one of accuracy as it is acknowledged that mediators are not neutral, inevitably having their own values, views, feelings, prejudices and interests, as the next contributor acknowledges in the context of family disputes:

> **Lorraine Schaffer:** I actually *do* think that what distinguishes the role of a mediator from any other role is that we are impartial. And I think it is actually essential to the role that we are. But it is how you define and how you look at impartiality. Because none of us can be non-judgmental inwardly. We do make judgments. We do bring our own histories and our own values and beliefs to mediation. But the important thing about the role in principle is that as a mediator you are not there to impose your views, to give people advice, to tell them what to do. And you are certainly not there to side with one person or the other. So in that respect, however you might debate what impartiality means and how possible it is, I think it is an absolutely essential quality of mediation.

The second problem is that claims to neutrality overstate what is possible, laying the mediator open to legitimate challenge. The third problem is that claims to neutrality could be dangerous if asserted in situations of manifest inequality (Haynes 1981).

Here the differences between impartiality and neutrality are examined in relation specifically to *outcomes* of the mediation process in the context of community and victim–offender mediation:

> **Marian Liebmann:** I will try and be impartial. I don't think that's quite the same as neutral... If somebody discloses that they have abused somebody or that they have been abused or that abuse is going on, I think in that sense I'm not neutral. I have to say, 'Well, that won't do.' So there are certain things. I remember Dale Bagshaw [Australian mediator, trainer and scholar] talking about the kind of difference between mediators who were totally impartial, totally neutral – whatever the parties did was OK. Whatever agreement they came to was OK. And at the other end there would be mediators who would say, if people didn't come to a just and fair agreement, then they would have none of it and call the thing to a close and go back to whatever the alternative process was.
>
> She asked us at the time to think about where we might be on the spectrum. I kind of thought I would probably be between the two. That's a typical mediator thing to say really. If somebody was making a flagrantly abusive agreement and somebody was just being coerced into it, I would stop the process. But if somebody was making an agreement that they seemed to agree to and yet I myself didn't particularly think it was very fair, I would check it out but I wouldn't necessarily stand in its way.

Realising impartiality in practice requires the demonstration of even-handedness by the mediator in relation both to the management of negotiations and in relation to the objectives of the parties (Davies and Roberts 1988). A commitment to impartiality, while essential, is one thing. One of the problems is that the mediator must not only *be* impartial but must be *seen to be* impartial. A number of factors can safeguard impartiality and its perception. For example, the mediator must give due weight to each party's views and objectives. The mediator must also avoid expressing a view that coincides with that of one party. The following family mediator describes the process of learning how to manage conflicting accounts of the 'truth'.

> **Lorraine Schaffer:** I think probably I'll always remember John Haynes... When first appointed I had the honour of being on a course of his at Bromley. And I think, as with a lot of people, what sticks with you is that kind of thing where there's no one truth and different perceptions of reality. I think it takes quite a while to actually learn what that means. So I always tell the story that I think it probably took me two years of mediating before I stopped worrying about who was telling the truth and who wasn't. And really realising that there

isn't a truth. And although people tell you diametrically opposed stories, in their perception it's their story and it's how they see it or how they feel about it. And it is not helpful as a mediator to try and establish truth because there isn't [a truth]. I think it's about helping people hear and understand. They may not have to agree with the other person's perception but at least if they can have a better understanding of it that often is a way to help them resolve differences.

The implications of demonstrating impartiality have gender, ethnic, cultural and racial dimensions, as illustrated in the context of organisational mediation:

Carl Reynolds: I think my other orientation is that I don't assume that because I think that I am neutral and impartial that people will perceive me that way… So I'm very open to people not being comfortable with me. I am quite upfront about that most of the time. Do you have a problem with the way I am? Or even what you assume about me being a mediator. You don't have to tell me what it is about me, but if they are not comfortable then that's fine and they can find somebody else. A couple of times they have [taken me up on this]. And once, I think, because it was important that one of the parties felt that there was somebody who might understand issues of race in a way that I wouldn't. So it wasn't that they wanted somebody who was like them; they just wanted somebody who may already have had experience in racism. And I suppose part of my political belief is, [as a] white male European, I can't really experience racism – at the top of the pile, so to speak, in terms of rank. So in one case I think that was very appropriate.

In another case where I stood down and did get somebody in who was black and also a woman, in this case, who was a colleague of mine. And she reported back to me later that, as far as she was concerned, that person was just using a delaying tactic. But again whatever's going on for them, is going on for them. So I suppose I really try and cultivate that notion that no matter what people do, it is just what they can do that moment. And that if they decide to leave or do something else then it's not for me to judge them. And I strive for that but I think that's important.

The protection of impartiality requires consideration being given to the structural arrangements that inform the model of practice adopted. It is far more difficult for impartiality to be seen to operate where, for example, the model of shuttle mediation (the mediator 'shuttling' between the parties each in separate rooms) is deployed. While the model of practice must be appropriate to the circumstances, the structural arrangements can enhance or diminish the risks of the mediator being perceived as partial, for example, in the situation of a multi-party environmental mediation:

Andrew Acland: I think…that the impartiality, the necessary impartiality of the third party is key. In the work I do, quite a lot of the principles – I do a lot of work in quite large groups often with people who have their own constituencies

> – are things like transparency. It is not like a commercial mediation where you are going into a caucus meeting or a private meeting with each side in turn, say. The vast majority of my work is done in plain view with both sides in the room; very often quite a lot of people. And therefore transparency, and transparency of record, is important. But this is very particular to the work I do at the moment.

Whatever form of 'non-partisanship' is adopted, consisting in equal distance or equal closeness, the achievement of impartiality imposes the greatest challenge to the effective practice of mediation, requiring thought, care and attention, practice over time, and skill.

Voluntariness of participation

There was a unanimous and unambiguous consensus expressed across every field of practice represented that, in principle and in practice, participation in mediation should be on a voluntary basis only. The manifold pressures threatening that principle were referred to as well. The next contributor's viewpoint about informed voluntary participation as one of the cardinal principles is typical, though the kind of justification expressed is unusual:

> **Carl Reynolds:** [Voluntariness is] absolutely fundamental. That people should choose to come into something. And tied to that is the notion that people understand exactly what it is that they are getting into. That kind of ties with my practice, I suppose in the sense I don't believe people shift from where they are until they've understood why they got there in the first place. And why the other person got there. And why what they did affected how the other person responded to them.

An unequivocal affirmation of the principle of voluntariness in one field of practice, that of community and elder mediation, highlights recognition of current challenges threatening another field of practice, that of family mediation:

> **Yvonne Craig:** There are of course the classic [principles] – of confidentiality, of impartiality, of following the ethical codes of mediation, the respect for people that one is dealing with… [and] it has to be voluntary. That of course is the whole issue because we know there is this question of mandatory mediation which we have had problems with in family mediation.

The field of family mediation is currently coming under strong but diffuse pressure to abandon its long-held commitment to the principle of voluntary participation. It is not at all surprising that this includes growing pressure from an overloaded family justice system having to deal with an increased number of litigants (many in person because of the stringencies of legal aid) and many complex and difficult family conflicts (for an explication of the arguments against compulsion in family mediation, see Roberts 2006).

In the next extract, it is possible to discern the impact of a different source of pressure, that coming from the family mediation profession itself, towards some form of compulsion, though important distinctions are also being drawn between acceptable and non-acceptable forms of compulsion:

> **Lorraine Schaffer:** I think voluntarism is a debatable issue, very current now. And it's interesting, I actually had around the group discussion with the students who are finishing the [mediation] certificate, asking how many people thought mediation should be totally voluntary and how many thought that there could be an element of mandation. I think the overall impression was, and it's one I probably agree with, is that until mediation is very established and understood by the public, which I don't think it is, in a way that counselling and therapy are, and because of the fact that, if people *are* in conflict, it is probably their natural tendency to want to avoid dealing with it. But I think (a) it's not going to be helpful to them to avoid it, and (b) using a third party such as a solicitor or somebody who is not going to facilitate them actually directly meeting with each other somehow, [that] somebody will also not resolve it, even if it goes through the courts. So I am not opposed to the idea of people being expected to at least come for an information meeting about mediation. I don't think they should be forced then to mediate if they choose not to. And I think if they are in mediation and they are not happy about it, they have the absolute right to stop mediating. So I think that's my view really about the voluntary side.

A flavour of the same debate, also taking place in Germany, is recalled below. The views of the contributor coincide with the content of recent draft legislation on the subject. This makes a clear distinction between a pre-mediation information meeting which can be mandatory, and mediation itself which remains voluntary (Law on the Reform of Proceedings in Family Cases and in Matters of Voluntary Jurisdiction, June, 2005, Section 144, Extra-judicial dispute settlement regarding the consequences of divorce).

> **Christoph Paul:** We don't have mandatory mediation in Germany. We are discussing mandatory mediation in Germany. A lot of people say it's *the* wonder of mediation, it helps a lot. I'm very sceptical about [mandation]. I personally recommend that there should be information about mediation, at whatever stage of the conflict, either before court or within court. And I think it should be the obligation of the judge to recommend the people at least to try it. It doesn't mean that they have to do it or that they lose the right to solve their conflicts in court without at least trying mediation. I think information about mediation would be helpful for a lot of people. That would be mandatory, just information.
>
> I think that the background of the discussion [now] is that mediators think that as soon as mediation is mandatory then a mediation boom will start. And I

think it's the wrong way. You can't wait for the judge to give clients to you. You have to convince people that they come before or when they realise that the judge doesn't help them. There is a discussion of a lot of people saying, no mediation is voluntary because they say people are in such a conflict, and what is then voluntary? But I think that's a different thing. I think every conflict is a catastrophe. It doesn't mean that when the people decide to go to mediation, it doesn't mean it is not very voluntary.

In considering the application of the principle of voluntary participation in relation to industrial disputes, the statutory framework is the critical context, though in practice this has its limits:

Roy Lewis: In the labour field there is no such thing as an involuntary mediation by and large. So you either have mediation on a voluntary basis or you simply don't have mediation. There is no court annexed system of mediation in this country to do with employment. Of course, having said that, you have got the ACAS role in the tribunals which is to try and promote settlement, but they can only achieve a settlement if the parties are prepared to agree one. So in fact here are two elements. If you are talking about compulsion or lack of voluntarism, the one is the process. Are you required to enter into a mediation process or conciliation process? And secondly, is the result of the mediation in any way compulsory? The answer to the second question is not at all. The answer to the first question is there may be some pressure from the system, at least in the sense that ACAS in the tribunal has got a role there. But they have only got a role as far as the parties are going to let them play that role. If the parties aren't interested in any kind of settlement, that's it. So it's just a statutory framework really.

That negotiations never occur in a vacuum is well established (Roberts and Palmer 2005). Mnookin and Kornhauser's seminal North American article describes all negotiations as 'bargaining in the shadow of the law' (1979, pp.978–9). It is clear across different areas of practice, from victim–offender mediation to the organisational and environmental sphere, that in relation to the principle of voluntariness, the impact, implicit and explicit, of that powerful coercive environment of litigation and adjudication is profound:

Andrew Acland: [Voluntary participation is] essential. An essential principle. I have always been very doubtful about any form of mandated mediation. I know that in very pragmatic terms a judge mandating a mediation probably gives it a better chance of happening at least. But there is something about the mandating of it which to me, the voluntariness is actually more important in a way. People should do it because they want to, not because they have been told to. But I'm probably at odds with others on that one.

This view, as it turns out, is in no way at odds with the views of other contributors. While the pressures and challenges that threaten its implementation were acknowledged, recognition of the paramouncy of the principle of voluntary participation was unanimous amongst contributors. This consensus unites therefore not only different fields of practice but current judicial opinion as well.[2]

Party control and mediator authority

In principle what distinguishes mediation and constitutes its chief benefit is respect for the parties' own decision-making authority. This defining principle is incompatible, in the first instance, with an approach that denies the parties the right to make their own informed decision as to whether or not they want to participate in the process in the first place (see above). Also fundamental to mediation is a presumption that the parties (notwithstanding stressful circumstances and personal vulnerability) are competent to be the architects of their own agreements and to make their own decisions. The following environmental mediator illustrates how implementation of the principle can occur in practice.

> **Andrew Acland:** Decision-making authority [is] always with the parties. And any authority, and I'm not sure it's quite the right word, that a third party has is derived from the parties. So you act with their consent...[and] I think trust is a consequence of what you do. I'm always rather worried by people who immediately say on first meeting 'I trust you,' because there's no basis for it. It's a very shallow form of trust. People will trust you when they have seen you in action for a bit. So the action is speaking louder than words. It is part of the transparency. Another part of the transparency, I suppose, is certainly again in my work, the principle is that you give the people you are working with some control over the agenda. Because I often work with large groups of people you tend to start with some sense of how you are going to run the process. In fact the design of the process, the process design is an absolutely critical function of the work of the large group. You have to know how you are going to structure the conversations, if you like. And one of the principles is that you involve the people you are working with in agreeing to that structure. So that you don't impose it upon them. It is actually their meeting. Actually that's a principle I think is important for all mediation. That it is actually *the parties'* mediation and not the mediator's mediation.

The parties therefore consent to participate with the mediator in the mediation process. The mediator is only there with the permission of the parties. To the extent that they are aware of their right not to participate if they so choose, the parties retain ultimate control. The authority of the mediator derives therefore from a tacit or explicit understanding between the parties and the mediator. That occurs expressly in the context of the mediation of labour disputes:

> **Roy Lewis:** I just start with my terms of reference. I'm not very philosophical. The one thing I never do is exceed my terms of reference. If it looks as if the terms of reference aren't going to be viable then we have got to get the parties' agreement to vary them. They define what the mediator is required to do. In broad terms that is to promote settlement of a dispute. But it may involve rather more than that. It may involve consideration of the merits; it may involve making positive suggestions. All that type of activity needs to be anticipated in the terms of reference.

Respect for the parties' authority for decision-making has equivalent significance in the field of workplace and other fields of mediation.

> **Carl Reynolds:** I think the notion that everyone's going to understand what's going on from their own perspective – that whoever I'm working with, I'm kind of paraphrasing, *people are capable of making their own decisions really*. If I'm working with them I'm working with them to try to help *them* make decisions rather than to discover what's diminished that capacity. Also the notion that to a degree I suppose we are all capable of co-operation or altruism to some degree and conflict also diminishes that. [Emphasis added.]

Consideration of the issue of party control cannot be separated, therefore, from questions about the authority and power of the mediator – first, how can the authority of the mediator be exercised in ways that serve the essential objectives of the process, in particular the objective of retaining party control? Second, when does the exercise of that authority cease to serve those objectives, becoming instead an abuse of power with the mediator exerting unacceptable pressures upon one or both of the parties who then act (or fail to act) in ways they would not otherwise have done?

Two primary principles essential in the context of international mediation are, according to the next contributor (Mark Hoffman), first, that a mediator must never get involved or drawn into a situation other than by the invitation to participate of those involved in the conflict themselves; and second, that a mediator must make a commitment to the individuals who are themselves involved in the conflict. Nevertheless the mediator has to recognise that even by not imposing oneself, and even by introducing a non-coercive process, the mediator may risk exerting 'subtle forms of power'. This requires a constant 'reflexivity' on the part of the mediator in order to monitor what kinds of interventions are being used round the table and how power is actually being exercised through those interventions in the process. These interlinked concerns are bound up with the distinction drawn, in this context, between the mediator and the facilitator:

Mark Hoffman: The difference is partly, again, something that the literature teases out — and it sets up almost dichotomous ideal types that probably break down in actual practice. The main distinction would be that mediation often takes a more formalised tighter structure: mediators often, at least at the international level, are presumed to bring with them certain kinds of resources that they can use. They often have interests in an outcome, a particular kind of outcome, to the conflict, and so to that extent a mediator at least in international conflict would be deemed to be somebody who is outcome-driven — they know more or less where they want to get the parties to, and how to assist to get the parties there. Whereas the facilitator is more…is process-driven and to a certain extent may have particular ideas about what might be useful or appropriate outcomes, but in a sense isn't wedded to a particular outcome, and indeed part of what they are trying to do is to explore a whole range of possible outcomes and foster a process of creative thinking on the part of the parties to the conflict.

But from our point of view — and the principle is in a sense derived from people like Burton and Curle — the solution has to lie with the parties themselves. It is not something that can be imposed from outside and so rather than bring them the solution and how to get them to it …it is drawing out of them what would be an acceptable solution between the various parties involved in the conflict that would make it work.

In the field of commercial mediation, a different style of mediation, less unobtrusive and 'low profile' perhaps, is not incompatible with a similar commitment to party control, a principle regarded as so fundamental that even stating it 'goes without saying'.

David Shapiro: My job is to catalyse the ability of parties to make their own decision. How do I come to this decision, which is my own, and what are the factors that I should take into account in coming to that decision? And what are the things which are important to me? And how can the mediator help me articulate that in a way which satisfies the basic requirement that the mediator does not make the decision, the parties make the decision for themselves with the mediator's assistance. I will not bang heads. I have yelled at parties in a mediation but I will not bang heads.

In the commercial field too, the subject matter of mediation may dictate a less idealistic, more pragmatic approach in practice. Issues of principle may well prevail, but it appears that many cases are 'money-driven' to a greater extent than in other mediation fields.

David Shapiro: The older I got I moved away from principled issues and basically, while still principled issues, they were really money-driven; I early came to the notion that every case has hair on it. Every case. Every case has got a problem with it. There is no perfect case anywhere. There is always going to be a problem.

And essentially what one tries to do is look if I can get a really good settlement for my client. Why start running risks I don't have to run?

You try to get the best settlement you can even though you are very prepared that they didn't come up with what you thought was a reasonable approach. Again you didn't go into this nonsense about positional bargaining. You said, look, this is what the case is worth, this is what I want. [Settlement seeking is the approach] generally because it's based on common sense. Why are we doing all of this crazy stuff with a legal system which has not delivered justice except on a fluke? When people can't sit down and work through a solution. Now there are cases for mediators which warm the cockles of their heart and cases which are strictly money. If for example the mediator had put together, had put back a fractured relationship, healed a fractured relationship, and everybody wins, nobody loses type of approach, I mean the mediator gives himself 12 brownie points for that. In a straight money case there are no brownie points, it's just a job.

A settlement approach can create a tension between conflicting interests. In the next example, in the context of community and victim–offender mediation, there is a tension between the mediator's interest in achieving 'success' in terms of an agreement, an 'outcome-driven' pressure referred to above in the international context, and that of the principle of party determination.

Marian Liebmann: I think empowerment, self-determination, those kinds of things [are important principles]. Quite humanistic principles really. The mediator is there to help the people concerned... It's very tempting to think that your reputation stands or falls by whether people come to agreement or not and I think that's a trap I fall into from time to time. I think ideally you shouldn't have a stake in the outcome – it should be up to the parties.

There are complex implications in practice of applying the principle of party control not only in connection with elder mediation.

Yvonne Craig: [Mediation] needs to be affirmative of people, to use the jargon word 'empowering'. That we act as reality agents to people rather than encourage them to develop fantasies about what they can or they can't do. I have to say in parentheses that I am very concerned about a lot of this pseudo empowerment, particularly of young people. But also of elderly people. That they have the rights and the ability to do anything they want. And then of course they find that they don't have the natural abilities to do things. There's a lot of rethinking that needs to be done about empowerment. I found it in my increasing special work with old people, which is appropriate because of my age, because gerontology is now telling old people that they should be empowered to do this, that and the other. They should be taking on the managers of the sheltered housing, industry. And a lot of the disputes I deal with are with older people who I think have been improperly counselled to be dominant in a sphere where they haven't got the competence because of their age and deficits undermining that.

Summation

The core principles of mediation are regarded as essential across fields of mediation practice for safeguarding a fair process and outcome and for protecting the parties. These principles are integral, sustaining and reinforcing one another – for example, in the demonstration of respect, of impartiality, of voluntary participation, and of party control. The vulnerability of the parties, the complexity of circumstances and the difficulties of the dispute, plus the unpredictable dynamics of the mediation process, complicate the realisation of these principles in practice, imposing an onerous responsibility on the mediator.

Notes

1. Shah-Kazemi (2000, p.305) affirms this core aspiration of mediation with an emphasis on the essential significance of the cultural and normative context that shapes the mediation process: 'The mediation process is predicated on achieving an initial consensus, which will ultimately succeed because of the mutual respect between not just the parties themselves but also between each party and mediator. This respect entails, at its most fundamental level, the acknowledgement of the universal human capacity to act with dignity in the pursuit of fairness, at the same time as being understandably orientated towards what is in their [and their dependents'] best interests. This respect can only be authentic when the cultural and ethical norms upon which it is based can be shared by both the mediator and the parties.'
2. See, for example Mackay, 1995, p.704: 'Compulsory mediation quite simply does not work and is a contradiction in terms'; Lord Woolf, Access to Justice (1996 ch.18, para.3): 'Despite these advantages [of ADR], I do not propose that ADR should be compulsory either as an alternative or as a preliminary to litigation'; and the Court of Appeal judgment in *Halsey v. Milton Keynes NHS Trust* [2004] 1WLR 3002, that the court's proper role is to encourage the parties to mediate but not compel them to do so.

7
Theory and Practice

> There is nothing so practical as a good theory.
>
> (Unknown)

All practice, it is argued, is inevitably informed by suppositions, ideas or frames of reference that explain phenomena and provide understandings of what is going on, so that, on one level, 'practice is never theory-free' (McGuigan and McMechan 2005). At the same time, mediation has often been described as a practice in search of a theory, a view epitomising a contrary view that mediation is a practice self-consciously lacking any framework of theoretical understanding. This scholar encapsulates the position with these words: 'Most analysis of mediation is essentially descriptive and pragmatic. There is little or no theory of mediation' (Stevens 1963, p.11).

On the other hand it is well recognised that a long-established, discrete and distinguished body of negotiation and mediation literature exists. This autonomous theoretical source can be distinguished from the range of distinct disciplines that are also considered to inform the broader study of conflict and dispute resolution – the academic literature, for example, of sociology, anthropology, economics, political science, peace studies, law, economics, communication, neuro-linguistics, international relations, socio-legal studies and social psychology. In addition, there is a school of thinking, characterising the legal profession, that mediation is but one of several dispute resolution tools that form part of a *lawyers'* toolbox. The practice of mediation is regarded not as one involving the adoption of a separate, autonomous mediator function, but as part of and as an adjunct to *legal* practice. There is, therefore, scant incentive to embrace other theoretical paradigms of understanding. The picture is confused by exhortations to *lawyers* to embrace a fuller understanding of the creative possibilities of dispute resolution that go 'beyond the adversarial model' and embrace 'process pluralism' (for example, Menkel-Meadow *et al.* 2005, p.xxxiii).

Theory and practice in mediation: A problematic relationship?

The field of ADR and mediation in particular is acknowledged to have been subject to extensive research study and critical commentary over decades, to an unusual degree. Despite, or perhaps because of this, again peculiarly in this field, the relationship between the theory and the practice of mediation has been characterised, by scholars and researchers, as a problematic one, involving a theory/practice divide (see for example Rifkin 1994). In particular, as already noted, the interaction between research and practice, and between academics and practitioners, has been perceived to be restricted – with exchanges unfortunately rare and with limited impact. When exchanges do occur, these are considered to be less than productive with a consequent loss of benefit to both groups.

Theoretical accounts and research studies are considered to have findings perceived to be threatening to practitioners – because they are critical of contemporary practice, for example, in raising concerns about issues of justice, of power, of coercion, and challenging purported mediator claims to neutrality. Notwithstanding, it is proclaimed that there exists an 'angst about the social implications of the field and about the micro-dynamics of good practice...', shared by researchers and practitioners alike (Rifkin 1994, p.204).

In North America, researchers have criticised mediation training programmes for being devoid of explicit theories of practice. These are alleged to focus, instead, exclusively on skill-building and practice techniques as hallmarks of good practice (Rifkin 1994). New theoretical and research perspectives, it is claimed, can create dilemmas and tensions for practitioners, including the risk of undermining chances of professional advancement because of the challenges posed to established training programmes and providers. In addition, some researchers relegate the value of what practitioners themselves contribute to their own knowledge base of theoretical understanding, of policy and of practice, to a rhetoric advanced to promote the expansion of an 'occupational jurisdiction' – and contrast this self-serving interest to the objective 'social scientific analysis' of the field by social scientists (Dingwall and Greatbatch 1993, p.367).

Other aspects of theory have been linked to problems associated with the development of mediation as a professional activity, involving the consolidation of standard-setting and the regulation of practice. The professionalisation trajectory itself (a predominantly mediator-driven project), it is argued, can create resistance to innovative theoretical approaches, with tensions arising both from a lack of consensus amongst practitioners about what constitutes good practice and the threat of change that is inevitably entailed in the endeavour (Rifkin 1994).[1]

Another problem has also been identified with the evolution of the professionalisation of mediation and the new significance that is attached to the importance of a core knowledge base and its transmission through training and education. Tensions arise, therefore, between the perceived objectives of professionalisation, including the control of entry into the field, and those areas of practice that are characterised by a volunteer, grassroots, lay and community ethos. These are some of the problems that discussion of theory raises in relation to mediation practice.

An alternative narrative posits a different, less oppositional, experience of the interaction between theory and practice in respect of mediation. The ADR field is acknowledged to be an 'experiential' field, exemplifying the concepts and practices of the 'theories-in-use' school in the development of professional education (for example, Schon 1983; Menkel-Meadow et al. 2005). The importance of 'grounded theory' highlights, too, the recognition that good practice and the reflections of experienced practitioners constitute a rich resource for the development of the best models and theories (Jones 2001, p.133). More particularly, developments in family mediation in the UK, for example, demonstrate the close collaboration of researchers and practitioners in joint working parties, constructing a range of policies and practice guidelines such as on domestic abuse, the role of children in mediation, cross-cultural mediation, mediator selection criteria and procedures, and mediation models for dealing comprehensively with all the decisions relating to family breakdown – those concerning finance and property as well as children.[2]

The concept of 'theory' too is one that requires some disentangling in this context (see below). Theoretical perspectives, research findings (empirical as well as theoretical), and scholarship and academic study all refer to aspects of understanding actors' *and* observers' templates that are usually distinguished from the domain of 'practice'.

This chapter draws on contributors' responses to questions relating to the impact of theory and research on their practice. Contributors' reflections explore whether and how implicit understandings become explicit, and whether the insights of research and theory confirm, enhance or change individual, tacit templates of practice. Three aspects are considered: first, the purpose of theory in relation to practice; second, those theories that are specifically identified as being of significance to practice; and third, in conclusion, practitioners' ideas about forms of theory and their realisation.

The purpose of a theoretical understanding of practice

Contributors testify to a common view that an understanding of *what* one does as a practitioner and *why* one does it is as necessary to good practice as knowing *how* to do it. This family mediator has written articles exhorting colleagues to attend more carefully to theoretically informed practice in order better to understand what they are doing:

> **Lorraine Schaffer:** Theory is about people having a better understanding of why they do what they do. Why people behave as they do. How to help people better. That is what I think theory is about. It's not about saying that you can't be a fantastically intuitive mediator who actually doesn't read a book. I think that happens too. Because people skills are part of any intervention. But I do think if you can't explain to somebody why you are doing what you are doing then I don't see you as being as competent as you could be. It doesn't mean that theory always helps you out of a bad situation when you have a tough case. I think theory becomes very unconscious. I think everyone needs theories, it's just whether they can name them or not.

The importance of a continuing process of clarification and self-conscious understanding of practice, particularly by the most experienced of practitioners, is highlighted by another family mediator who regularly observes his supervisees in action.

> **Tony Whatling:** I think you may become a very good intuitive worker, but an intuitive worker isn't necessarily developing strategies that might make [their practice] even better. I see an example of this when I am watching highly experienced mediators, but they are simply not summarising. And I see the clients behaving in ways that are demonstrating that they are not being understood. They [the mediators] can be more conscious of doing it in future which will improve their practice. What matters is their practice would be sharpened and enhanced if they were aware enough. Intuitive practice on its own is not enough.

This importance of theory for good practice is shared in the context of the environmental and organisation field where teaching and training have sharpened understanding.

> **Andrew Acland:** Who was it who said there's nothing so practical as a good theory? I think it *is* important that people understand some of the theory. You need a good grasp of theory to understand what your experience is I think, so you have something against which to measure and some way to frame it. One thing I found enormously helpful, is that over the years I have done an awful lot of teaching and training in this field. And I think that has helped me hugely in understanding. There's nothing like having to explain something to others to really force you to get your own thoughts in order; having written endless sets of training notes on the same subjects and constantly coming at the same things over and over again.

Theoretical input in training (in labour relations mediation in this instance) can generate a critical approach to practice.

Roy Lewis: Well, you start off with a theory not just of mediation but you start off with a theory of what you are resolving. So you start off with a theory of conflict in fact. All their stuff comes from what's been worked out in the Harvard Law School. And it is a distinctive theory. The value of it is not that you just take it in uncritically and therefore try and apply that. But it helps if you have some education of that nature. You might be critical of it and react to it but I think it helps to make you more conscious of what you are doing to have some kind of training.

A theoretical framework, however useful for conceptualising reality, has its limitations and should not become a substitute for or be mistaken for that reality – as this perspective from the field of international mediation illustrates.

Diana Francis: I think theory can be very helpful in enabling you to sort ideas into shapes, or realities into shapes that make them 'handleable', and one of a facilitator's roles is being able to help people conceptualise so that they can get round and manage competing realities that they are trying to deal with. To that extent it is important. I think it's equally important to say that theory is not reality and can never actually represent or substitute for reality. If it's been as instrumental, I think it's fine... As a way of kind of hijacking or controlling other people's ideas, I think it's a disaster. Certainly expounding on theory is no substitute for listening to people and helping them engage in and learn from their own experience and knowledge. I love the kind of theoretical discussion which is really wrestling and trying to improve theory.

Awareness of the academic literature can serve a specific purpose in the practice of mediation in the international arena, in fostering reflexivity, and self and team awareness. The limits of relying on theory are clear too if the danger of imposed outcomes is to be avoided.

Mark Hoffman: Some sense of theory is probably useful – I'm not sure it's essential... I think probably what is most important is actually having a capacity for reflexivity on the part of the facilitator/mediator themselves – to have a kind of critical self-evaluation. I've worked with individuals who know the theory and are quite skilled in the process because they've learned the process, but have not a critical bone in their body in terms of being able to stand back, particularly to talk about power dynamics. And I think that capacity for a kind of critical self-reflection would be fostered by looking at the academic and theoretical literature.

[And critical] mutual reflection. That's where putting together a good facilitation team becomes important. You can't be a prima donna about what you do. *You* have be able to work as a team [and] be honest [about] dynamics of the team. So it has to be something that works both at the level of the individual and the team. Certainly not having a huge ego helps. I've worked with a couple of individuals who had huge egos. These people were interested in process but they knew where the process was going to go and they would get frustrated when the parties weren't behaving in the way they were meant to according to the rule book – Day 3, we should be here and not there.

[People] who are *so* professional that the process itself dictates what they're doing and a particular idealised, almost recipe-book understanding of the process can get in the way. And I think that can be really unhealthy because it becomes frustrating for the participants, because they feel they are being steered towards something. And probably unproductive in terms of outcomes because they have a certain artificial quality. So that capacity for reflexivity becomes important. And that's why it may take a while to work out what's going to be a good team.

The following approach in a different area of mediation practice, the commercial field, is consonant, suggesting that the scope for superimposing abstract models of theory can be equally unhelpful. Also of importance is the need for there to be reflection about practice and its application in ways that are *demonstrably* effective.

Tony Willis: I don't think I'm very good at the theory. I think I've got a sufficient grounding – I pick at it. If you examined me now on the Harvard Negotiation Model[3] I'd fail – I really would fail. I think that the mediators who could achieve an A star in the Harvard Negotiation Model are actually rather bad mediators. There are then people who probably wouldn't know what the Harvard Model smells like if they fell over it in the street, who are damn good mediators. And so I think there's a continuum which must be the case if my theory about the primacy of respect for the individual is right, which can encompass all those different kinds and traditions of people. And so I hope the answer is no. It [theory] helps; it helps to be interested; it is *necessary* to be interested; and it is *necessary* to have done quite a lot of thinking about it; and it is *necessary* to have made the processes work, to have demonstrated to yourself that you understand how the process works. But I think a *detailed* theoretical knowledge is not necessarily something that is high on the list of requirements.

Limitations of theory for practice

The limits of the significance of theory was noted in certain areas of practice, peer mediation by children, for example.

Marian Liebmann: I think principles are very important. But whether you need to know loads of theory I doubt. Because, after all, you can teach mediation to eight-year-olds. You can get nursery age children to mediate.

There are others who are deemed not to need theory in order to be effective mediators.

Yvonne Craig: In specialist areas I do think you need to be very competently trained. However in my many years with Camden Mediation Service, which to its credit has taken in and trained a lot of grassroots people... I mean that with no disrespect. What they bring are other skills and resonances which mean that when we are mediating in one of the situations I have already described, in council houses, when two different races or cultures are living close to one another, they can provide excellent mediation. And it is not necessary in that context. It is not necessary in some community contexts for people to have a knowledge of the theoretical literature.

The next international mediator was of the view that no particular theory played a part in his practice. Pragmatic influences, finding things out for oneself and building relationships with people were important.

Adam Curle: No, I don't think [theory was any influence]. What I've tried to do was to find out what was driving people and to look for, to search with them for alternatives or ways of getting out of situations. Actually I've never been a successful mediator.

Well, I can only think of really two things where I think, *I think* I've played a part. And I'll tell you approximately what I've done. First of all, India and Pakistan... Nigeria, yes something did happen. I felt that I *was* able to contribute something of note and you know one never knows exactly. You can have a relationship with people, like I did in Nigeria. The main thing which I think I was able [to do] was to suggest something positive to Gowan, the Nigerian Federal President. [What has influenced practice was not specific research but]...oh I suppose, lots of things, lots of people. But I can't think of anything specific. A lot of little bits and pieces which come together which have to come together over maybe a long period of time. I don't think of mediation as being settling some particular dispute. I think it must be a slow, it must be slow, it must be part slow, part fast, certain activities or circumstances, ideas.

Theories about the dynamics of political conflict can assist in understanding influences that affect the timing and capacity for intervention, particularly in situations of international violence.

Diana Francis: Here I feel myself falling immediately into theory, for example, theories that save you thinking. [There] is this hourglass image that before widespread violence and after widespread violence, you have big opportunities, but at the point of acute violence there is rather little to be done. The truth is that even at the point of acute violence, there would be people constantly working away to try and find beginnings of possibilities for dialogue and so on, but when violence is extreme, it is very hard to think in terms of mediation. More theory here. Various theories about the dynamics of conflict and polarisation. Typically the

> space for communication gets vastly reduced while violence is high and escalating. And sometimes, it is when there is a lull or a diminution of actual violence that the openings come.

While affirming 'absolutely' that a sound grasp of theory is essential for excellence of practice, another perspective, from the commercial field, confirms a consistent view of the nature of the detailed, multi-faceted complexity of practice of mediation, and its unpredictability.

> **David Shapiro:** It is primarily pragmatic. I would say one might be able to come up with a philosophical angle. But it is so overwhelmed by the pragmatics of the situation. The funny thing about the pragmatics of the situation, you can take a mediation involving the same set of facts and one will succeed and one will fail. The reason is that each individual comes into it with an approach to the problem as a zero sum...it starts all over again. And there is no pattern to any of this because the personalities of the disputants will change the equation entirely.
>
> No [particular writing has informed my practice]. As a matter of fact *my* writings mostly informed other people's views of practice. One is 'Pushing the envelope' – basically a modern term which in effect says you are moving out from the standard stuff. You are moving into different notions of how you do a thing. At the time it came out the people were shocked. And now many of them are using the same techniques. And the other [piece of writing] is 'Tough talking'.

Then there is a view that there are mediators who are so naturally talented they do not to require any extra input in the way of theory. A German family mediator and a British commercial mediator give their views:

> **Christoph Paul:** I think there are people who can do it without any theoretical background. I think there are talents. I'm pretty sure there are. For example, I think especially if we are talking about political mediators. I think there are people who probably never read a line about mediation and they are wonderful in the most complicated situations, the most terrifying conflicts; they can handle them. But this is not the general mediator. I think for a general mediator it is necessary to be well trained. I think the training needs theoretical training especially, and some experience and you have to know a lot about yourself. You have to know what a crying mother in front of you is for you, or a father who doesn't say a word and always looks like a stone.

The necessity for natural talent for the task *plus* experience, was rated of great relevance. At the same time doubt is expressed by the next British commercial mediator about the extent to which theory is or is not important.

> **Philip Naughton:** People say that you need to have 50 mediations under your belt before you reach a level of competence. Which makes you a successful senior mediator. I think that some people just make good mediators provided they know enough about the pitfalls of mediation more than the opportunities of mediation – to avoid putting their foot in it. Natural talent? I think so – and I'm really not sure how important theory is.

Theories of relevance[4]

Contributors draw on many sources for learning about their work. Examples include the literature of psychology, anthropology and sociology; family therapy and systems theory; theories of conflict and theories of negotiation. Those who were pioneering mediators had to draw on what was available at the time, making their own contributions to the literature in the process.

> **Andrew Acland:** It's been empirical and experiential. Largely because when I started, there really wasn't a great deal of literature, or if there was, I wasn't aware of it. And certainly I can't remember the first book I read on mediation. It was probably after I'd written on it myself.[5] There wasn't that much around. So actually most of the early influence, when I first started really thinking seriously and writing about it, was actually taking ideas from other fields, from social sciences or from psychology or from group dynamics and things like that. And from history to a certain extent. So there was no canon of literature. I suppose [there was a theological background]. Because, although my role at Lambeth Palace was strictly secular, and I only got drafted to write sermons when we were really desperate, I did of course read quite a lot around it. And I have always found a sort of theological idea of mediation actually quite intriguing. Partly because I have such severe doubts, I think, about so much theology that actually something that can ground it in the human experience is rather appealing.

A more recent example, from the German experience, illustrates not only the continuing relevance of one's own experience for advancing theoretical development and evolving effective practice, but the range of sources drawn on – training material, reading, discussion, conferencing, cross-disciplinary teaching research and writing.

> **Christoph Paul:** [Research] did change my practice. I trained from 1994 to 1996, two years, 200 theoretical hours. Then I had to write all these things. If I would have stopped my theoretical reading about mediation at that level it would have been very difficult for me, I think, to practise at the level I am practising now. It helped me a lot – reading, discussing, going to congresses and teaching as well. Because I am teaching together with a psychotherapist so all the teaching we discuss in advance. How to handle it. How it affects the mediation. How it affects the people we are training.

A practitioner in the field of community and victim–offender mediation regards her own efforts at writing about the subject as important for learning as any reading of others' works.

> **Marian Liebmann:** I'm not a brilliant reader to be honest. I'm a better writer. People sometimes think I read tons because I write so much, but actually I find writing easier than reading which is strange.

Limitations of a different kind in respect of some of the literature exist for the following commercial mediator whose strong views are expressed with characteristic bluntness. Theory that deals with 'pragmatics' can be invaluable.

> **David Shapiro:** Let me say that some of the more academic articles that one reads in the journal and so forth, I think academic crap… Because half the time I don't know what they're talking about. And I think I'm reasonably intelligent. I can read this stuff… What's he saying? What's he talking about? It's gone. It's a language I don't understand. There are other articles that deal with the pragmatics of the stuff that are absolutely invaluable, like, for example, the whole question of the role of confidentiality.

For many mediators initial introduction to the knowledge base came in mediation training. That is not enough however and continuing education is regarded as essential to keep understanding and skills alive.

> **Roy Lewis:** Yes, there were [theories taught in training]. Not in any kind of great quantity or economic sense, but there was a theory of negotiation that was a starting point of the entire theory of mediation. And of course if you are dealing with collective negotiations then you are always looking at these things with that in the back of your mind. It is just helpful to have exposure to anything that might give you any kind of additional insight. So I'm not saying that as far as what I do there's a big theoretical basis in it. But I have to say I think education and continuing education is of assistance to mediators. And I think most practitioners do it by attending seminars.

The value of a particular training handbook, used in the original education of this victim–offender mediator, still stands the test of time.

> **Marian Liebmann:** Well I mentioned the Friends Suburban Project in Philadelphia. They did a weekend in London. Their manual is called *A Mediator's Handbook*, I think. It is just a model of clarity, openness and user friendliness really. Even though I was heavily involved in the *Mediation UK Manual* which is a lot more complex, has a lot more material and was really good. And also does something which the *Mediator's Handbook* doesn't do, which is about indirect mediation. It doesn't do anything about preparation, just people coming to the meeting and starting…which I think is a limitation. The *Mediation UK Manual*,

which I was heavily involved in, has a lot more about the actual stages. Christopher Moore, I've read bits of his... There probably are other books but I can't tell you. John Paul Lederach is somebody that I have read lots of in the cross-cultural field.

The direct influence of teachers, as theoreticians and practitioners, can play a powerful part in generating fresh and analytic approaches to practice as this example in the international field illustrates.

Diana Francis: I've mentioned the thinking of active non-violence, and I tend to put in the active just to avoid misunderstanding. All that I have received [has come] more on the hoof than through books. It's very much part of my way of thinking. Jean and Hildegarde Goss-Mayr. She's Austrian and he's French. They were a married couple working for IFOR [International Fellowship of Reconciliation] for quite a lot of years in various functions and did an extraordinary amount of pioneering work, training and supporting people in very violent situations and taking non-violent action. It was very much part of the preparation for the overthrow of President Marcos in the Philippines. They did a lot of important work in America too and Africa. He's dead now but Hildegarde is still active. They were my kind of non-violence teachers, both as models and as theoreticians... It was in workshops. It was really face to face. And they did write and they had particular analytical tools that they used, which I use very much still and that people find very useful.

While a Quaker theoretical frame informs approaches in the fields of community and international mediation, a Gandhian influence, albeit indirect, informs another approach in family mediation.

Fred Gibbons: Coogler, to me, his book opens up with a tribute to the work of Gandhi and peacemaking, and how he almost changed the world.[6] The significance in terms of [the] history of Gandhi. And he talks about all the energy that can go into negative activity and what positive views and co-operation can do in shaping people's lives. So that's the opening statement. I was very interested to see the power. If people can change what can be achieved [when] all that energy is going in the right direction. So that was a starting point. Then he [Coogler] talks about the importance of structure. Of erecting a structure carefully step by step. And he lays great stress, as I know you do, on preserving dignity and how people, if they are helped in mediation to be able to explain their point of view, free of intimidation, are much better at negotiating. The more comfortable they are, the more progress they can make and feel valued in that session. And so structure became the key. It had to be structured. I suppose ground rules would be crucial to ensuring the structure.

It also needed a team and it needed even the cleaner to understand exactly what was going on, the whole team – secretaries, administrators were involved in team meetings every week to look at the progress of a project, to express their

> views and make changes based on what was recommended. If there was a [mediation] meeting in progress then you didn't knock on the door. Everybody had to [show] respect. You didn't always get it. Mediation was taking place. It had to be quiet and [there had to be] respect for people trying to work through a family problem. And the whole team had to share it.

The value – and the limitations – of the application of a specific theoretical concept, in realising the core objectives of mediation, is articulated in two areas of practice, first in relation to the international scene.

> **Diana Francis:** Then another concept which I find terribly useful is Johan Galtung's notion of cultural violence, but his relating that to structural violence and direct violence. So using those three categories I find enormously useful and explanatory for people. Not that they're the truth, because you could have any other three categories, but I find those very useful.
>
> I use as a tool, very often, 'needs and fears mapping'. This is all in that book, that which comes from Cornelius and Faire. And I don't like the win–win language. It's much too happy clappy. You can't talk about that with people when you've gone to hell and back, and probably not back. But as a tool I find it useful in dialogue workshops. I might ask people in the first place to tell each other about their positions, i.e. what they think should happen and how they understand the conflict – which I take to be part of their position. So your story and your demands. So to allow people to do that, make space for that, which is very tough, and then to invite them to do a new piece of analysis and presentation in relation to their needs and fears. It is an extraordinary experience to see the degree of, well, the experience and recognition of common humanity that that can facilitate.
>
> Of course it's not a magic wand. I once tried using it, going straight into needs and fears, without allowing... I don't mean allowing, I didn't try to prevent...without *inviting* them to present their position. One side really played the game and did it and the other side put their position and so then the other side felt terribly wronged and exposed. So that was a lesson hard learned. In the course of five days it was well recovered from, but very uncomfortable, and I didn't feel clever about it.

In the arena of victim–offender mediation, a second example illustrates similarly how the theoretical component is seen to be integral to the realisation of core aspirations of mediators.

> **Yvonne Craig:** [Research has influenced my practice] a great deal. I have spoken of your work, of Simon Robert's work and of course the impetus that was given by the early American work on mediation. Perhaps I haven't indicated enough that it is important to me that I have always been amongst those people who, in talking about mediation, have argued very strongly that mediation is not second-class justice. And this is not only because as a magistrate I was concerned with

> justice, but also because of the great influence of people like Martin Wright [on] restorative justice, [and] Tony Marshall, who, of course, had both pioneered the victim/offender reparation thing within the criminal justice system. And that has been tremendously successful and influential. And I think it has been very important because mediation has not been [seen as] a process of justice and fairness. So it is true to say that the restorative justice strand in mediation theory is always very important. Restoring just relations between people. It's a theme that is harmless so far as I'm concerned. It isn't only harmless, again from a global perspective it is peace and justice. Peace and justice have to go together globally as they do in inter-personal relations. In other words you cannot mediate an agreement that is unjust.

It is not the theory that poses problems for practice; on the contrary, a rich source of theory, generating new intellectual and experiential insights, is welcomed for providing fresh and imaginative directions for thinking about the field. At the same time, there is tension, unexplained here but common in the field, that can arise between the academic and the practitioner.

> **Andrew Acland:** I'm just trying to think what research I have been reading recently which might have affected [my practice]. I've got very interested recently for example in research into the nature of intuition. Because if you are running a fairly fast-moving process, you don't actually have a lot of time sometimes to make very reasoned decisions. And I've got interested in how people make those kind of intuitive decisions. And the more I read about it, the more I realise that a lot of them are not intuition in some mysterious sense. It is actually experience-based and in some ways it is, I don't think scientific is quite the right word, but it is. So that kind of research I do find interesting. If I read theory it tends to be organisation and psychology rather than in mediation *per se*, and there are some very interesting things coming out ranging from the very scientific and academic right through to the frankly mystical.
>
> There's quite a lot of theory now on group processes, participation theory and things like that but a lot of it is frankly pretty turgid. I think one of the problems is that there's always been a great tension between academics and practitioners in this field. One of my standard questions to any academic is, you know, have you actually run a meeting about parking meters or dog poo on a wet Friday evening in a community centre. Because you don't need a theory, you need crowd control.

Mediation as a staged process is a recurring theme. The analysis of mediation as a staged process of negotiation is famously theorised by Gulliver (1979). This theoretical framework of the two interlocking processes, developmental and cyclical, constitutes one of the fundamental planks of understanding about mediation. This is based on phases of a developmental model that are not 'merely the constructs of the observer, rather the phases arise out of the dynamics of the interaction itself' (Gulliver 1979, p.184).

> **Marian Liebmann:** But I think there are certain principles. To me one of the most important principles is that it is a staged process. The most common reason why things don't work out and when people are arguing is that they are not listening to each other. And the first time somebody says something you get off on that particular tack, but you never get the full story on the table. So it's good to have some kind of stages. I know it's different in commercial mediation. They only meet at the beginning…and do it all in shuttle and meet together to sign something. But I think the fact that you have to go through certain stages seems to be important. You have to help people to listen to each other. If you haven't got all the information it's no wonder you are in conflict because you haven't got time to stop and think about it.
>
> I have seen people train in mediation without giving any kind of staged process at all. I found that amazing that you would actually be training people like this. This is in workplace mediation. Well, you just kind of invent it, you just kind of do it. So they did stuff around skills but to me the skills hang on a framework. When I train people in victim–offender mediation, we spend a day or so looking at restorative justice theory and things about offenders and victims. And then we do indirect mediation because that's how you start anyway. And I know some people disagree with that because they say you are carrying messages to and fro and you can't be certain but I still think that is a valid thing to do.
>
> And then I train the stages of the face-to-face meeting. But each stage introduces some more skills. It's all pegged onto this process. Without that, even if it doesn't go according to plan, even if you go round in circles you can think, 'Oh well, we've been through two rounds of uninterrupted time and questions and so on and what is it that we need now, things are still not sorted. I think we need some separate meetings.' So you've got this kind of structure to hang on to that helps me think about where I am in the process and what it is that is needed next. And it's not so much like a fixed rigid thing. If people haven't listened to each other they are never going to work out how to reach agreement. Certain things have to come before certain other things.

An Italian perspective affirms the value of a clear theoretical and methodological framework of reference for practice. The 'negotiation model' of mediation, its centrality undisputed, is nevertheless located within a method of practice that values additional therapeutic understandings as necessary for effective practice in the family field.

> **Costanza Marzotto:** The principles that inform my approach in family mediation practice come from a theoretical and methodological framework of reference, [and] are known as the *'relational–symbolic'* approach in a psycho-social and clinical perspective… From my practice I draw [on] the efficacy of the use of the *genogramme* as an instrument to understand the implication of many generations

in the process of divorce and [of] the indissolubility of the parent–children bond. When I trace a line from husband and wife, and another, different line between parents and children, I can remark [on] the impact in the daily life, of a theoretical concept: you live as parent during *all* [of] life.

When I [see] the rush of the couple to go directly or speedily to negotiation, without enough exploration of [the] history of the couple, I register the difficulty to sign the final arrangements, to change the attitude in front of the other parent and to recognise his value.

In my practice I can find a confirmation of the theoretical model. On the other side, the actions 'here and now' are more comprehensible [in] the light of the theory. A very important contribution comes from the research: the results coming from a scientific analysis of the practice give me new direction for my practice.

A progression of thinking, in culturally diverse directions and involving fresh, flexible and relevant approaches to practice, is recounted by the next mediator. Recognition of the need for innovation arose as the result of decades of experience as a practitioner, trainer of mediators, and supervisor observing other experienced mediators' practice.

Tony Whatling: I think it is that route by which I came [into mediation] that clearly bears on the way I do it, and very much that strong influence of task-centred, time-limited, client-centred, client problem-solving models that don't try to get inside the person's psyche. And inevitably when I came into this business I became influenced by the Fisher and Ury [1981] *Getting to Yes* negotiation and dispute resolution frameworks. The Haynsian[7] future-focus, Western, problem-solving [approach] made sense at the time. And was comfortable for me in terms of that background. And so the future focus was terribly important to me at the time and to family mediation in this country. Yes [I've moved on from that].

From papers at conferences that I've given in the last couple of years – one size does not fit all. What I am saying about it now is that it is still valid. It is entirely valid but not for all potential clients in mediation. And to say come in to this shop and this is the product, as it were, take it or leave it, isn't good enough. Off-the-peg suits look good on some people... So I think, for example, without going into models yet, I became increasingly concerned, once I started thinking, about gender. Once you begin to unpack the issues around the way men and women think differently and act differently... I'm very fortunate that I spend a lot of time doing a lot of observation of practice as a professional practice consultant. What happened was that I was actually able to observe these sorts of issues very much more objectively than being in the chair as a mediator. And I could see these extraordinary communication problems. Deborah Tannen says all male/female communication is cross-cultural. And I could see sometimes women struggling with this model in the room but at other times I could see men struggling with two female mediators and their ex [partner], trying to arrive at a common language.

And this whole business of the past…[and Haynes'] mantra about emotion is that it is ['unuseful'] and we can't change the past, we only have to change the future, was for some couples fine, but for others the past has got to be talked about, it's got to be unpacked.

Then there's stuff around apology and forgiveness. It's calling for a bigger toolbox… But what's very fascinating for me is that some mediators admit to it almost on the side, as though it's a little bit of a secret. 'I know I'm not supposed to be doing that. I know I'm not supposed to be facilitating emotional discussions of the past. But I find it helpful.' There's that purist paradox.

Again in the family mediation field, North American writings and research have been extensive and of great influence in the UK. Two British family mediators reflect on both the benefits and limits of the impact of this body of theory on their family mediation practice. The greater the theoretical range, the more responsive the mediator can be to differing needs.

Lorraine Schaffer: There is family therapy which is based on systematic practice. Obviously that's been an influence on me. And I think there are quite a lot of overlaps with what systemic family therapists do and what mediators do. And there are a lot of skills that we can learn from each other. So I don't feel I know enough about family therapy because I'm not a trained family therapist, but there are ideas that I have found useful. And I think as a social worker too, to be able to think about systems… Although you may have two people in the room with you, I think it is important to be aware of all the other background influences, extended family, children obviously.

So I think if you think systemically, it is useful rather than just saying everything is located with that person or with two people. I also think the needs theorists are quite useful. I think Maslow's hierarchy of needs is a useful way of trying to understand where people are coming from. So if their basic human needs are not met then they are usually not going to be in a position to be very self-reflective or anything else. I think you need to know that. And I do like the way Bernie Mayer has adapted the needs theory to looking at conflict resolution. He postulates a 'Wheel of Conflict' which puts needs at the centre and then has things around it like communication, values, structure, emotion and history. I think the idea that there are these dimensions of conflict, the cognitive, emotional and behavioural, is very useful. Thinking about where people are and how deep to go and whether you need to resolve conflict on all those planes. It's useful to think there are these different levels. So I think that needs theories are helpful.

Just recently we have had this workshop with John Winslade on narrative mediation, and although I have been reading the book, he did bring it more to life. I think there are useful ideas from that as well. Useful in terms of how you can actually ask questions in mediation. I don't totally buy the post-modern social constructivist theoretical views because I actually do think there are some values that are more absolute in society. But I think the point about reading and theory is that it makes you think and I think if you stop thinking and stop learning as a mediator, your practice is going to go stale. But I learned to be eclectic as a social worker and I think I'm eclectic as a mediator. I think one of the problems with Bush and Folger's transformative mediation, from what I've heard, people and services can go very gungho, that it's only *that* way to do it, or there's only one way of mediating or only one model and I don't agree. I think the more models, the more theories you have, the more you can be responsive to different people and different needs.

Questions can arise, of course, about the quality of research whatever its influence, and how best to deploy it. Consumer studies are seen to be of particular value.

Tony Whatling: I think [research] matters desperately. To what extent is the research informative? It's not my field of expertise but I am endlessly fascinated by client-centred studies, in terms of what they can tell us about what we do well and what we don't do well. I, and probably others, were somewhat damaged in the early days by *Surviving the Break Up* [Wallerstein and Kelly 1980] – its dogma and somewhat dubious methodology. And also I think by a lot of studies which told us how badly parents had done in the past. I am now increasingly interested in sharing research with clients, not in a directive way but in an informative way... Having the direct hands-on experience of working with the Ismailis, there's nothing quite like that. Being in the room with it...is a much more experiential route to the theory rather than a theoretical route. It's all begun to come together...getting an increasing understanding of the values that they bring into the room, primarily through training, but inevitably many many hours of conversations and [recognising] that there are differences that it is important to understand and to draw out. I never believe that I know it all, as it were.

Testimony to the considerable impact of some research on practice, manifesting in the improvement both of intellectual understanding and in practice skills, possibly at the same time, is evidenced by this experience in the labour relations field.

Roy Lewis: Other than this one general point, given my starting point and origins in collective labour relations, I obviously started with a notion of what collective bargaining is about. So to that extent the answer is yes [research has been influential]. To put it in a nutshell I suppose it could be reduced to one sentence. The notion of collective negotiation activity that most appeals to *me* is what Otto Kahn-Freund called a dialectic of collective bargaining. On the one hand it expresses the conflict between the parties, and practically, on the other hand, it provided a means of resolving it. And then the third-party role comes along and is a gloss essentially on that process. So this is all reducing it to a couple of sentences. Kahn-Freund spent his life trying to work this out. In a nutshell this would be my starting point as someone who comes from a background of the study of collective labour relations.

Not all research has proved invaluable and there are gaps of understanding begging to be filled by further research on relevant topics, as emerges in the following view about the subject in the context of family mediation.

> **Lorraine Schaffer:** I think Joan Kelly's research has been helpful. The idea of parallel parenting has really stayed with me and I've actually used that, because in a way it's accepting the reality that there are some parents who are not able to get on with each other for whatever reason, simply cannot bear each other, perhaps they have remarried or have new partners, as long as they are not openly in conflict, as long as they accept each other as parents, the children can actually go between two homes where there is not a lot of communication, but not a lot of conflict, and that will work. And I think that was quite freeing to think that you don't always have to get people to be nice to each other, to be able to talk.
>
> I think, because the research is mostly from America, I do think we do have to have research in England, because we are a different culture. I think it would be very useful. Certainly there has been the research about contact issues and quite frankly what I have read is so commonsensical that I'm not sure how helpful it is. You know, people in conflict are going to have a hard time with contact. So fine, we know that. What we don't know is what actually works for people. Does mediation work? What do they need, what do they want, does it last? Those are the questions I think somebody needs to research in England.

The most valuable research, in terms of its impact on improving practice, may be that conducted by the practitioner him/herself. This view involves no diminution of the import of other researchers' contribution to the field, in this case international relations.

> **Diana Francis:** I think I mentioned the [works] that are really important to me and they are really important. What I say now makes this sound more important than that. The research that influenced me most was my own action research.[8] Because it was precisely four years of challenging myself minutely about everything I thought, said and did. It is part of why I find it very hard to give a short answer to any questions... My data was created by my accounts, my minute by minute accounts almost, of processes that I facilitated over two to three years. It just does open so many questions and makes you challenge your own assumptions constantly. Just going through that process at this very radical action research centre in Bath really made it. It's called the Centre for Action Research in Professional Practice (CARPP). And it's about habits of self-challenge as a professional...

Summation

That theory and research do have significance in practitioners' understandings about their work and how they practise is affirmed by contributors, though a minority questioned the extent of that significance. Striking too is the broad consensus that conceiving of 'theory' in any narrow terms, such as an academic text, is not necessarily considered to be helpful. Rather a rich variety of sources and forms of theory are perceived to be of value in influencing, informing and advancing understanding and therefore practice experience.

For all contributors the culture of collegiate exchange, through peer discussion, at seminars, workshops and conferences, and above all through feedback from clients, creates a most effective environment for learning, one corresponding to that of the guildhall of craftsmen where regular exposure to other practitioners, apprentice and proficient, is encouraged even required (Pou 2003).

It is quite clear, too, that mediators, in practising as well as teaching, training, researching and writing about their work, inevitably reflect upon it. That induces personally and mutually generated processes of explication and conceptualisation resulting in knowledge, including self-knowledge, as well as skill-building. Exposure to fresh thinking can result not only in improved theoretical understanding but also in the adoption of appropriately flexible, even radically different practice approaches. The direct influence of teachers as well as in teaching itself, especially co-teaching across disciplines, can, for some, be more productive in enhancing theoretical understanding and gaining insights than the reading of any books or articles. For others the literature dealing with 'pragmatic' issues is rated more highly than 'academic articles'.

Finally, it would be misleading to postulate any notion that a conceptual let alone practical opposition exists between the spheres of empirical, pragmatic knowledge and of theoretical knowledge. Theory can take many forms, interweaving constructively with practice in a recursive relationship of mutual influence and significance.

Notes

1. Ogus (1998), on the other hand, highlights the advantages of self-regulation, compared to external regulation, for *protecting* greater consensual standard-setting, flexibility and creativity.
2. Leading researchers from the Universities of Bradford, Bristol, Exeter and Newcastle, and the Roehampton Institute, have contributed directly to these joint working parties. In addition, the research of Gulliver (1979), Cobb and Rifkin (1991), Grillo (1991), Kelly and Duryee (1992), and others has significantly informed family mediation thinking on training and practice in the UK.
3. This refers to the celebrated negotiation programme attached to the Law School of Harvard University.
4. See Further Reading for a list of books and articles and other writings expressly recommended by contributors.

5. *A Sudden Outbreak of Common Sense: Managing Conflict through Mediation* (1990).
6. O.J. Coogler (1978) inscribes his book with a quote from Mahatma Gandhi: '*I have learnt through bitter experience that one supreme lesson, to conserve my anger, and as heat conserved is transmuted into energy, even so our anger can be transmuted into a power which can move the world.*' Coogler continues with these words: 'This system of structured mediation is, therefore, my anger transmuted into what I hope is a power to move toward a more humane world for those who find themselves following in my footsteps.'
7. The late Dr John Haynes, distinguished North American trainer, teacher and practitioner, promoted particular tenets of mediation practice, including focusing on the tasks in order to reduce emotional pain and turbulence, and eschewing any exploration of the past – in his view the past is where the problem is so focus on the future where the solution lies.
8. Ph.D entitled 'Respect in Cross-Cultural Conflict Resolution Training'; Diana Francis' book *People, Peace and Power* was based on it.

The Task

8
Practice Experience: Styles and Models

> He never sought to influence the outcome of the negotiations beyond a passionate appeal to both sides never to walk away. He was, they said, the orchestrator of their music without knowing the lyric of their meaning.
>
> (Jane Corbin, 1994, writing of the unique atmosphere of respect and friendship engendered by the Norwegian mediator, Terje Rod Larsen, in *Gaza First: the Secret Norway Channel to Peace between Israel and the PLO*, pp.8–9)

The mediation world has accepted, over many years, that there is no one best way to practise, and this had been confirmed in empirical studies. A rigorous approach to clarity about the nature and purpose of mediation and to adherence to mediator codes of ethics and the core principles of mediation has co-existed with a catholic mix of practice styles and models. Diversity of style and of model is usually considered to be one of the main strengths of mediation, welcomed for the benefits of flexibility, of cultural sensitivity, of creativity and of consumer choice (Conneely 2002). Vivid examples, captured at a particular moment, the late 1980s, in the USA, are those rich and diverse individual profiles of distinguished practitioners mediating in various fields (Kolb *et al.* 1994).

Multiple factors, apart from mediator style and model, also give rise to the different forms of practice, for example, the institutional and organisational context (including the relationship of mediation to the public justice system); the kind of dispute being negotiated; the expectations of the parties; and whether lawyer representatives are present during mediation. Such diversity, and the 'ideology of choice' that it engenders in theory, can be problematic in practice, creating potential confusion for the public and the risk that the intervener fails to make clear, and therefore, prospective parties fail to understand, essential distinctions of role and function, and critical differences between models of practice (Menkel-Meadow 1995, p.124). If, therefore, engagement in the mediation process is to have the parties' fully informed and voluntary consent (and, in relevant areas of practice, that of their lawyer representatives) and, if discrepant expectations are to be avoided, a heavy duty lies on a mediator to disclose in advance his or her preferred practice model and style. This is necessary too because of the danger, possible in any profession, of complacency arising from a conviction of benignity in one's own intervention, for example: 'Even given the diversity of styles now practiced, many believe that few mediators have strayed far from basic principles, or maintain that few mediators, unlike brain surgeons or criminal lawyers, are in a position to cause real harm to clients' (Pou 2003, p.203).

Styles of practice

> ...the primary function of the mediator...is not to propose rules to the parties and to secure their acceptance of them, but to induce the mutual trust and understanding that will enable the parties to work out their own rules. The creation of rules is a process that cannot itself be rule-bound; it must be guided by a sense of shared responsibility and a realization that the adversary aspects of the operation are part of a large collaborative undertaking. (Fuller 1971, p.326)

In the theoretical endeavour to address disparate and ambiguous forms of mediation practice, different schemes of categorisation have been constructed. Silbey and Merry (1986), for example, categorised a 'bargaining' and 'therapeutic' conceptualisation of mediation practice; and Riskin (1994) devised a grid of descriptors of key 'mediator orientations', a system of classification based on two principal questions, one of problem definition and the other of mediator role – that is, whether *the mediator* defines the problem narrowly or broadly, and whether the *mediator's* primary objective is either to *evaluate*, assess and predict the grounds for settlement, or to *facilitate* the parties' negotiations without evaluating.

More recent developments, also in the USA, take this polarisation process further. Differences of practice approaches, it is now argued, are not 'just a matter of style', but reflect fundamental contrasts of value, principle and philosophy (Charbonneau 2001, p.39). Moreover, one mode of practice, the Transformative Mediation Framework, lays claim to be 'a qualitatively distinct approach' to mediation, in comparison with others, the problem-solving approach in particular. This framework, it is postulated, has the potential for generating transformative effects (moral and more ethical ways of being) in the parties and in society, but only if mediators concentrate on the opportunities for party 'empowerment' and inter-party 'recognition' that arise in the process (Charbonneau 2001, p.42; Folger and Bush 2001). At a stroke, the Transformative Framework assumes the entire mantle of mediation, not only appropriating traditionally acknowledged hallmarks of good mediation practice as its own, but also premising their exclusive realisation on a transformative 'mindset' (Folger and Bush 2001, p.23).

No reference to or acknowledgment is made in the literature on Transformative Mediation, of the universal, empirically substantiated cross-cultural delineation of the core nature of the mediation process that confounds the divisive dualities inherent in the transformative framework of mediation (Gulliver 1979). The analytic clarity of this delineation of process is of value precisely because the dynamic reality of mediated negotiations is one of complexity and inherent unpredictability. If the mediator fails to understand this universal process, negotiations could be prolonged, or damaged, or fail. In addition, mediating under time constraints and with limited information can be like 'stepping lightly across a minefield. If [the mediator] accidentally steps in the wrong place the entire process can blow up in his face' (Saposnek 1983, p.27).

Gulliver (1977, 1979) has highlighted two concepts fundamental to an understanding of mediation and the role of the mediator:

- Mediation serves a negotiation process.
- The role of the mediator is understandable only within an understanding of that process.

The fundamental skill of the mediator lies in knowing how to set up and orchestrate other people's negotiations and, in particular, to manage that crucial information exchange that moves the parties progressively through the developmental phases of the mediation process towards a mutually agreed outcome. This has been the traditional skill of the mediator in other cultures and times (Gulliver 1979). The most important of the mediator's functions, therefore, are first, to facilitate constructive communication exchange between the parties; and second, to recognise and manage the critical transitions between the successive phases of the process.

The intervention of the mediator is most needed (and most problematic therefore) at moments of transition. The most problematic of these is the transition between the early phase ('exploring the field'), when differences and extreme assertions are more likely to be expressed and when consequently the distance, insecurity and hostility between the parties is greatest, and the more constructive phases when differences narrow and the potential arises for exploring common interests and possible options for co-operative endeavour and consensual decision-making. How that change is brought about is critical and is best illuminated in the style, the manner and the timing of the mediator's interventions. It is recognised that different strategies will be required at different phases and the relevance of the strategy that a mediator deploys relates crucially to its timing within the process. What may be appropriate at an early stage may be totally inappropriate at a later stage and vice versa. An understanding of the meaning of the strategy can only occur within an understanding of the context of the process it serves. Nor, as the literature makes clear, are parties the passive recipients of the mediator's interventions. The strategies of the parties themselves combine with those of the mediator in a dynamic and fluid situation of 'reciprocal influence' (Kressel and Pruitt 1985, p.196).

An inattention to this fundamental processual dimension for thinking about mediation characterises a peculiarly North American preoccupation with strategy, technique and a position/interest-based approach that dominates mediation thinking and training programmes there (see for example, Fisher and Ury 1981). It is on the basis of these assumptions about mediation that the Transformative Mediation Framework has come to be defined and contrasted (Beal and Saul 2001). Other aspects of practice, relating both to descriptions of models (the 'standard problem-solving practice') and to delineations of process (the 'standard stage models of the mediation process') are characterised, without empirical substantiation, as *intentionally or inadvertently* fostering 'disempowerment', over-directiveness, settlement-driven approaches, pressurisation, a judgmental stance or coercion (see for example, Folger and Bush 2001, pp.2, 25; Della Noce, Bush and Folger 2001). In addition, insufficient distinction is drawn between the notion of settlement (the legal disposal of the case) and that of agreement (the individual parties' reciprocal and consensual resolution of *their* issues, legal, ethical or psychological).

As the 'ownership' of mediation becomes the new and controversial focus of debate, a hierarchy of practice models is constructed. The combination of different theoretical and practice approaches is labelled a 'myth'. No combination of approaches is possible, it is asserted, as each approach mutually invalidates the other and the 'incompatible' theoretical frameworks, and practice habits that underpin their difference, make it impossible to 'do both' (Folger and Bush 2001; Della Noce *et al.* 2001, pp.53, 54). 'To choose any approach to practice is to choose a set of values. We inevitably assume that the values we are choosing are the ones that mediation should be built on' (Della Noce *et al.* 2001, p.54). Thus the Transformative Mediation Framework recognises and empowers itself.

This chapter explores the subject matter of mediator styles and practice models as reflected in the contributors' descriptions drawn from their direct experience. The scope and variety of professional and personal practice paradigms represented in the UK and in Europe are at once rich, contradictory and more modest than those revealed in contemporary North American literature (see Bush and Folger 1994; Lang and Taylor 2000). A singular contrast is the North American propensity to define practice in rigid terms of either/or dichotomies. These 'simplistic taxonomies' do not appear to constrain thinking in the UK or Europe in respect of the complexity and multi-layered textures of practice experience (Menkel-Meadow 2001, p.126).

As the contributors' reflections on this topic reveal, a question about a practitioner's style of practice raises new questions rather than provides concrete answers. The description of style involves defining an individuality of practice approach which cannot be separated from other issues – the perceived purpose and management of the mediation process; the parties and other participants including lawyer representatives; the subject matter of negotiation; and the structural arrangements framing the organisation of the session. Additional factors too, internal and external to the process, have an impact, such as the statutory framework. Of less relevance is the gender or profession of origin of the mediator, except in the commercial context.

General approach to the question of style of practice

It is interesting, in the light of current North American debates on the subject, that several of the contributors not only did not articulate their approach in terms of any particular style or framework but also, regardless of field of practice, found the question of their 'style' itself a puzzle. There appeared, too, a strong resistance to any attempt to pigeonhole practice approaches and a readiness to challenge simplistic definitions of style.

> **Philip Naughton:** I don't know quite how to answer that [question about individual style]. No particular style. I think you'll have to ask others. What styles are there? There is the bully. There is the confidante. There is the cerebral. There is the sociable man or woman. I don't think I've ever attempted to be the cerebral. I will rarely, I don't think I have ever bullied clients though I sometimes bully lawyers. Most of the time what I'm trying to do is to work with each party and become part of each party's team. The perennial problem is how far you go in pressing parties in respect of the merits. No successful facilitative mediator is truly facilitative. You're not doing your job unless you press a party with questions, mainly in the form of observations which test the propositions being relied upon by each party. And getting that right is quite a skill.

In the commercial context in particular, it is necessary to distinguish the mediating of negotiations involving representatives of legal teams, from mediating between the individual parties themselves. In this case the mediator adopts a different approach in respect of the negotiating participants. It is worth speculating that the firmness the mediator is able to adopt in relation to the lawyer representatives in the process is likely to be tolerated because that mediator has established credibility with those lawyers. Credibility derives from several sources: a shared professional background; equality of professional standing; acknowledged expertise in the relevant law; mediation reputation; energy and creativity; success rate; a demonstrated capacity for hard work; and the ability to get on together personally (Menkel-Meadow *et al.* 1995; Watson 2002).

In a similar vein, in the community and elder mediation field, categorising one's practice approach in terms of individual style could be seen as a limitation, inhibiting responsiveness to the specific circumstances.

> **Yvonne Craig:** I don't like to think that I have a style. I like to be responsive to what seems to me to be the needs of others. In other words my listening or my attentiveness begins from the moment that I read my case papers about the problem to when I open the door and see [the parties]. I did at one stage when I was young. I nearly went on the stage. Therefore I think perhaps I have a natural ability, as I understand actors have, to forget themselves and to enter into other people. I adapt myself to what I see to be necessary.

This deliberate reluctance to categorise style is matched by the difficulty of specifying one's unique style of practice particularly when a mix of styles is common. Another's perception (such as that of a co-worker) may illuminate aspects of an individual's style that may be atypical or unrecognised, as is illustrated in this reflection in community mediation.

> **Marian Liebmann:** Describing my style is really difficult. I think mostly I'm fairly quiet and considered. At the last one I did, which was a face-to-face session, my co-mediator said she saw evidence of a kind of assertiveness and steel that she hadn't actually known that I possessed. So needs must. I actually told people to shut up and that they weren't getting anywhere in this particular direction. That was one mediation where I actually thought the legal position was important. So I said, look, the legal position *is this*. It's no good you waving your papers and saying you are going to law because there's nothing for you to gain. So can we put all that to one side and get on with the actual issues that we *can* agree or disagree about.

This example also illustrates the clear but fine line that mediators draw between the giving of legal advice, which is inseparable from a partisan relationship of representation and is, therefore, not appropriate, and the giving of legal information, setting out information as an impartial resource to both parties, which is appropriate in mediation. Informed consent as to the nature and objective of the professional relationship protects the parties, and the lawyer, when acting as a mediator (Riskin 1984).

Two themes emerge from contributors' reflections. First, the mediator's style of practice can be associated with a range of other significant factors – the parties' needs and wishes; the dynamics of the situation; the practice context; the field of dispute; the stage in the mediation process; and the individual personality of the practitioner. So what may even be described as an *absence* of individual style, can also be perceived as one seamlessly adapted to these requirements. Second, whatever way the contributors describe their approaches, these correspond with that well-documented continuum representing the range of strengths identified cross-culturally in the literature (for example, Gulliver 1979). These range from virtual passivity to 'chairman' to 'enunciator' to 'prompter' to 'leader' to virtual arbitrator. 'These terms are not proposed as principally typological of interventions but rather as useful indices along that continuum: Actual roles and associated strategies can be displayed as more or less resembling, more or less near to, one or other of these indices. This, of course, states nothing about the effectiveness of the strategies' (Gulliver 1979, pp.220–21).

Style of practice linked to a party focus

The way in which differing styles of practice are deliberately adopted in relation to the parties' attributes and needs is exemplified in the teachings of the distinguished North American mediator and teacher, the late Dr John Haynes, renowned for his charismatic persona and the specific strategies that comprised his explicit tenets of practice (for example, the mutual, neutral problem definition, the process interruption strategies and his brilliant use of questioning techniques). He also explicitly modified his style according to the perceived personalities and dynamics of the parties, adopting, for example, a more assertive, directive stance with those he regarded as powerful parties (that is, good negotiators, articulate, well-educated and resourced) and a gentler, less directive approach with those he regarded as fragile and more vulnerable, personally, socially and economically. For different reasons, several mediators, in different fields of practice similarly linked their stylistic approaches directly to the particular attributes of the parties to the process. This mediator in the family field with experience of working (including extensive training abroad) in a culturally diverse context, is particularly sensitive to the dangers of ethnocentric and gender bias in styles and models of practice.

> **Tony Whatling:** I suppose it [describing my style] would be things like relaxed, non-directive, all the sorts of things I've already said. I want to try and get as soon as possible to a position with the couple where they experience my respect and therefore I have earned mine. Mediators earn trust. They use it all the time in training. I see it as an intensely inter-personal activity with clients. I don't think it's done well often. So as soon as possible I like to get on to a level, call it a relationship if you like, where they know I am concerned about them, interested in them and want to understand them. We can have some challenging conversation, in which I'm never directive, I'm very much facilitative mediator. Of course we don't know what [dress code is] appropriate to the role. But for me it's not casual. So although I'm very well known for wearing extravagant waistcoats when I'm training, I would not wear those waistcoats for a mediation. Not always a tie, but certainly a smart shirt. I think it is important that first five minutes. And the whole manner, the calmness of my manner, creates an atmosphere in the room.

> I'm going to demonstrate, if necessary, that I'm going to manage this process, but at the same time I'm going to be authoritative with a small 'a'.

Notwithstanding that the following labour mediator's description of his style represents the opposite end of the continuum of intervention, the same primary responsibility is attached to the focus on behaving respectfully as well as *being* respectful towards the parties.

> **Roy Lewis:** [My style can be described as] directive I suppose, fairly informal. But you can't go too far. The one thing you daren't do is crack jokes actually. A sense of humour can be misinterpreted so you have to be very careful about witty remarks. A sense of humour can help [but] you really have to be careful what remarks you make, I think, because they can easily be misinterpreted. You always want to maintain not just a veneer but the reality of being fair minded and courteous to people as well.

Style and the processual shape of negotiations

The optimism of hope that a mediator can bring to parties floundering in the midst of conflict and stress inheres frequently in a faith in the parties' own positive capacities for change, as the following family mediator testifies. Optimism, born of trust in the parties, can be enhanced by trust in the mediation process itself, acquired by the mediator as a result of understanding and experiencing the processual shape of negotiations. At the same time, limited follow-up information, both consumer feedback and research, inevitably creates uncertainties about outcomes.

> **Lorraine Schaffer:** I think, although I'm hard on myself and critical, I think that people I work with, I actually genuinely believe that everybody has something good in them. I actually genuinely think people can change if they want to. I actually think when I'm with people I'm very positive about them and I think, as a mediator, I can give people the idea that there is some hope at the end of the tunnel, and there are ways that they can move forward and not be stuck. Even if they stay stuck you have at least given them some glimmer that maybe there are other ways they could deal with it. And I think sometimes we will never know, because mediation is a very short-term intervention. Although cases might not finish satisfactorily at the time, we will never know really. On occasion I have heard on the grapevine of people in my neighbourhood that have been to mediation, I've actually heard it did have a big effect. We do need that research and that follow-up. We would get much more idea about what effect we do have. The one research project that was done by Janet Walker, was done a number of years ago, and mediation practice has improved a great deal. I would like to see somebody doing some more in-depth research like Robin Emery did, in that longitudinal study in Virginia, which was actually very positive.

One central tension in the role of the mediator is that existing between the need to settle a dispute and the lack of power to do so – what has been termed 'the mediator's dilemma' – the dilemma of how to settle a case without imposing a decision (Silbey and Merry 1986, p.7). This study examines the repertoire of strategies employed by mediators in their attempt to resolve this tension. This same family mediator wrestles with the common dilemma of trying to reconcile strength of intervention with the maintenance of respect for party authority, highlighting the constraints involved, both practical (such as the limited time available) and professional (balancing theoretical preference with professional judgement).

> **Lorraine Schaffer:** If you are a good mediator, if people come up with ideas and plans and proposals, if they think it belongs to them, then I think you've done the job well. But I would say that there are times, if people are floundering and truly stuck, then I do think I can take a more directive role as a mediator, in the sense of asking whether they have thought this, that or the other. Some mediators are very purist and they think you should never suggest any options. But I think if people are having a lot of trouble, then it can be helpful to, say, come up with ideas – 'Have you thought of it this way?' So I wouldn't say I was a passive mediator at all. It's important to get the balance right. So I think sometimes I do wish I would sit back more and give people more space to engage with each other. I think that's a very good mediator who maybe can really give space and time to enable people to talk to each other. I'd like to stop coming in maybe sometimes. But I do think it's necessary. If we are there to do nothing, then why are they coming to us? We have something to offer and can do that.

Style and practice context

Different perspectives inform the vexed subject of how interventionist it is proper for a mediator to be. In the labour relations context above, the directive style connotes a positive approach appropriate to the tough circumstances of labour negotiations. Such a mediation approach may be consistent with the link to the arbitration role where mediators may act in either capacity depending on the terms of reference. The style of mediators who also work as arbitrators is recognised to be similar. The style of the distinguished North American labour mediator, William Hopgood, is typical, as described by a colleague: 'Bill doesn't confuse mediation with arbitration. He doesn't push people, make pronouncements, or use pressure tactics to get them to compromise. He uses question to get at their interests' (Kolb *et al.* 1994, p.150).

One of the advantages of mediation and one of the major factors distinguishing mediation from arbitration is 'the latitude a mediator has to move beyond the issue of who is right and who is wrong', enabling the mediator to move from:

this kind of black-and-white approach to one where the focus is on the parties' interests'. This involves 'getting a fix on things because you've been there before. That's why the parties want you. Anybody who says that mediation is a pure, free-form process, that mediation is not content-driven, is wrong. You have to begin forming a vision early on. That doesn't mean that everything is all mapped out, that you have the strategies and tactics all set. Or that you think that just because you have a fix on things, the parties will agree. You have to condition them [to get used to new ideas] – that's what the process is all about. The parties are buying more than a conference leader. (William Hopgood, quoted in Kolb *et al.* 1994, pp.159, 170–71)

In the context of organisational and community mediation, even the 'conference leader' approach may be a directive step too far, involving a clear departure from the norms of good practice where, although a 'low profile' is the preferred style, differences emerge its interpretation.

> **Carl Reynolds:** I have met people who have described themselves as facilitative mediators, having heard my description, who would say it is OK to offer to people who are stuck, to offer them options to think through things. So I think there is a huge debate that is in the field about where are the boundaries about practice. Now when I started, I would certainly get very dogmatic and say you're not mediating if you are offering options. Now I am much more relaxed about it. It is much more about as long as people understand the type of mediation they're going to be working with then that's fine, because they're making choices about what they're coming to.
>
> On a broad scale I'd say if mediation is alternative dispute resolution, then we should avoid any form of advocacy even it it's the offering of options because otherwise it is not an alternative. Because you know everybody else will offer you advice, suggestions, ways forward and so on. So I suppose on a grand scale I have the view that if it's got to the point where you think people are stuck and you feel no other option as a mediator but to offer options, then you might want to ask yourself, what it is about my practice that has prevented these people from making a decision for themselves. On the one hand. And on the other hand, why is it that I feel that they *have* to make a decision at this moment in time. In other words am I oriented towards wanting them to reach an outcome and therefore I'm overly intervening – Andrew Acland coined the term – 'facipulating'. That's why you need reflective practice because if we don't reflect on what we do then we must get into bad habits...so my default is to say what is it that I have not done to help them to decide for themselves what it is they want to do.

These reflections mirror others which emphasise the primary focus on respect for the parties and their objectives as well as the evolving nature of actual practice experience – from the purity of training principles and the dogmatism and rigidity associated often with the insecurity of the novice, to the more fluid responsiveness and adaptability of the experienced practitioner. Such an evolution is summed up below, as 'and then you make the journey'. There is a similar reluctance to label personal style, as already noted, common to several contexts of practice. Differences of style relate to context, the hard-nosed business context, in particular, where lawyer representatives are normally present in mediation.

> **Tony Willis:** I don't think I can really [describe my style]. Well, I'll pick some rocks off the plain [though] this is not giving you the whole picture. I try to be business-like as these are mostly business disputes; and respect the individuals and their views whatever they may be – to understand why they're doing [what they're doing]. I try to be reasonably brisk in terms of moving things along – I'm bad at doing it and it runs counter to the idea of giving them rope when needed. And I try to be realistic and pragmatic – not get hung up on things they get hung up on; try to see round the edges, the bigger context all the time. [So] I don't know what my style is – it is the style of someone who has done my kind of work and is used to dealing with professionals.
>
> I'm like most mediators, commercial mediators who do this a lot. You get trained as a process interventionist but in subject matter non-interventionist. You get trained to be non-judgemental; you get trained in all these things and then you make the journey. And the journey takes you to being occasionally *extraordinarily* interventionist and *very* directive if you think that's the right thing to do. You try and do it in a very careful way. So if you see a lawyer behaving like an idiot, if there are occasions when you take a lawyer into a room and say, 'You're behaving like a complete prat. Explain to me, this appears to be the case, what the hell are you trying to achieve?' You may take a lawyer into a room and say, 'That point, you damn well know, is absolutely hopeless, isn't it? *Isn't it?*' I'm expressing it in a way that leaves no escape.
>
> So the idea that there is a school of mediation that is directive and a school that is not, in our sort of context, is just impossibly naïve. Occasionally I felt that I could have been a cardboard cut-out. What they needed was a cipher. And I was it. And I recognised that and played the part of a cardboard cut-out. And it worked. But that's very rare. Most of the time I really am running the process pretty tightly and I'm being fairly interventionist and I'm being fairly judgmental when one needs to be – once they've been allowed to play in the sandpit and do what they want to do.

In the field of international mediation, an 'elicitive' approach is preferred, one that draws on the parties' perspectives and meanings rather than on externally imposed expertise.

> **Diana Francis:** On the kind of obvious one [of style], I put myself on the elicitive side of things. So not heavily presentation based, try to start from participants' own perspectives and experiences and bring in theory, any knowledge that *I* want to contribute, as a function of dealing with their experience, and

> using concepts in a functional way for them. I will bring in a tool because I feel it is specifically useful, not because this is what I do. I would always design any workshop from scratch. Never this is what I do in a situation. Always what is the context? What is the group? What are they asking for specifically? I am eclectic. I certainly use far more of other people's ideas and theories, because why would you impoverish what you can offer to people by sticking only to the things you thought of? And it all goes around. I mean nobody's thinking is independent in this sphere. Some of the ideas that people bring are very simple, like John Paul Lederach's pyramid on different levels. Very, very simple things. It happens to be useful. Just as a way of ordering thinking.

Another international mediator (involved, for example, in bilateral workshop discussions in Moldova) also described his style of practice as 'elicitive', that is, combining flexibility with some element of purpose and structure – being able to recognise when the conversation is not being productive and 'trying gently to steer it back to something that is' (Mark Hoffman).

Style and mediator personality and preferences

More textured complexities relating to style manifest themselves in the discrepancies that can arise between the reputation a mediator may acquire and even be proud of – as a tough, no-nonsense mediator, or as cerebral and quiet, for example – and a mediator's own perception of his or her style. The appropriateness of a flexible approach, responsive to the persons and the issues, is again manifest in the commercial context. The personality of the individual mediator is another critical variable in understanding their style of practice.

> **David Shapiro:** Personally I like it [my reputation as a tough, no-nonsense mediator], OK. But it's not true. There is no question that I am very direct. Quite clearly my approach to the problem will vary depending on the issues, the people involved. For example we have done four mediations involving X company and Y firm. And each case they are arguing over peanuts. The lawyer on the other side is constantly pushing all kinds of crazy arguments. And I said to him, 'That's bullshit. It's always been bullshit. I told you it was bullshit the first time you raised it. I'm not paying any attention to it.' I told the other side I was not paying attention to it. 'It's wrong as a matter of law. Stop doing it.' Then he said to me at the third meeting, 'Will you stop me from running the argument?' I said, 'If you wish to run the argument, go ahead. But forget it.' Well, they were back to me for further meetings, four and five…and essentially the next mediation is going to be very interesting. It is basically the same issues involved. It is just the personalities that are going to be different.
>
> I don't think that any mediator, no matter how hard he tries, can get away from who he is. It has to [influence the performance]. Take, for example, mediator S. [He] is a very laid back, cerebral kind of mediator. Very understated. Very

quiet. He has as many successes and failures as I do. I have a totally different personality. Some guy described it in this recent article as 'He takes over the room,' something like that... It's fair to say that that's who I am. It is not fair to say that that's who I want to be in any particular mediation.

Structure and clarity assume particular significance in the way this mediator prefers to work (in relation organisational and environmental matters).

Andrew Acland: For me [style] is all about clarity and structure. I think that ours is a very language-intense business and I really like to get the meaning of words clear and to structure things. I like ideas and issues to be very, very clearly structured and to give people very clear anchors about where they are in dealing with them. I know that some of my colleagues use a more relaxed discursive approach; others, I think, probably are even more prescriptive. So I try and find a balance between being fairly loose and fairly disciplined, but with the structure always in the background.

In contrast to a brisk and business-like style and a clear and highly structured style, appropriate to the worlds of commerce and organisations, a different style may be more appropriate depending on the context, professional background, and/or culture. In the case of the following Italian family mediator, her personal style may reflect both the context of family and inter-personal relationships and her professional background as a psychologist. Her readiness to use humour may be compared to the labour field (see above). She, like other contributors, is unapologetic in describing her own style as 'directive'.

Costanza Marzotto: My individual style is warm, oriented to listening [to] the subjects, but also [to] the family vicissitudes; not only the problems [arising] during the cohabitation, but also the nice memories before the crisis; I use often humour and witty remarks, on my self and about the clients' situation.

I try to discover the symbolic [aspects] of the events, of the objects, of the relations: in order to achieve this objective I ask a lot, I put many questions and at the same time I am directive. On a scale of 1 to 10, I put myself at 7.

Change of style and experience

In the practice of family mediation in Germany, the experience of the following mediator charts a change similar to that described by mediators working in other fields and countries. As a consequence of increasing experience in both child-related and financial issues, his adoption of a more 'liberal' style allows him the freedom to depart from the prescribed 'high principles' of practice laid down in training, the minimilist style in particular, and to explore new approaches, including, on occasion, a greater strength of intervention. In teasing out what is meant by a 'directive' approach, it is clear that for this mediator, it means stating directly where he thinks responsibility for decision-making lies, i.e. with the parties, rather than telling them what to do. At the same time there is an explicit focus on their needs and wishes.

> **Christoph Paul:** It [my style] has changed a lot. I have been much more, is liberal the right word, I don't know if it is. In Germany one of the high principles in mediation has been, and has been taught, a kind of abstinence. You leave it all to the clients and if they don't get along, just give them a second session and a third and a fourth and a fifth. And leave everything to them. And I changed that because I was tired of that.
>
> I get more and more directive, the more experience I have. For example, I say, 'Well, you have a responsibility, you have a child, you have to look for a solution. You have a responsibility towards each other. You have to look for a solution. You can't treat your wife or you can't treat your husband like that.' More directive. And I find it helpful. Sometimes I've been shocked about myself. What am I saying? You know. Then finally I realise that [what] I was saying was liked. At the end of every session I ask what was helpful, what was less helpful. I get the feedback that these directives were accepted as very helpful. [I say] but I think *you* [the parties] have to be clear for yourself. What do *you* need now? I think you need something. So tell me what *you* need now. And I tell them they have a responsibility to find a solution. To find *their* solution. And I address it more directly than I did at the very beginning.

Summary of reflections on style

These reflections comprise a rich narrative that expresses a complex variety of mediator styles influenced by multiple and interconnected variables that determine individual practice. These mediators do not claim to practise in one or other 'style' nor do they find it helpful to classify their practice in any specified way. Indeed there is an express reluctance to categorise and label practice styles, and in most cases, a combination of styles is regarded as a positive option, adapted to meet the contingencies of the situation, the context and above all, the parties' needs. That central focus, on respect for the parties, their objectives and meanings, emerges in all the fields of practice represented and whatever style of practice is deployed.

Contributors might willingly change their style to enhance effective practice especially with greater experience. The concern to eschew any labelling of style contrasts with the dominant North American approach that categorises and dichotomise styles of practice resulting, in some instances, in the creation of divisive dualities. The analytic project, valuable as it must be in its attempt to conceptualise the messy world of practice, inevitably involves the construction of convenient typologies designed to clarify practice. But this project should not diminish an understanding of the complexity, variety, ambiguity, contradiction and unpredictability that make up actual practice.

Adopting a 'directive' style, which several practitioners claimed to do where appropriate, was associated with a range of purposes and meanings. Managing difficult transitions in the process is acknowledged to present one of the central challenges for mediators, for example, at an early stage when maximal demands are likely to be made and when the distance between the parties is greatest, so the shift of attitude required of them is also the greatest, requiring therefore an increased strength of mediator intervention. This can constitute one of the central challenges to the role of the mediator – how to control potentially destructive exchanges effectively and, at the same time, remain impartial and non-directive. The interventions of the mediator have to be understood, therefore, not only in terms of *what* they contain but *how* and *when* they take place.

'Directive' behaviour took different forms: adopting a business-like or assertive stance; contributing ideas about options; engaging in 'reality testing'; and reminding the parties of their responsibility for making decisions. The 'directive' style described was not regarded as involving any departure from good practice principles, such as pressurisation, manipulation or coercion of the parties. Rather, the epithet 'directive' was associated with the readiness to assert a greater strength of intervention where necessary. On the other hand, the unobtrusive style, termed variously elicitive, facilitative and 'laid back', conveyed different forms of mediator behaviour as well – an 'abstinence'; a quiet and considered demeanour; and a calmness of manner. Some mediators adopted both styles and other possible styles, sometimes in the same session.

There is little in these reflections that sheds any particular light on the gender implications of mediator style. No discernable differences of approach reflected the gender of the practitioner, male and female equally unobtrusive and minimalist, and equally ready to assert themselves where it appeared to make professional sense. Nor did the professional background of the mediator appear to have any explicit significance, though it did appear to be assumed in the commercial field that those acting as mediators shared the same background as the lawyers acting as representatives in mediation. What was of relevance was the substantive expertise of the mediator in these and other fields, in labour disputes in particular.

Questions remain about the relevance of the style of the mediators to their success. No empirical research reveals any consensus on what exactly constitutes 'style'. A continuum of interventions is apparent with combinations of style rather than any clear-cut divisions or consistency of identification (McDermott 2005). What empirical studies do show is that success in mediation is a function of the pre-existing characteristics of the dispute and the disputants, as well as the degree to which the parties perceive the mediator to have accomplished the primary tasks of mediation, namely, providing information about mediation, establishing ground rules, gaining the informed commitment of the parties, focusing on the full range of issues raised by the parties, maintaining control of pace, balancing power, opening up communication between the parties, providing the opportunity to be heard, gaining information and understanding, reducing tension and anger, and ensuring that the parties feel responsible for and content with the outcome (Thoennes and Pearson 1985). Realising all these goals depends on the competence of the mediator rather than on the style of practice.

Models of practice

> I shall try to persuade you that fairness in procedures for resolving conflicts is the fundamental kind of fairness and that it is acknowledged as a value in most cultures, places and times: fairness in procedure is an invariable value, a constant in human nature. (Hampshire 2000, p.4)

This section focuses on models of practice, that is, those structural features that frame the mediation process. The usual raison d'etre of an effective model of practice is that it promotes the realisation of a constructive and a fair process. There are additional ways in which these objectives in mediation may be safeguarded (though not necessarily guaranteed), which include the skill and integrity of the mediator; professional training, accreditation and the monitoring of practice; the principle of voluntariness; independent review; etc.

Fuller has famously stated: 'For of mediation one is tempted to say that it is all process and no structure' (1971, p.307). What this observation serves to highlight is the difference between the processes involved in mediation and those involved in adjudication. The latter are characterised by institutional rules, formal procedures and clearly demarcated roles and authority that make up the formal pattern of due process for dealing with disputes. No such institutional framework occurs in negotiation processes where the parties seek to sort their dispute by voluntary exchanges. Where the parties cannot manage this on their own and resort to mediation, certain structural changes become inevitable. First, a simple bilateral process is transformed by the presence of a third party. Second, the very presence of that third party imposes the rudiments of a structure upon the encounter – who is to participate and where, and the time to be made available, for example. Mediated negotiations require this minimum of rules at least, although cross-culturally mediation differs greatly in the way it is organised, the degree of formality, and the number and kind of rules imposed upon the negotiations (Roberts 1983).

In another classic statement, Fuller states that '[t]he central quality of mediation [is] its capacity to reorient the parties towards each other...by helping them to achieve a new and shared perception of their relationship' (1971, pp.305, 325). Toward that objective the structural framework or model of mediation ideally serves two main purposes:

- It enables the parties to negotiate together in a way that would not have been possible on their own. Ground rules usually embody the values that underpin mediation – mutual respect, equity of exchange, for example – and make rational communication possible.

- The framework is designed to secure fairness. Rules of procedure are designed to make possible equal opportunities for full and confidential expression, to offset mediator power or bias, and to enhance party authority for decision-making.

The interwoven nature of structure and process is a conspicuous feature of mediation – the structure encompasses the process and the process informs the structure.

There are a variety of structural arrangements or models that can be used to frame the mediation process, some of which are set out below:

- pre-mediation/preparation or intake sessions
- plenary or joint meetings
- caucus
- separate meetings
- shuttle mediation – the mediator acts as a go-between or conduit, shuttling between the parties who may be physically or temporally apart
- co-mediation
- single or plural meetings
- conferences
- combinations of any of the above.

In addition, practical arrangements can contribute to the effectiveness of the model – for example, separate waiting rooms for the parties to ensure safety and avoid heightening conflict; seating arrangements that limit confrontation and encourage relaxed and open exchange; and plentiful, suitable refreshments to ease tension and reflect an attitude of consideration (Coogler 1978; Haynes 1981; Folberg and Taylor 1984).

Contributors describe using a number of different models of practice, some consistently, others in combination, still others eclectically and in two cases, *sui generis* models are devised to reflect the unique requirements of each situation. Factors that have an impact on the kind of model that is adopted include the number, role and status (representatives or individuals) of the parties; their personalities, needs and behaviour; the kinds of issues to be negotiated; the cultural, physical and institutional context; and the gender of the mediators. No single field of practice appears to be associated with any one particular model of practice, though in the international field several structural arrangements – workshops, fact-finding exercises, etc. – may be deployed concurrently in order to address specific complexities and, indeed, dangers of the situation.

It is interesting to note that the major differences in practice models that emerged were *within* the same context of practice – that of the family and of the commercial context – rather than between different mediation fields.

Preparation for mediation

Most contributors cited the first stage of the preparation of the ground prior to mediation as very important, in the interests of both the mediator and the parties. The normal practice is to set aside separate time with each party, in direct face-to-face meetings or on the telephone. Preparation may serve two purposes – better informing both the mediator, to engage more effectively in the process, and the parties, to decide whether or not to participate. Two stages of preparation may be discerned – the stage involving the making of the decision as to whether or not to mediate; and the stage where the decision to mediate has been taken, but how the mediator proposes to proceed has yet to be determined with reference to the parties and the specific circumstances. What may constitute 'normal' practice across fields and across some countries may not, however, be approved practice in another country, as the following family mediator records how his departure from the accepted German approach – which is never to engage with the parties separately – may be perceived. It is not only in Germany that this professional debate generates major controversy (see Roberts 2005).

Christoph Paul: In Germany we have the sessions only together in family [mediation]. In business mediations it is different. In family mediation [the parties are seen] only together. More and more I dare to try things out. Like separate sessions. For example in Germany there is this model that you should not talk to people on the phone, only organise the date and do everything with the two in front of you. And I think it's not helpful. For example, for me it is much more helpful to just know at least a little bit before on the phone. For different reasons. *I* feel better prepared. For example with this [case of a] young child, the mother is very complicated, the father says she is a borderline personality. I don't know whether it's true or not. She is [said to be] very aggressive and the family therapist terminated the therapy because of too much aggression in the wife. I don't know if it's true but it's very helpful for me knowing it. For example, I am thinking of making this a co-mediation with a female mediator with psycho-social qualifications, which might be helpful. For this purpose it is necessary for me to have telephone calls in advance, to know a little bit about this, which is by German standards very strange.

Advance access to information of this sort helps this mediator equip himself to mediate in the way he sees to be most effective, in this case by engaging a suitably qualified co-mediator to complement his legal expertise. Preparatory meetings prior to mediation also serve the purpose of equipping *the parties* to make fully informed choices as to whether to engage in the process. This is the way the preparation stage is seen to assist in the context of elder mediation.

Yvonne Craig: But of course mediation is always offered, having received first the invitation to mediate. The invitation very often comes from Age Concern. Sometimes the old people directly themselves. And when you respond, first of all in writing, you tell them what mediation is so that they can review it. We give them information about that and whether it will cost them anything. We say we are available. What we like to do is to spend an hour at least with each person who is party to the dispute to listen to what they want to tell us and how they would like to see the matter resolved. We see each one individually. And we tell them about this in our correspondence and we say that after we have met each of you individually and listen to what you have said, what we would encourage you then is to share with us in the joint meeting. And again what we always do, we do our visits in the morning, [have] a sandwich lunch ourselves, and then meet them after lunch generally on the same day.

The preparation stage can serve several different purposes: in respect of community mediation, concretely informing the mediator about the situation, and in respect of victim–offender mediation, ensuring not only the suitability of the proposed encounter and the informed consent of the participants, but also their physical and psychological safety.

Marian Liebmann: First of all it's an initial interview with both sides, separately. I know in family mediation, you started off with a joint model and then you introduced separate interviews because of the domestic violence issues. Community mediators go to people separately and victim–offender mediators do too. For different reasons I suppose. For community mediators it's really good to interview people in their own homes because people are actually saying, 'Listen, you can hear the neighbours, that wall is paper-thin.' You can look at it. Or they say, 'Look at the garden fence' or something. You can actually see what the problem is. You are engaging people on their own territory if you like.

In victim–offender mediation I think it is important to go to people, again in their own homes, or to see them separately, because you don't know what issues there are. You don't know if there are any issues of intimidation or whatever that would make it dangerous for them to meet. So there is a preparation stage. If things go really well and both people are keen to meet and it seems to be the right way forward, then you have a preparation meeting with each side and then we go to a joint meeting. But if there are things to be sorted out or people are not sure, you may need to pay more visits to one side or the other and especially with

> the victim–offender work because sometimes there are messages to pass on that are really important before the meeting happens.
>
> So, yes, preparation time is really important. Somebody once said it's a bit like the icing on the cake. You haven't got to do so much in the preparation that there is nothing left to do, but you have got to be fairly sure that you've built enough cake that the icing will sit on there and will do the job. And it depends very much what the issues are as to what the joint meeting can do. Sometimes it is obvious that only a joint meeting has got any possibility of resolution. Sometimes it is the contrary.

The preparatory meeting, conducted effectively, also allows the parties the time, early on in the process, to begin to think about what it is they really want. This can have the advantage of generating the possibility of positive change – as occurred in the following account of a neighbour dispute.

> **Marian Liebmann:** One thing that really interests me is that sometimes things really shift between the preparatory meetings and the mediation. I remember bracing myself for a really stormy evening once with two families who just really hated each other and thought the other would take the piss. I think I had been quite persuasive to try and get them together, because I thought nothing else is going to help here. They have done all the other things. They have been to the housing association. They won't get anywhere with the law because there's nothing legal here. And one of them said beforehand, 'We are only going to stay for ten minutes,' taking a position near the door and so on.
>
> We started proceedings in the usual way reminding them of the process rules and ground rules and then opened the discussion. And the ones who had been most vociferous said, 'Well, you know, I think it's time we acted like grown ups. The kids will be kids and I think we just need to talk to each other when something goes wrong.' And we tried for half an hour to get some more stuff but it didn't come. They had really sorted it. So I think sometimes things actually happen because people start thinking about things. In the preparatory meeting you really want to help people to think about what they want to say and do at the meeting. You don't want to script it all for them. But you want them to be thinking about what it is they really want.

Separate time with each party, prior to mediation (sometimes termed 'intake meetings') and throughout the process, in order to screen for domestic abuse (affecting not only the parties but also any children and any other significant family members) is now considered to be a requirement of good practice in family mediation (see Domestic Abuse Screening Policy, UK College of Family Mediators 2000). Principles of screening stipulate that this must take place separately with each participant; that each participant must make an unrushed, fully informed and voluntary decision to enter mediation; and that in cases where the abused person has made an informed choice to use mediation, the mediator has a responsibility to ensure that appropriate safety arrangements are in place, such as safe waiting areas, safe termination, etc. (UK College of Family Mediators 2000, sections B.1; D.1.2; 5). There are, of course, additional reasons why mediation may not be suitable – relating to the parties, the dispute or the circumstances. The following family mediator describes how the practice model in her service evolved in respect of preparing the parties for family mediation.

Lorraine Schaffer: Since I was trained in the Bromley model,[1] although we didn't start this way, I think when we moved to the separate intake system, I found that to be much preferable. When I came here to the Institute [of Family Therapy Mediation Service], there was a systemic model being used which meant that people, unless there was reason otherwise, came for a joint intake or a joint session and had only maybe ten minutes with the mediator to check out the risk factors and do the financial [assessment for legal aid]. And I really have transformed the system here so that we do have separate intakes for everybody with very few exceptions. Because I think people need to come separately without the pressure of the other person being there to tell the mediator their story. And I think, although you are not using what they tell you when they come to mediation, I think it prepares people better. So I do actually think that the separate session is very useful having seen the other system operate.

The same mediator has to do both intakes. Times when that hasn't happened it has been very problematical. So they have to assess the case, whether it is suitable for mediation. If people say they are willing obviously we have to have the final say. If there are mental health problems or drug problems, or one person is frightened of the other person – all of those things. I think it gives the mediator the ability to assess it. The same mediator has to see both. At [another not-for-profit service] they have intake workers so when I mediate there I have not done the intake. And I think that's OK too. When people come to mediation for a joint session then that's where it starts.

Preparation meetings, which are common in commercial and other mediation fields can also be valuable once the decision to mediate has been taken – whether it is a meeting of the lawyer representatives to discuss the best way to conduct the mediation, or others who will be playing a significant part in the proceeding negotiations. The following mediator describes the trajectory of one preparatory meeting, highlighting his uniquely flexible approach to devising the appropriate model of practice.

Andrew Acland: I did a lot of work with some of the key people in advance. And we produced a rough format for the meeting, which we abandoned almost immediately, which is very often the way in a situation like this. And then it is a case of letting it flow, and letting it become clear what to do next. The point about all the planning and preparation in advance, is not to come up with the perfect process, but to become thoroughly familiar with all the options and

> possibilities and what you might want to do in different circumstances. Then, if you do need to change direction, you can do so calmly and confidently. I find people really value this willingness to be flexible and responsive to the needs of the situation.

Working models of mediation

Despite crucial differences between contexts of practice, mediation models do not appear to show context-linked features. Individual mediator preferences for ways of working appear to be decisive, however.

The plenary or joint mediation model

A plenary or joint session involves the presence of all the disputants at the mediation meeting. Powerful arguments can be made as to why mediation is best conducted in the presence of all parties. Joint meetings enable the mediator 'to observe the parties in their direct relationships with each other' and thereby gain a clearer understanding of the issues in dispute (ACAS, no date, paras 38 and 39). Direct communication between parties is more likely to be encouraged. This objective is what determines four contributors – two commercial, one international and one family mediator – in their preference for using plenary sessions.

In commercial mediation, one factor that distinguishes it from other fields is the routine involvement of legal representatives in mediated negotiations. As already noted, commercial mediators have no hesitation in adopting a firm approach in managing lawyer representatives compared to the parties, controlling the nature and extent of their participation in the negotiating process (Coyne 1999). The following commercial mediator makes it clear why he prefers to adopt plenary meetings (not exclusively, also resorting to caucus meetings where necessary). This is because these meetings enhance the opportunity both for party self-expression (of the issues that are important to *them*) and for inter-party dialogue between the parties. It is noteworthy, in a field of mediation practice dominated by lawyers, and where the interests of lawyer representatives (primarily in the legal disposal of the case or in a monetary settlement) often prevail, how much importance is attached to giving the parties their own voice in the negotiation process and attending to their needs and interests. The literature on lawyer negotiations highlights how unusual this may be (Menkel-Meadow 1993; Coyne 1999; Golann 2000).

> **David Shapiro:** Let me tell you what I like to do. If I am prepared, OK, I will tell both sides; I do not want any openings from the lawyers. The clients can get something off their chests, fine – 15 minutes. Let them get it out. If the lawyer's going to do it, I tell him forget it – unless I am not fully prepared on the facts and

> I need their opening...to make damn sure I didn't miss anything. Normally I will say, forget it. If the client wants to say something, get something off their chest.
> A guy can spew out all this hate, all this that and the other – the sense of injustice – in 15 minutes. You get more of that OK and you turn the other side off. So that's the one thing. The next thing is, suppose I don't have an opening at all from anybody there. I will open and do the usual mediator opening. It's all confidential, blah, blah, blah. Caucus rules. All of the stuff. Then I will say OK. As I understand it, what you're saying is so and so. Mr X, do you agree with that, or not? And I'll start a dialogue. And I will keep those people in the room with the dialogue going as long as I find that they are exchanging views. And maybe rationalising arguments. [I try and encourage the dialogue] as much as possible. As much as possible...to get them talking directly, not through the mediator. I think that's a much more effective way than using the mediator as a shuttlecock. It doesn't always work that way... it could work that way and I think OK there's a better chance of real communication done that way than doing it through the mediator.

The opportunity afforded by the plenary meeting allows *all* those present to have their say and communicate with one another, not only the parties, as is evident in the description by another commercial mediator who adopts a mixed model with separate time as well with 'subsets' of participants. Each party can be talked to privately as can the teams of lawyers. It is necessary, as already illustrated (Shapiro, p.142), that the propensity of the lawyer representatives to dominate the exchanges be kept in check. What might appear a surprising feature of these commercial mediation exchanges where clients may be corporate bodies with legal representation, is the emotional intensity of exchanges, more commonly associated with the inter-personal disputes of family and neighbourhood mediation.

> **Tony Willis:** On occasions I've kept people in plenary session from beginning to pretty close to the end. There's quite a lot of people who say that you'll be doing that more – I think I agree with that intellectually... [And occasionally that does happen.] The plenary session is very constructive; it goes on a long time; and you see the bones of the [matter] on the table.
> I always have them all together, with almost no exception. Once, in one or two cases and I think I shouldn't have done actually with hindsight. Where they've said, 'We're so angry, we hate each other so much,' and I know the feelings are mutual. Oh it happens, yes...and I then shuttle.

The authority of the mediator to deal effectively with lawyers requires, as already noted, sufficient credibility. This commercial mediator acknowledges the importance of reputation in this respect. Yet the exercise of a degree of care is essential too.

Tony Willis: I don't think anyone's ever complained about it [seeing the parties on their own]. I've been conscious that once or twice people feel a little uncomfortable with it but they've never complained about it. And I do understand the sense of it. I think it's because they know who the hell I am and they know my reputation. And I'm pretty careful to say, 'Would you mind awfully if I talk to your clients?' So I try and deal with it fairly gently.

The shuttle model of mediation

Shuttle mediation refers to the way the mediator may function as a go-between, shuttling between the parties who remain physically (possibly temporarily) apart. The mediator may act as a simple conduit, passing messages back and forth, or may negotiate actively on behalf of those disputants who obviously cannot negotiate directly. Shuttle mediation is commonly used in international disputes, and occasionally in community, environmental, family and labour relations disputes. There are three main purposes behind the use of shuttle mediation:

- It aims to avoid confrontation both for the parties and for the mediator where the level of conflict is high.
- It allows the parties to disclose confidential information to the mediator that they do not want revealed to the other party.
- It gives the mediator the opportunity to discuss matters that would be uncomfortable to raise if the parties were together

(Folberg and Taylor 1984).

There are disadvantages too in the shuttle model – impartiality cannot be seen to operate; the power of the mediator is increased as total control over the process of communication can lead to control over the substance of that communication; the parties are denied the information derived from direct experience of each other; and protection of confidentiality is problematic (Roberts 1997).

Only one contributor, Professor Adam Curle, describes his model of shuttle mediation, a model dictated by the circumstances of working *over years* in conflicts between India and Pakistan; in Sri Lanka and in Zimbabwe as well as, for shorter periods, in Rwanda; and in the war between Nigeria and Biafra:

Adam Curle: I found Biafra very stressful because [it was] very dangerous. And I dreaded going back every time, not so much for myself, partly of course, but for my family. But I knew I had to do it.

He described his first (of two) mediations in Sri Lanka as the 'oddest', involving not the Tamils with whom a temporary peace had been struck, but the new President caught up with a rebellion of impoverished students and others in the south. The mediator's good personal relationship with the President enabled the 'strange truth' to come out that he was himself of humble birth, coming from the same background as the rebels and therefore sympathetic to their cause, and was desperate to reach some kind of peaceful accommodation. In appalling circumstances of conflict 'reeking with blood and horror and piles of smouldering corpses and rivers clotted with bodies' mediation enabled the two sides to make contact in clandestine meetings and come together.

The caucus

The caucus, a North American term, involves the mediator meeting individually with one side or a subset of a participant group (for example, lawyers only or clients only). The primary purpose of the caucus is to enable the mediator to gain access to information and insights that cannot be obtained in the joint meeting (Stulberg 1987). The caucus can be used effectively for purposes of breaking an impasse in negotiations, for educating a party in their negotiation style, and for exploring possibilities of compromise. In family disputes the caucus allows the parties to reveal information to the mediator that they do not wish to disclose to the other party, to explore personal feelings about the issues, and discuss matters too uncomfortable or risky to raise in the joint meeting (Folberg and Milne 1988). Confidential exchanges, whilst one of the main advantages of the caucus, are also fraught with difficulty requiring considerable skill on the part of the mediator in keeping track of what is known, how that knowledge was obtained and from whom, and any constraints attaching to it (Menkel-Meadow *et al.* 2005). Disputants, for example, have no means of knowing whether confidentiality has been breached, if that topic crops up spontaneously anyway.

Three dominant approaches, depending on mediator philosophy, have been identified in relation to the use of the caucus: never caucus; the selective use of the caucus; and always and mostly caucus (Menkel-Meadow *et al.* 2005).

This commercial mediator who adopts the third approach and almost always uses the caucus explains why it is his preferred model.

> **Philip Naughton:** Yes, I am of the view that caucusing – not that I like the expression – is more successful than open sessions. And open sessions are, I say unkindly, are at least sometimes the time where the mediator catches up with what he should have prepared before. That's unkind. Plenary sessions are very valuable, but where I get the work done is in private sessions. What I will often do is to call a pre-mediation meeting of lawyers only to discuss how we're going to do it.
>
> Quite different from...quite a lot of others who will spend more time in open session trying to resolve differences as to interpretation of contract and succession of fact, whatever it be. But I just like to get in there and start working with the teams.

Whilst the literature confirms the usefulness of the caucus – in generating confidence, intimacy and encouragement in the negotiations – this pragmatic explanation, as a way of working effectively with the teams, is not usually cited. In family mediation there is the added necessity of the caucus – the continuing need, in some cases, to screen for domestic abuse, and for protecting fairness (Roberts 2005). The disadvantages are those already referred to in respect of shuttle mediation – including the increase in mediator power, the absence of direct interaction between the parties, and the added time it takes.

Eclectic models of mediation

Many mediators, and the majority of the contributors whatever their field of practice, use a mix of models, most involving a combination of plenary and caucus sessions devised to meet the requirements of the particular situation and the parties' needs and objectives. The following examples illustrate the different kinds of considerations that influence a mediator's approach to structuring the session.

In labour relations a number of factors are relevant: first, the statutory and organisational framework exerts a powerful influence on the way in which mediation is practised. Different processes and procedures – consultancy, mediation and arbitration – impinge and overlap in problematic ways. The long-term aspect of some of the mediated negotiations highlights that broader objectives, such as improving relationships for the future, that are often at stake, rather than monetary settlement or the resolution of a particular dispute. The plenary model is more likely to realise that end. It can consolidate consensual decision-making and limit the risk of tactical reneging on what has been agreed.

> **Roy Lewis:** Typical would be a one-day mediation. But it's sometimes much bigger than that. In fact industrial relations mediation overlaps with consultancy and so you are talking about things that could be longer term, could be designed to improve the entire relationship. It can involve several separate meetings with the parties, separately and together. It would then involve a draft report which you then bring them back to discuss.
>
> Assuming you are working towards a settlement or heads of settlement, there will be a time when they come back. And you say this is what we seem to be on the verge of agreeing here. Then you leave them all there, so that no-one can then turn round and say no, that's not what we were saying. You may have other joint ones or groups.
>
> It may be a combined process [mediation and consultancy]. Sometimes that's what the parties want. The other extreme is somebody's suing someone for sex discrimination, it's due for a couple of weeks in the tribunal in a few weeks time. Let's spend a day trying to see if we can resolve it without doing that if it's in the parties' interests to do so.

> I'm absolutely insistent they have to go into the terms of reference from the outset so that everyone's agreed what the nature of the process is. I'm not worried about a mediation/consultancy overlap. But I would be worried about, or more worried about – though I actually do it – but I'm worried about a mediation/decision-maker role. I find that is much more difficult. Not just mediator/arbitrator. I'm involved in some procedures which involve adjudication and mediation.

This family mediator adopts an entirely flexible approach to his model of working – a confidence to experiment that has been acquired with experience. His practice is clearly unorthodox in the German family mediation context.

> **Christoph Paul:** I am absolutely flexible. For example in inheritance mediations if there are more heirs than four, I never work on my own. I always take at least somebody who is assisting me. Because I think with more than four, I haven't the equivalent training to work in groups. I don't feel so secure working with groups and I think it is very helpful to have someone there.
>
> I have and I do [talk to children]. And I like to...and I find it very helpful. I offer it always at the very beginning when children are on board, that it might come the moment when it is helpful that the children might be within the mediation. I will leave it to the parents and just saying this, that there might be the moment, gives another awareness to the parents that the children are a part of the mediation. In practice when children are involved I think it is not more than 5 per cent. But what I do, I work with chairs representing the children. And what I also do is I ask the parents if they would like to try out changing chairs, sit on the chairs of the children – if they want to try it out. Most of them don't do it but just asking it is sufficient. I am very flexible. I love to try things out. I love it. [My colleagues] say here comes Christoph again. Ask him what he tried out last time.

After decades of thinking in terms of a western 'client-centred, client-empowering' model, a new eclecticism transforms the following family mediator's approach since his recent involvement with the international Ismaili community, participating in devising and presenting mediation training programmes in many countries throughout the world. 'Intellectual understanding derived from direct hands-on experience' has been instrumental in his realisation of the necessity for adopting innovative models more appropriate to a non-western communitarian cultural heritage.

> **Tony Whatling:** I think the difference between the individual and the collectivist is so profoundly important to the way we try to work as mediators that we ignore it at our peril... I think there's no doubt that what I discovered quite quickly was an arbitration style mediation. They [traditional Ismaili conciliators] had never had any training so what they were doing was I suppose a derivation of the early history models of dispute resolution, informal justice systems where you take your problems to a spiritual leader or wise person. And each side

represents their case. And then the wise person or the spiritual leader will tell you what they think should be done.

In the first country I did the programme, Pakistan, people were saying this is wonderful what you are giving us. What I was doing was taking what I knew how to do, which was an individualist, Western model, saying this is how to do it. They were saying to me, 'This is fascinating but our problem is going to be, if we take this model, this approach to a mountain region of Pakistan, we are likely to be judged by the disputants as incompetent.' Apparently in many of those regions the disputants would 'be happy', be satisfied with a judgment even if it went against them. As long as they felt that that historical cultural style had been [observed], they would feel that justice had been done, I suppose.

It has been a running dilemma for me…because it seemed to me that what I had to try to do was to constantly [attend to] the extent to which the model could be adapted to be more culturally sensitive. I'm still working at it week by week. How far it will be adapted to be more culturally sensitive without at the same time bending it so far that it is no longer mediation in terms of its fundamental principles.

In the international context, the danger of imposing 'Western' expertise is recognised to be one of the many pitfalls to be avoided, by trainers in particular, in the context of peace-building and conflict transformation initiatives (Francis 2002). Equally it is recognised that trainers must be aware of uncritical acceptance of 'traditional' methods which can embody their own oppressive elements, particularly in respect of gender. In this context the fundamental importance of respect – for individuals and for other cultures – takes on particular significance in relation to inter-group political mediation at whatever level. Mediatory interventions can take a variety of forms, specific to each situation, and additional to those operating at the high elite political level already described in respect of the shuttle mediation between leaders in Sri Lanka. The plenary model has the chief benefit of keeping all participants communicating around the table rather than breaking into small groups. Parallel pieces of work – workshops; study visits; fact-finding on the ground for 'reality' checking; bilateral conversations with individual participants; multi-layered discussion within the facilitation team itself; bringing in external expertise (for example, for constitutional advice) – all these combine, in a complex interplay of plenary, caucus and co-working models, to contribute to the lengthy and complicated process that mediation in these circumstances entails. This complex of structures reflects the variety of intermediary roles and functions that third-party actors, as individuals and as teams or panels, need to fulfil – for example, convenor, 'enskiller', reconciler, monitor and guarantor (Mitchell 1993, as quoted in Francis 2002). This is the way this international mediator describes her approach in mediating between middle-level leaders from different political sides, striving always to bring people together to draw on 'their common humanity' in a joint meeting based on clear ground rules.

Diana Francis: [In] my mediatory kind of work, what I say is that I would take into account people's need, in the first place, to seem very friendly to each other. And this is probably not typical of inter-personal mediation. But there would be a need to stress commonalities and a resistance to looking at the issues which divide. Well, I would be trying to do introductory things that were in the first place allowing people to get to know each other probably at a superficial level at that stage. Although we might try and do it in rather common humanity terms like tell people what *you* would like them to know about yourself as a person or whatever. So we would be making a place for a kind of common humanity, getting to know each other. Because knowing that will provide some basis and also people will feel comfortable with it in the first analysis. And establishing very clear ground rules in a plenary together.

I would usually ask people to say what they are hoping for and what they are afraid of, and making a case for the importance of talking about what they are afraid of. And surfacing some things and then relating people's fears and hopes both to the agenda, which will probably have been conceived of in fairly limited terms, and be introduced as provisional. And also relating people's hopes and fears to ground rules: so if these are some of the things you are hoping and you are afraid of, what kind of working agreements could we make that would give us all a sense of that's where we might be heading?

[On emphasising the importance of the joint meeting] I'm not saying you couldn't [shuttle between groups], but I would be being more ambitious than that. It's not to say you might not end up having to do that, but I never have. I mean it would be part of my mental repertoire that that's what you can do. For instance I can remember years ago, when the Balkans wars were still ongoing, having a women's workshop with people from different territories meeting together in Hungary. They'd say, I hope nobody will get angry, I hope there won't be any conflict and then I would say, forget that hope. But the important thing is to know that we can handle it and that we *will*, if conflict comes up. In that workshop somebody very early on accused somebody else of being a spy and there was a huge rumpus. And then I did have separate meetings with the two key people.

Curiously enough once there has been some heat and it has been managed, people become much more confident. And although it's not very pleasant for the people involved, while it's happening it really can be quite constructive for the group. So I would always say well, we will have conflict. We can't talk about these things without anybody getting heated or upset. But the important thing to know is that people survive these things and do something that they feel is worthwhile. And we are here to make it as manageable as possible.

The co-mediation model

This occurs when two mediators, ideally one male and one female, mediate together. There can be distinct advantages in this model in certain situations – for example, where there are a number of parties, there is high conflict or particularly difficult circumstances, or where additional, complementary expertise is needed. The disadvantages of co-mediation have also been identified – in particular the risk of gender bias and imbalance where two mediators of same sex co-mediate in family disputes (Roberts 1997). Other problems can arise – of authority; status and control can arise between two mediators of different professional backgrounds; of confusion arising from conflicting styles and approaches; and of an increase in the risk of exerting pressure on the parties (Dingwall 1988).

Two examples of the successful deployment of the co-working model are illustrated by their application to the international and the commercial mediation scenes. The following example demonstrates how mediators can share the demanding task, stimulating and supporting one another, providing complementary expertise, and setting the tone for courteous exchange and an example of how to negotiate. The negotiation of respective interventions creates its own tensions and inhibitions, however. Co-working also minimises the dangers of egotism, as another mediator noted about one of the desirable attributes for teamworking in international mediation: 'Certainly not having a huge ego helps.'

> **Diana Francis:** I like, very much, working with co-workers, particularly if they are regular colleagues. That makes it easier. But I like working with new people too. I think there's much less danger of your being a guru if you are a co-worker. You are somehow modelling collegiality, co-operation, and I think that's very good for the workshops. It's harder work because instead of just *you* doing the thinking, which takes long enough, you're doing it with someone else. Because the other thing is, I'll probably plan roughly the whole of the thing, but every night I would reckon to say, 'Do we stick with our plan, do we adapt it or do we throw it out and make a new one?' And doing that with somebody else is very supportive and takes an awful long time because you start looking at all the options there are, whereas if you are on your own you don't have so much stimulus, so you think, I'm pretty confident this would work. And sometimes in terms of collegiality I know that I'm giving up on what [I think] because this is not a negotiation process. I'm giving up on what *I* think is the best way of doing it to accommodate somebody else.
>
> It is quite hard work. If it's meant to be absolutely equal, both in terms of function and in terms of experience. If you have different functions it's easier. I can remember co-facilitating once with an Indian colleague who is wonderful. I mean she had all the local knowledge from Asia. I was *very* dependent on her. She had the presence, she had the organisational clout. In terms of thinking out the agenda, she was actually terribly slow and left it mostly to me which, because it

wasn't acknowledged, felt the exact opposite of what I was hoping for in terms of possible colonial preconceptions. Whereas if we had been really clear that we had these different functions, it wouldn't have had that impact.

Or I'm working in Tbilisi with a colleague, she is my boss, but I'm her consultant. So if I play the lead on dreaming up the agenda according to her specifications and then we co-facilitate, it's a very equal relationship, plus she has the language and I don't. But at the same time it allows for different functions and I get a bit more of a clear run. It's a mixture, but I do like co-facilitation. I mean, it's so 'heads together' and what you learn! And then I think how did I do this 15 years ago? I didn't know a quarter of what I do now, so was I rubbish then? Am I rubbish now? If I am still functional in ten years? Perhaps also you can only do so much.

For the following commercial mediator, on the rare occasions when he has co-mediated, it has not always worked well, largely because, notwithstanding immense respect and liking for the co-mediator, styles of mediation were too different. This account tells of a very difficult mediation involving a number of parties which was successfully co-mediated. However successful a co-mediation may be, as expressed already in the context of political co-mediating, it inevitably involves the surrender of some independence of thinking and action.

Tony Willis: The reason we got on well was because we just bring different strengths to it. And I have been doing this much longer than he had. I'm older and therefore have got more cuts and bruises and scar tissue than he's got. He, on the other hand, is intellectually much brighter than I am and he had a very clear understanding of the legal decision…which hasn't been my particular specialism – which was of very great help. So he and I would do all sorts of things. We would play hard cop, soft cop. We'd play the primary negotiator, he's the lawyer trip. We did all sorts of things. And it worked superbly. Of course he's a very charismatic, fine chap and we just got on like a house on fire. So it can work very well but *mostly* I don't do that and *mostly* it's just me. And *mostly* that's the way I prefer to work.

I'm afraid I'm a selfish bugger. And also because what I mean by being selfish when I'm with someone, I obviously have to involve them in my thought processes about what I'm doing and why I'm doing it and so on. And I find that slows me down. And like lots of people who do things all the time, you get to it very quickly – and I've been doing this for years of course – and very quickly you get into the stage when you're not entirely sure why the hell you are there – it's very plain to you instinctively and then I want to do it and so recognise…and if someone paused and said why you are doing this, I said 'I haven't the foggiest idea, it seems the right thing to do.' Whereas when I'm with someone, it takes time; and it distracts; and I find it slows me down immensely; and I find I lose the thread instinctively…whereas you need to learn from that and to trust the

> instincts...so if you have to explain it, as I'm not very good at explaining things, I find I just then...I fall off the edge and lose it.

In this example of 'reflection-in-action', the thinking and the doing are complementary: 'continuity of inquiry entails a continual interweaving of thinking and doing' (Schon 1983, p.280). Co-mediation can interrupt this process, exposing the possible gap between intuitive 'knowing-in-action' (knowing that is tacit and implicit in patterns of action), and its description (Schon 1983).

The *sui generis* model of mediation

The most flexible combinations of approaches to and models of mediation practice have already been explored. One contributor went further in describing the paradox of his 'no model' approach, in effect constructing unique models of practice for every separate occasion, taking into account considerations such as power and culture.

> **Andrew Acland:** It is actually trying to think through what needs to be covered and what is the best way of doing it. And very much, particularly in large groups of people, you really have to think about the power issues. Are people going to be inhibited or excluded because of the nature of the meeting? For example there are some people who will be much happier working in smaller groups than larger groups so you have to bear that in mind. There are also cultural issues. You may have people from cultures where there is not the habit of speaking out loud in public. For example if you are running a meeting in Japan you can't run it the same way you run a meeting in London. If you are working with people in a local community where possibly English is a second language or the people are not particularly educated, then you have to be wary of using the very word-heavy process. You have to do your homework, you have to understand the situation. You have to understand the nature of the stakeholders you have in the room. If you fail to prepare you prepare to fail. Very boring. But it's true. The scoping and design process is actually the key to it.
>
> [There are no archetypal models.] Absolutely not. Each one is a one-off, absolutely one-off design. Compared with, say, commercial mediation where you might have an opening statement on each side and then caucuses coming back together, no. Every meeting is absolutely individual *sui generis*. And that is actually the fun. The bit about this work which I most enjoy is taking a complex problem and a complex group of people and saying, how can *these* people, with all their differences and divisions, talk about *these* issues in a way which will get them from where they are to where they want to be. And that is the challenge. What combination of small group meetings or revolving meetings or chaotic meetings or private conversations is actually going to crack this problem... Normally, once you get in a room you will start with some kind of formal introduction, making sure people know who each other is, setting out some ground rules, running through an outline of the agenda you think you might pursue.

> Telling people when lunch is, things like that. Basic, absolutely essential. And giving a rough sense of what order you think you are going to approach the thing. But I try and keep that as loose as possible because you almost always have to change tack in the process of doing it.

As the following example reveals, the task is a complex one, intellectually and emotionally – managing the numbers of participants (25); organising the complicated subject matter; structuring the session constructively; and facilitating the expression of strong and hostile feelings.

> **Andrew Acland:** The session is organised but also particularly the ways in which people address the issues. So, for example, last week I ran a three-day meeting for an international organisation with a federal structure which is becoming dysfunctional for a mixture of personal, historical and purely organisational reasons. And it is a difficult situation because there were a range of activities which the organisation gets into, some of which are organised centrally and internationally, some of which are organised by their country affiliate organisations. And they wanted to talk about how to change. And they also wanted to talk about organisation. So the direction and purpose of the organisation. Now of course there are different models of organisation which would work better with different purposes and directions of the organisation. So immediately you have a number of variables, each combination of which would lead to a different conclusion. Now in that situation you have to work out, do you tackle the direction first, or do you tackle the organisational model first, and which is the sort of controlling point? How do you actually deal with this mix of variables in a way which is going to be most useful? It's an intellectually challenging thing to do, quite apart from managing a group of highly intelligent and motivated, and very cross 25 people.

Summary of reflections on models of mediation

Mediation can be structured in a wide variety of ways to accommodate the requirements of the parties, the dispute and all the circumstances. No one model of practice fits all. Many variables – including the cultural, judicial and institutional context of practice – have a direct impact on possible structural arrangements. Some factors determine structure – in family disputes, for example, continuing screening for domestic abuse requires there to be separate time with the parties. It could be argued that some structural features better than others promote the realisation of a constructive and fair process (Roberts 2005).

The preferences of the mediator strongly influence the model they deploy. Amongst the contributors, the greatest differences of approach appear *within* the same field of practice. Amongst the commercial mediators, one main difference lies in the preference for joint or separate meetings. In that field, too, another difference is the extent to which reliance is placed on advance comprehensive documentary preparation for mediation. One of the commercial mediators regards five pages of paperwork as more than adequate and a large amount of case documentation largely irrelevant. Amongst family mediators, a heated international debate currently rages over whether or not the parties should have separate time with the mediator. That difference of view was manifest in the reflections of the contributors. While one contributor (British) regarded the separate structuring as a 'gem', another (Italian) regarded it as undermining transparency and encouraging 'secrets'. The unanimity of the British contributors on this matter may not be typical of other mediators in this country, many of whom (lawyer mediators in the main) have strong objections to seeing the parties separately.

Summation

The reflections of the contributors are their own accounts of how they practise, their styles (should they choose to define these), and the structural arrangements they deploy to frame their practice. What emerges are the rich, uncertain and unique realities of practice. There is no indication that dominant North American theoretical formulations about mediation practice, in particular the narrow parameters of the bargaining/therapeutic, evaluative/facilitative or problem-solving/transformative dualities constrain thinking about practice in the UK and Europe, nor does it appear, either, that practice is fitted into moulds derived from theoretical research generally.

The dimensions of style and of model described in this chapter illustrate some of the many strands that nurture mediation as 'a protean social practice' (Menkel-Meadow 1995, p.119).

Note

1. The way mediation is structured at the SE London Family Mediation Bureau, situated in Bromley, constitutes the foundation of a practice model based on the Coogler Model of Structured Mediation devised by O.J. Coogler, one of the founding fathers of family mediation in the USA. The significance of the Coogler Model is two-fold: first, central issues of party autonomy, mediator authority and power and the protection of the process are explicitly addressed by means of structure, composed of the integration of three structural components – procedural, value and psychological; second, is the way these issues are addressed in practice, namely, the focus on the 'modest' profile of the mediator, advance agreement on the 'rules' of engagement, etc.

9
Problems of Practice

> There is no intractable problem.
>
> (Desmond Tutu)

Mediation occurs in a political, legal, economic and professional environment, the competing tensions and heavy pressures of which bear directly on practice. This impact is inevitable and considerable. The mediation process has the potential of unique benefit over the adversarial legal system but also of risk, in particular, that the more powerful interests will prevail over the weaker. Questions of fairness, of justice, of mediator authority, and of the exercise of power within the process (not only by the parties but also by the mediator) preoccupy not only researchers but also practitioners. Of course, these questions, properly raised in connection with mediation, apply equally to all methods of dispute resolution – private negotiations, solicitor negotiations, door-of-the-court settlements or adjudication.

While court intervention is likely to be most appropriate 'in a setting where conflict occurs among unequal strangers, when a court can, at least in theory, rectify an imbalance by extending the formalities of equal protection to weaker parties', research exposes the fact that this ideal of equal justice of the law is incompatible with the social and economic realities of unequal wealth, power and opportunity: 'The austere neutrality of the law is constantly eroded by the special protection that its form and substance provide to privileged members of society' (Auerbach 1983, p.120, pp.143–4). It is fair to say, therefore, that 'No dispute resolution mechanism is devoid of problems concerning fair outcomes and none of the alternatives is best for every dispute' (Folberg and Taylor 1984, p.247). The main problems, dilemmas and challenges of mediation raised by the contributors reflected these abiding concerns manifest in the two domains of the environment of practice and of practice itself.

The Environment
Political tensions
The early trajectory of the growth of the alternative dispute resolution movement is well documented (Menkel Meadow *et al.* 2005; Roberts and Palmer 2005). Emerging in the 1970s as a new way of thinking about disputes, it embodied a self-conscious aspiration to seek 'a better way' of addressing quarrels (Davis 1984). In the UK, enthusiasm for mediation, notwithstanding the reservations of a few British academics (Freeman 1984; Davis and Bader 1985; Bottomley 1984, 1985; Matthews 1988) was not diminished by more widespread criticisms expressed in the USA at the time (for example, Abel 1982; Auerbach 1983; Fiss 1984). These critiques, examining the political implications of 'informal justice', identified a range of concerns associated with the growth of private ordering. Fiss, for example, worried about the impact of power disparities on settlement processes, asserted the social value of the courts as public institutions devoted primarily, not to resolving disputes, but to giving meaning and 'operational content' to the values of society (for example, liberty, equality, due process and freedom of speech): 'Adjudication is the process by which judges give meaning to our public values' (Fiss 1984, p.2). ADR could be seen as an attempt to privatise the courts, trivialising their role and avoiding public accountability.

Abel's findings, focusing on public mediation programmes in the USA, suggested that in some cases alternative dispute agencies, such as Small Claims Courts and Landlord and Tenant Courts, served to divert the legitimate claims of the more vulnerable groups in society (the poor, black people, and women) away from legal channels into forms of second-class justice that lacked the safeguards of due process and increased the risk of covert state regulation. While 'informal justice', it was claimed, processed the small claims and minor disputes of the poor, justice according to the law was reserved for the rich. Ironically, concerns were also directed at private fee-for-service family mediation in the USA, only available to the rich.

Justice and fairness
An important dimension of the political critique of mediation revolves around the debate about justice and fairness in mediation. Justice in western cultures is symbolised by a blind goddess holding the sword of state power in one hand and in the other, balancing the scale of justice exactly. Justice is thus understood as impartial, rule-determined, consistent and state-sanctioned third-party decision-making. Strictly speaking justice, involving a judgment as it does, is not applicable to mediation where authority for decision-making lies with the parties themselves. On the other hand, fairness is regarded as a matter of central importance in mediation – that the parties feel that they have been treated fairly

and that the outcome they reach is fair, or as fair as is practicable in the circumstances.

Because mediation is held in private, its procedures informal and flexible, and the safeguards of due process do not apply, it is recognised that there is always the danger that more powerful interests could prevail over the weaker. Where legal representatives participate in mediation, these risks are, to some extent, reduced. Unlike justice, fairness, determined by the parties themselves, involves personal, ethical and well as legal norms. The future as well as the past is relevant in considering fairness.

Like scholars and researchers, the contributors emphasise the importance of issues of justice and fairness in mediation. This community and elder mediator makes clear the impact North American thinking has had on her practice in this connection.

> **Yvonne Craig:** Perhaps I haven't indicated enough that it [the early American work on mediation] is important to me. I have always been amongst those people who, in talking about mediation, have argued very strongly that mediation is not second-class justice. And this is not only because as a magistrate I was concerned with justice, but also because of the great influence of people like Martin Wright, restorative justice, [and] Tony Marshall who of course had both pioneered the victim–offender reparation thing within the criminal justice system. And that has been tremendously successful and influential. And I think it has been very important because [some say that] mediation has not been a process of justice and fairness... rather that advocacy is the process of justice. It is true to say that the restorative justice strand in mediation theory is always very important. Restoring just relations between people. It is a theme that is harmless so far as I am concerned. It isn't only important, again from a global perspective it is peace *and* justice. Peace and justice have to go together globally and they do in inter-personal relations. In other words you cannot mediate an agreement that is unjust.

While equal significance is attached to the subject of justice and fairness in mediation, this commercial mediator contributes a different perspective, one highlighting the power of the traditional environment of adversariality governing dispute resolution.

> **Tony Willis:** The one [issue of importance] that I can put my finger on, and I have spoken endlessly about it in the past because I believe it quite strongly, and I don't express it clearly enough, and it is a big subject, and is quite difficult to get a handle on it, and that is the fact that society is built on adversarial lines. And there are many respects in which that is highly desirable and *good*, but it is so all-pervasive that it gets in people's way and gets in mediators' way and gets in the way of a solution... because people almost have an adversarial win/lose gene in their DNA... But this belief that why should I agree because the bastard is

wrong and why should I agree because the judges could find me wrong or right really does influence the way people behave. So it is a problem.

In addition, the ethos of individual rights associated with the pursuit of legal interests exists in tension with the ethic of collaboration, reciprocity and consensual agreement associated with mediation (Gilligan 1982).

Tony Willis: You persuade people to agree, you persuade them to persuade themselves to agree when you know there is quite a big issue of principle behind it and someone probably is right and someone is probably wrong and yet you are persuading them that the pragmatic course is to agree, which will mean that that principle [is abandoned]. So that is the philosophic rock underneath us really and I do worry about it. In other words you are helping people to achieve a result which recognises that life is not fair and the legal system is extremely imperfect. And proving the principles of adversarial justice is an extremely risky and dangerous thing to do... But then you say, 'Hang on, what about the principle? Does it mean the principle doesn't get proved? Does it mean the principle can be discarded? Does it mean you can behave in such a way that you can ignore the principle?' One thinks about these things.

It is only rarely the case that people say but I'm right! And yes, the discussion does go on. Why the hell should I? They're bastards and they're wrong and I'll damn well show the judge that I'm right. Followed by a discussion of what the costs could be and what would be the outcome if the judge disagrees with them. And how strongly you feel about it when the judge says you are wrong. And then you have to go into a discussion about how imperfect, because it's a human construct, the legal system is. And how there's no perfection.

A colleague, a former partner, asked, 'Yes, but is it justice?' Of course it's not justice. It's not designed to achieve justice in the sense that he meant it, in the broader philosophical sense. It may be justice in the sense of what is realistically achievable. But he meant it in quite a different way. But of course we all must be concerned about notions of justice and fairness and so on. So I mean you're asking me what were the issues and there are thousands of them I could trot out. I do think it is quite a serious issue.

The debate about justice and fairness is complicated further in its application to international mediation, where understandings about power, its distribution and dynamic, take complex and contradictory forms.

Diana Francis: For a conflict to be mediable, I think there needs to be enough incentive on both sides, whatever the source of the incentive, for a co-operative problem-solving approach to have any mileage. And the power might come from the misery of a mutually hurting stalemate. But that does presuppose that both sides have the capacity to make each other's lives wretched, basically. And then I wouldn't want to be found a mediator in a situation where power and justice somehow went unacknowledged.

In practice, if you are mediating between a specific collection of people within a wider conflict, the power relations in that interaction won't be the same as the power relations in the external conflict or the big conflict, if you like. And sometimes they are even reversed in the dynamics of the group. So I facilitated, with different colleagues, a dialogue process between young people from Serbia proper, Serbs from Kosovo as it was, and Albanians from Kosovo as it was. And the power in that interaction was very much with the victims, or the people belonging to the group that felt itself entitled to call itself the victim group. And victim-hood is a very big power in a dynamic. And certainly the people in that process who were on the back foot, as it were, were the Serbs. And obviously they were there [participating in the dialogue] because they were aware of the moral issues as well as having personal needs and perspectives.

And if I were asked to mediate something in the Middle East of a similar nature, probably that reality would also be present and that kind of contradiction of power, if you like... I was trying to think back to neighbour mediation and thinking, well, if it's somebody who makes a terrific racket and an old person next door whose life is made a misery, if the person making the racket is completely unaffected by the old person's misery they won't be coming to mediation. It's only at the point where either they've got a bit of a conscience *or* the harassment factor starts messing up their life, so that to just put a stop to being harassed that they will come... And that's where the ring-holding function of a mediator comes in very much. In the context where I am working it tends to be the victim who's making the running.

Autonomy and external intervention

Kressel (1985) has drawn attention to the lofty and extensive nature of the mediator's goals – in relation to the parties, to the process and to the outcome. The fulfilment of these goals in themselves would constitute no mean achievement and have to be striven for in circumstances that are fraught and many-layered, usually at a time of enormous personal, political, social and economic difficulty, in whatever field of practice. At the same time, the intervention of the mediator is a modest one and limited (except in some international mediations) within a short and specific dimension of time. Mediation in its nature fills a space which no existing service – advisory, welfare or therapeutic on the one hand or legal and the courts on the other – could in their nature fill. Mediation cannot nor should substitute for these other services and must be clearly distinguished from their important but quite different help. The limits of mediation are clear too, requiring practitioners to have a proper regard for priorities and boundaries.

In the family field, mediators have had to resist unrealistic external pressures to provide for the unmet needs of children coping with separation and divorce – for counselling, advice-giving, information, assessment and therapy – all vital interventions but ones which should not be confused with mediation or attempted at the same time by the same person. This is why it is recognised that mediation should not be criticised for failing to remedy those ills which it cannot and never set out to solve in the first place (Felstiner and Williams 1985). Exactly this kind of distortion is feared in the context of community and victim–offender mediation where a culture of official encouragement for mediation, and an espousal of the virtue of 'participation', appear to co-exist, paradoxically, with a culture of official ignorance and resistance to mediation, particularly in respect of funding.

> **Marian Liebmann:** I think as mediation becomes more mainstream, there is a danger of it being used by statutory authorities to do jobs it was never meant to do. Some of it is OK, it depends on how you frame up the surroundings. It seems to me to be perfectly fine, say, to offer mediation in neighbour disputes before you go down the Anti-Social Behaviour Order route. It seems a very good idea to me. And it seems very good to offer mediation for homeless people, and for children who have run away from home, but it so easily gets drawn into who is a problem child. If I give you an example from the X project. I and one or two others could see that it was doomed to failure from the start because it was seen to be a very blatant attempt by the housing department to avoid rehousing 16-year-olds which they had suddenly acquired a legal obligation to do. And so they wanted to force them all to go to mediation first. There are areas where this kind of mediation is going on very successfully. The housing department seemed to think they could shuffle things off to mediation but they wanted everything to happen immediately. So I think they have now taken it back in-house, which, given the way they work, is probably the best thing to do.
>
> So I think there are a number of traps where they are mainly to do with mediation being set up to serve some other end, in particular to save money. And I think the target culture doesn't help. Because whatever targets you set are open to manipulation… So it is actually very hard, I think, for mediation particularly to get targets that are set up in such a way that they don't apply pressure to one group or the other, or don't subsume the process into a coercive statutory procedure. So I think that's one of the biggest challenges. I think generally being part of the system and not being independent is an issue.

The public funding of family mediation in 1996 has brought to the fore, too, the powerful dilemmas of external regulation. Eternally introduced notions of success, defined in terms only of cost-effectiveness and reflecting government priorities of reducing the heavy cost of legal aid expenditure, have their impact on practice. One concern is that more evaluative settlement approaches, those traditionally practised by lawyers, appear likely to be rewarded financially, in the context of mediation, according to standards invented by and accepted by lawyers (Davis *et al.* 2000). These pressures combine to diminish more elusive, but no less important 'process' benefits, precisely those that distinguish mediation. This can be more costly, in all respects, for the parties in the longer term in the experience of this family mediator.

Tony Whatling: I mean the pressure on mediation in this country today is to be faster. I was there when it kicked off, when the Lord Chancellor was saying, I want mediation now to be at the centre of divorce rather than legal processes. Move mediation to the centre. We all wanted to hear that, but what we didn't want to hear was when he said there will be no new money.

Then I think we have been through a period where the Legal Services Commission did not know how to franchise mediation. They had great experience of franchising legal services. So in a sense there was a sort of wilderness which was quite favourable to mediation, after which of course [the LSC is] increasingly looking for economies of scale, ever increased pressure towards joint intake, a pressure towards reducing the number of sessions which you spend with a couple. All of which encourages faster activity...[and more work that is] evaluative, directive. It's between those schools – evaluative and directive mediation. That's a very different philosophy from what we were brought up with, which was that alternative where the parties [decide], it's their money, it's their children, their pensions. So I'm worried about that pressure... I'm very concerned some of those quick fix couples who go through that evaluative model could well be very unhappy. They may well not have sorted it out.

I think repeatedly that parties whose greatest problem is that there has not been the opportunity prior to mediation, and they may not be using mediation, to talk about 'it'. And at some point that may need to be talked about. I mean, 'the affair', 'the betrayal', 'the crisis'. They have never talked about it, they have behaved around it, but they had never actually sat down and unpacked it. Too frightened to even try. So they behave around it by needling each other, screaming and shouting but they don't talk about it.

I think some of those couples who come through a quick fix model, two years down the road, three years, five years, are still fighting, quarterly, monthly over contact [over children]. Quite often one of the causes may be that it has never been addressed. They haven't had the experience in the process, not only of addressing it, but also the experience of exploring their differences, of being the architects of their own [decisions]. If you ask a lot of lawyers they will say it is a legal process. For me I would say it is a psycho-social transition of the same order as those other psycho-social transitions – going out to work, leaving home, getting married, getting divorced.

Funding pressures similarly affect the international field in the way that outcomes are determined and success defined. Again the pre-eminence attached to measurable indices of success displaces the significance of other, more intangible, values. As one international mediator identifies, one of the difficulties associated with 'second track' international work and the serious amount of donor money involved (although relatively low cost compared to other types of intervention), is how it demonstrates outcomes given the paucity of evidence of obvious 'success'. Donors ask, 'What do we get for all this money?' While there is now a growing literature about evaluation methodologies, there is still a question about how to measure the usefulness of the process.

> **Mark Hoffman:** And because you're often working at the level of relationships, ideas, concepts, perceptions, it's actually very difficult to measure this. I remember after one of the first workshops we did in Moldova, we went back and we had a communication from the then Head of OSC (Organisation for Security and Co-operation in Europe) saying, 'I don't know what you did with these guys but you completely rearranged their mental furniture. They are now talking with each other in a different way and are using a different kind of language.' But you can't measure that.

The legal framework

The dangers of the co-option of mediation, not only by government but by large business interests and the professional agendas, of lawyers in particular, have played their part too in shaping the growth and development of the ADR movement (Roberts and Palmer 2005).

From the 1990s, official enthusiasm for mediation has transformed the civil and family justice systems (Woolf 1996; Mackay 1995).[1] As Galanter observed a decade earlier in the USA (1984), two intertwined themes provide the impetus for such enthusiasm. The 'warm theme' celebrates mediation as a superior method of dispute resolution exemplified in the 'impulse to replace adversary conflict by a process of conciliation to bring the parties into mutual accord'. The 'cool theme' emphasises administrative efficiency and cost savings at a time when expenditure on civil legal aid amounts to nearly £850 million (of which 38 per cent supports people undergoing separation and divorce) and the civil justice system indicted by its then most senior judge as being too expensive, too slow, too complex and too unequal (Woolf 1996).

With such endorsement of mediation, it is not surprising that lawyers, mainly solicitors initially, began in their hundreds to train as mediators fearing the growing challenge to their monopoly of control as specialists in dispute resolution. The attempt by the Law Society to appropriate mediation as 'simply another area of specialism within what are otherwise *normal* areas of practice for a solicitor' [emphasis added] highlights the extent to which lawyers are willingly abandoning, notwithstanding the resulting confusion for the public, the exclusive partisan, advisory and representative role that they have historically monopolised (ACLEC Report 1999, p.58, para. 4.50: Roberts 2002). These same partisans are now presented as best equipped to be professional neutrals. In this way control is claimed over a new and potentially lucrative area of professional practice, and established boundaries and core understandings relating to the nature both of legal practice and of mediation, as a distinct, discrete and autonomous form of intervention, are challenged.

Challenges therefore to lawyers' monopoly of control over dispute resolution result in intense professional hostility typified in the experience of the following German family mediator, himself a lawyer, for whom the relative novelty of and concomitant ignorance about mediation combine with the traditional dominance of an adversarial legal system, to ensure a hostile environment for mediation practice. This suspicion transfers itself into the mediation, creating professional tensions amongst mediators, lawyer mediators privileging their profession of origin over others in respect of training needs and status.

> **Christoph Paul:** There are a couple of dilemmas even I feel. One dilemma is mediation still is not well known in Germany. That is a problem. The clients tend immediately to go to court and not go to the mediator if there is conflict. That's the traditional way. Then there are a lot of tensions between my profession as a lawyer, there are incredible tensions. There is a lot of aggression against me from other lawyers. They think, well, I am a traitor, and they think, well, you take away our clients. These clients litigating could be very helpful for their income. And if I am helping them without going to court and litigating over years? So there is still an enormous tension and there is a tension between the mediators with a psycho-social background and with a law background. There is enormous tension, which is not my personal problem because I am trained by more psychotherapeutic rather than lawyer trainers. But I know there is this tension.
>
> I don't know much about English lawyers or lawyer mediators. I know that there is this idea that lawyers know everything and if you are a lawyer you can do everything. And mediation is something they have always been doing, something similar to that. So they take a course a couple of weekends and they call themselves mediators. And the name 'mediator' is not a protected profession in our country. Which means that many mediators call themselves mediators, especially lawyer mediators who are not very well trained. I think another problem is, if you're talking about conflicts, another problem is training. You have the so-called well trained and the people who say, well, we are so well trained we don't want the others who aren't as well trained as we. Or we have those who say it is not a matter of training, it is a matter of personality. So there is a lot of conflict.

Professional practice

Many of the problems, challenges and dilemmas identified by contributors concerned mediation practice itself – problems inherent in the nature of the process, inevitable in relation to the parties and to the role and function of the mediator. Ethical and practical repercussions on those who are not participants in the process but who are directly affected by its outcomes are significant particularly in the practice of family and environmental mediation. Strong views were expressed in two main directions, relating to the parties to mediation and mediators themselves.

The parties

The significance of the internal dynamics of the process of negotiation in driving forward the mediation process towards a mutually agreed outcome has been cogently delineated by Gulliver (1979). Gulliver also describes, in general terms, three other important factors that overlie and give direction to these processual dynamics. First, there is the endeavour by the parties to use the available resources that afford each negotiating strength – what is usually described as the potential power of the parties; second, there are the guiding principles and ethical frames of reference that govern the parties' standards for assessing disputed issues; and third, the 'impingement of the outside world' upon the parties, those interested third persons and 'macrosocial conditions and trends' that constrain or advantage the parties (Gulliver 1979, p.187).

Despite these and other factors – including personal aspects such as motivation, personality, levels of hostility and emotional states – having such an influence on the mediation process, there is, in fact, little research that addresses their interaction in practice. In addition, it is recognised that these matters are not easily susceptible to analysis and explanation and that the concept of power in particular, while generating rich debate and little consensus amongst scholars, creates 'considerable ambiguity and great operational difficulty' when used to explain the parties' convergence on an agreed outcome (Gulliver 1979, p.190). It has long been recognised, therefore, that the parties are by no means passive recipients of the mediator's interventions, their strategies combining with those of the mediator in a fluid situation of 'reciprocal influence' (Kressel 1985, p.196). The parties:

> bring with them to the table, not only perceptible bodies and cognisable personalities, but freely moving unbounded, infinite potentialities for interchange of energies which are not contained, much less molded by any conceptions which start with conventional 'space' and 'time' as features of the universe of thought to be employed. (Douglas 1962, p.160)

Contributors' reflections on the parties' role in mediation reveal consistent concerns across fields of practice. For mediation to be effective, importance attaches to the parties' commitment to and good faith in participating in mediation, precisely because of the absence of direct or official compulsion to mediate. Three problematic aspects of this issue can be discerned in the examples described: (a) a party's reluctance or unwillingness to participate; (b) a party's exploitation or manipulation of the process; and (c) a party's capacity to participate. Examples of each of these aspects are illustrated below.

Party reluctance

This is seen to be *the* problem raised in the context of mediation in labour disputes.

Roy Lewis: I only find there's a real problem if the parties don't want it. So if the parties don't want it you've got a structural problem there that is difficult to overcome. You might be able to change their minds during the course of the mediation so that they are more inclined to be constructive than when they started. So that's a fundamental problem, I suppose, if the parties are just going through the motions.

Party exploitation and manipulation of the process

For trust to be gained in mediation, as in any professional intervention, it has to be earned, building from some minimum starting threshold (Davis and Gadlin 1988). Four dimensions of trust have been identified in relation to mediation – first, trust in the mediator. This requires there to be recognition of the legitimacy of party scepticism and possible resistance about what it is being offered, as well as the fact that race, class, gender and age all have a bearing on the issue of trust. Second, there needs to be trust in the process; third, trust in oneself as participant in the process; and finally, trust in the parties, their good faith, personal competence and common interests (Davis and Gadlin 1988). A lack of trust by the mediator in the parties is regarded as a serious impediment to any possibility of progress in the process and generates a strong response from contributors, in the first instance in relation to commercial mediation.

Philip Naughton: Problems arise and I suppose some of them at least could be put into categories which repeat. Off the top of my head one of the problems that I have is knowing whether to believe what people are telling me. The relationship of trust in mediations should go both ways and it is actually as important, the way which is not normally talked about, which is the degree of trust which the mediator has in the parties and their representatives. But knowing whether I'm being strung a line is quite difficult and there are some people who one trusts and there are some people who one mistrusts in terms of repeat players. Which is a delight when you work with someone who is entirely upfront and obviously so. So that's a big problem area.

[In order to deal with the problem of mistrust] the only thing one can do, really, is to make sure that you communicate what they say, on the basis that it is communicable, in pretty precise terms. What you can't do, in those circumstances, is put any gloss on the message you're communicating whereas quite often you are putting a gloss on it. Mediations change during the day. They start off normally, not always, with the lawyers taking the leading role and they nearly always finish with the clients taking the leading role. They get more confident. And I try to deflect the focus away from the lawyers towards the parties.

Since the 1980s and 1990s, the problem of mistrust appears to be a growing one, associated with the increasing involvement, as repeat players, of lawyer representatives in commercial mediation. Another commercial mediator, also recognising the need for care in the use of language and adopting a typical no-nonsense approach to dealing with the problem of mistrust, differentiates between the lawyers and the parties.

> **David Shapiro:** When people really want to litigate, they are coming into the mediation process to win, not to achieve a result. You see the interesting part about this is that when they [the lawyers] come in, [they are] in love with the case. In 40 per cent of those cases – this is the amazing thing – one side or the other, mostly on the solicitors, have missed the key issue in the case. The biggest problem that we have in solicitors dealing with mediation is a failure of issue identification, legal and factual…issues important to the lawyers because this goes to their evaluation of the case… I got to the point [where] I was there to help the parties no matter what. No matter what they said to me or not said to me. Parties come in and they lie to me. You've got to expect that. That's what they do.
>
> My problem has been to be careful what you say to people because they're going to take you at your word. And if you tell me that there is no way you're going to settle this thing under any circumstances, 'they're a bunch of bastards', and the other side say, 'you're not going to settle, they're a bunch of thieves'. And you say that to me, I'm terminating this mediation. I will take you at your word. We did that in a case – the mediation lasted an hour because I was fed up with this posturing stuff. I said 'Enough, that's it. I'm not going to do that. Are you sure you haven't anything else you want to say to me? No.' And they were furious and I terminated the mediation. [My authority] is the only thing I got. They were furious. I'd worked on this case for 40 hours. It was a very complicated case. And there was a way to go and they just wanted out of it. [They] refused to pay my fee. They were going to sue me, blah blah. Five weeks later they got settled. Basically it's my problem.
>
> Other mediators will take on more than the fact that these guys are posturing, they're lying, they're not paying attention, they're not listening, they have their own agendas. That's the biggest problem for me… I am holding people to a higher standard. I'm an old man. I'll be 77 years old in June. You are coming to me. You want me to help you. I'll help. It's hard work. I'm willing to do everything but don't you dare lie to me.

In commercial mediation too, a problem already noted in respect of bilateral lawyer negotiations (that lawyers' interests do not necessarily coincide with those of the parties) may be being replicated in mediation as lawyers' involvement as representatives becomes more routine (Menkel-Meadow 1993).

> **David Shapiro:** It may be that part of the problem, lawyers maybe, are a bit more savvy when it comes to mediation. They have been in mediations before, and that combined with coming to mediation with an attitude of not really

wanting to settle, now perhaps they have the knowledge and the tools of knowing how they can play so that they can waste time and not actually settle, whereas before perhaps they didn't have that experience…to manipulate the mediation.

The same problem of party commitment to mediation, but in situations of international political violence, has repercussions of an entirely different, new and alarming kind, not least, the relevance at all of peaceful negotiations.

Mark Hoffman: The interesting thing in terms of the academic literature…for facilitation and problem-solving…is there's a literature that has developed in the last five or six years, people at the LSE like David Keen, Mark Duffy and others, which focuses on the political economies of civil conflict. And this is particularly looking at contemporary conflicts in Africa… And their argument is that there are certain kinds of situations, conflicts, where you find people making recourse to violence not because they're using the violence as a way of trying to address a particular set of political grievances…and [as] the way of expressing them…this kind of argument [is that] there are now people who actually will use or mobilise political violence because it serves a certain function in terms of promoting their political and economic interests. And so they're mobilising on the basis of *greed*, economic and political greed, rather than a set of genuine political grievances. And *their* argument is that this has to explain why it was, for example, so difficult to reach negotiated peace agreements in the Balkans or in Sierra Leone or in other parts of Africa. It is because you could *negotiate* with these people. They would sign an agreement. But because they had no genuine interest in pursuing solutions or achieving peace.

So the interesting thing for these people is that in this kind of analysis, violence is not a kind of pathological feature of society that you can get rid of through a consultation process in a negotiated settlement because dispute resolution using violence is a different kind of rationality and functionality. And so, to that extent, they become spoilers in the peace process because they have no interest in the genuine process. And the challenge that that then poses for people doing mediation and facilitation work, starting with the assumption that violence is an expression of a set of political grievances, is you may be putting in place a process that has very little chance of success because the people are not genuinely committed to a political outcome.

Part of this argument is that features of globalisation contribute to this because warlords are now able to make connections to an international set of economic structures in terms of globalised capitalism. That means they can simply side-step the state. So the arguments [are] that we're actually getting new political and economic formations that have nothing to do with the traditional sovereign state and most conflict resolution processes are about somehow putting back together some kind of functioning nation state. So it is very interesting and very challenging.

Party capacity to participate

Unique circumstances affect the parties in the context of elder mediation. Their circumstances – widowed or separated (increasingly), lacking the status of employment, living far away from family and friends, having sold their own home and now living in a 'little box of a room' in residential accommodation – create and exacerbate dispute. In some situations, unresolved conflict, for example between a resident and a warden, can even lead to allegations of neglect or abuse. The next mediator has written of the complexity of the problem of elder abuse and its many causes and considers that mediation at an early stage can contribute to its prevention in some cases. She draws attention to some of the typical difficulties attending elder mediation – of capacity and confidentiality in particular.

> **Yvonne Craig:** It is, of course, this question of mental health. As people get older, large numbers of them suffer from psychiatric, psycho-geriatric obsessions and depression and indeed more serious mental illnesses. And not only does one have to ask whether one can have informed consent, but even if people do not have a dementia, whether they have the capacity for keeping any agreement which they reach in mediation. And an even greater problem is the question of disclosure, if we are mediating between two elderly people in a sheltered housing context, and we hear certain things which management ought to know. We find out that one of the elderly persons is an alcoholic and hides the bottles and management doesn't know. We have the ethical problems of how far the management has responsibility for the whole community. One can, of course, approach it by trying to get the old person to share their problem with the management but alcoholics deny [their problem]. So there are all of those kinds of problems of disclosure.
>
> There is also the problem with mental health, of when people do not know that they are being obsessive or they are acutely depressed. And what one wants to do as a human person is to say, 'Have you talked to your doctor about the feelings that you have?' One can to a certain extent ask that question. Because it is a question which is inviting them to look at their situation. But it is almost impossible without going into counselling/therapy, and yet what one knows is that the root of the dispute, the conflict, does have these kinds of origins, and that possibly medical treatment can help. And it is going to be an increasing [problem].
>
> Another ethical problem is the problem of conflict in which older people feel that they have a right and a duty to improve the life of all of the other people in that community. They feel that they have the right to tell the management how to do their job better. We can transform situations hopefully by helping people to act in different ways. But you can't transform people. And so although, let us say, we patch up some of these very bitter disagreements, what one feels is that these older people coming from a job, the loss of a large house, the loss of a family, they are coping with 'aging deficit' problems that mediation, on its own, cannot fix.

> And one last thing, if I may, because it adds just a bit of lightness to it, we think about dear old people, but the hatred and bitterness I have found is unbelievable, and it becomes accentuated because [of] living in a box.

The mediator

Mediators have had to face, squarely, their potential to affect the substance of communication by their control over the process of that communication (Silbey and Merry 1986). As already mentioned, a large body of work exists to illustrate the complex and subtle ways in which the mediator is acknowledged to exercise influence within the process. Possibilities exist at every level of intervention – from the most minimal to the strongest – for the mediator to exert influence, for example, in rephrasing or reformulating, in summarising, in editing, in the making of suggestions, in the raising of an eyebrow (as one commercial mediator has already noted). It is because the issue of party authority is so central to mediation that the dangers posed by exercise of mediator power, especially in its covert guises, need to be recognised and restricted. The question to be asked by practitioners is when does the exercise of a mediator's authority cease to serve the essential objectives of the process and become, instead, an abuse of power so that the parties, one or more, are put under such pressure that they then act (or fail to act) in ways they would not otherwise have done.

Power and responsibility

Many contributors – across fields – referred to mediator power as one of the main problems of practice. The following example illustrates, in the environmental context, recognition of the crucial relationship between the power of the mediator and the parties' authority for decision-making. There is recognition too both of the need for careful exploration, with the parties, of the issue of power, and of the practical limits and constraints, of time, of the difficulty, of the weight, and of the complexity of the issue. This responsibility is magnified in relation to non-participant third persons, those not directly involved in the mediation process, but whose lives will be affected by the decisions taken there. In the particular circumstances described below, that responsibility could be overwhelming.

Andrew Acland: I think the main tensions for me [as mediator] come down to the responsibility of the third party for the welfare of the other parties. I can sit here and say it is actually the responsibility of the parties, they make their own decisions. And that is right. But that is really in many ways to slightly gloss over and dilute the power which you have as a third party.

I can design a meeting to work in a certain way, and it almost certainly won't go according to design because they never do, but the purpose of doing the design is to really think through what might happen and to work out what you are going to do if it doesn't. While you make decisions on process but not on content, the reality is that the process decisions you make can determine how the content comes out and how it is discussed.

So if I have concerns around it, it is about a power which you never quite have sufficient time to explore with the parties and to explain. And I think the mediators are very much aware of this, but I think, because there is never really time to go into it properly, one never really gets to tease it all out. So one of the things I always try to do before I go into a meeting, to a certain extent, is not exactly to lower expectations, because if you did that you would possibly reduce their confidence that you were doing a decent job for them, but it is to try and manage the expectations so that they are very mindful about the situation they are in and what they are doing. And this is particularly true where you've got people who are working for a constituency which is not in the room. For example, I do a lot of work in the environmental and sustainability fields, and there, you know there are constituencies unborn, whose interests you have to keep in mind to a certain extent.

You know if you have got people in the room and the process you are using is leading people, however much you may not intend it to, to a certain conclusion, then you have a responsibility for people two or three generations hence who will have to live with that conclusion. And that is quite alarming. And of course it isn't *really* your responsibility but can feel like it... It's sometimes called 'transgenerational equity'. In other words, the interests of succeeding generations. So for example, a couple of years ago I was working on undersea carbon sequestration which is taking carbon dioxide and burying it in the seabed. The idea is to reduce carbon dioxide releases to the atmosphere to prevent global warming. But the suspicion is that carbon sequestration will only last for a thousand years. So you are actually trying to think, is it a good idea that people should be discussing a solution which is only going to last for a thousand years? Now that *is* actually an extreme example.

If it is a particular trait, I think I probably try and take responsibility for far too much. And that of course is not your, the intervener's responsibility. It is the responsibility of the parties because they are the ones making the decisions. Well, at the same time, it's something you need to have in your head. And you have to make sure that it is talked about. That's where the responsibility comes in. You have to make sure that the things that need to be on the agenda are on the agenda.

Children's interests

Of a different order but no less important, family mediators have long wrestled with the consequences for children of parental decision-making in mediation, a subject that has generated much debate over decades (Roberts, forthcoming). One of the special features of family disputes over children is that the two disputants involved are the parents in most cases. Another special feature is that they are bound together through their children in a continuing and interdependent relationship, for life, whether they like it or not. 'The two parties are locked in a relationship that is virtually one of "bilateral monopoly"; each is dependent for its very existence on some collaboration with the other (Fuller 1971, p.310). This intermeshing of interests is likely to be of an intensity sufficient to induce in the parents a willingness, however minimal or reluctant, to collaborate in their reaching some sort of accommodation. Children provide, therefore, the common interest and the mutual inducement for that collaborative effort. They may be simultaneously the cause of dispute, the main casualties of dispute and, consequently, the best reason for ending the dispute (Davis and Roberts 1988).

How mediators have reacted to their responsibility in this respect has changed. In the early years (the 1980s) discussion was characterised by two features: a polarisation of positions for and against the direct involvement of children in the process; and the importation into family mediation of child-saving and paternalist aspects of social work and family therapy practice. The situation nowadays is informed by the joint work of researchers and practitioners of the 1990s. An informed understanding on the delicate and complex role of children in mediation is now embodied in the UK College of Family Mediators' Policy on Children and Young People (2002). Nevertheless, dilemmas associated with the determination of what is in the best interests of children continue to challenge practitioners.

Tony Whatling: I'm very disinclined to take a position on people; it's how I am as a person. It's probably not disconnected to why I came into social work. When I needed to make child protection judgments I made them and I took children away. And I admitted people to psychiatric hospitals. I hated it but I was able to make a judgment about behaviour and say that cannot go on. But I don't write off the person in the process. I've come to a point in my mediation work when, for instance, we talk about the best interests of the child. And I meet mediators who have quite powerful personal positions on that which I have a problem with because they are too dogmatic for me.

I've come to the point of thinking that, in general, for most of the people I work with, what is in the best interests of their children is what the two of them come to decide. Is it in the best interests of their children? That's the question for me. It's not about hours of contact or any of that, but it's about reinventing the decision-making process... It's not for me to say.

I've worked with couples where the children moved back and forward between their parents every three weeks. The school's in between. The mother was in a same-sex relationship and the father was in a heterosexual relationship. None of that detail is an issue for me. It's not my business. It's quite clear from the children that there is nothing [problematic] whatsoever about the domestic arrangements. It is almost as if they thought that is what all separated children did. It's not a problem for me. I don't have a feeling of its rightness or wrongness. I'm more interested in whether they can make it work.

Maintaining a non-judgmental approach

For another contributor, maintaining a non-judgmental approach is the major challenge in family mediation in the light of changing family structures and values.

Fred Gibbons: An aspect of the work now which must be managed is the movement of people in and out of relationships which leave children [vulnerable], as I have experienced, with perhaps one of the partners being married four times by the age of 30, or [there are] four children by four different fathers. I find that difficult. That is a big adjustment I have had to make. I do the best I can with that situation. There are no roots any more. They haven't got the commitment to the relationship but I've got to do the mediation. [You can't] if you haven't got that strength. When I came in it was unusual to find anybody that had been married twice.

Gender

One problem referred to in the context of international mediation was the minimal involvement of women in the higher echelons of decision-making.

Diana Francis: I think this is partly a gender issue. But I notice that the world that I work in is as gendered as any other. Because typically leaders are men – not always, but still typically. Look at any copy of the Guardian to see who's there in their suits. People who work at the political level tend to be male. So that's part of it. Also I quite often get to do women only work which tends to be middle level, community level and not political for the same reasons.

Recently I was working for an organisation in Sri Lanka and did a gender study for them. And they said they wanted to be gender inclusive. And I said if you want to be gender inclusive – that was the outcome of my study – there are huge issues here. There is a big gender dimension and it would mean that you had to work at the community level as well as your track 1 and 2 interface. And they notably discontinued all their community level work... And I don't do work there any more.

So gender has quite a lot to do with it. I wrote a paper incidentally which is about gender and conflict transformation. This reminds me that if you are talking about people's voices and power relations within workshops it is very much dominated by male voices. Women are not saying the same things and are not speaking up so much. It's probably changing a bit. Just recently a female colleague and I had an episode where there was a very macho male in one of these Georgian workshops. We were standing up facilitating. He got to his feet and said, 'Why don't you sit down?' I mean pretending to be courteous but clearly because it was kind of seen as a power play. And the pathetic thing was that we both sat down. Not for long. We were completely gobsmacked. Good fun anyway.

Another manifestation of gender inequality is in the issue of payment in international work. This can be seen to operate at several financial levels with ambiguous implications depending on the context – here the discrepancy between western salaries and local money values.

Diana Francis: One of the biggest ethical issues for me is not organisational success, or funding, or aggrandisement or anything else, but is financial, because although I'm paid modest fees and make a very modest income, I know that in terms of local money values, I am highly paid. And that personal dimension of the global dilemma about monetary relationships is very unimportant. I've worked as a pure volunteer most of my life so I'm used to dealing with it, partly my sense of justice. They are on modest western salaries but they do get salaries, though why do I think I have to be different. But because it comes up every time you do a piece of work it is so in your face and of course, then there's discussion – and then there's British aid, the proportion of it that's going to international consultants. You think, 'How awful!' I'm paid peanuts. It's possible for me because I'm married. And of course it depends on the standard of living. I mean if I weren't so busy being a political activist I would probably look around for some really well-paid work to carry my badly-paid work.

Stress

The inherent tension of the mediator's role is derived from three principal and inter-related sources, identified by Kressel (1985) as:

- the lofty and at times contradictory and ambiguous demands of the role itself
- the intermediate position the mediator occupies between the parties
- the objectively difficult circumstances in which negotiations typically occur.

The goal of the mediator, and what could be more ambitious in the circumstances, is to embody that principle of objectivity and reasonableness that transforms the parties' interaction (Simmel 1908a). The mediator is expected, therefore, to maintain a calm, disinterested, rational and creative presence in the midst of the parties' stress and distress. At the same time the mediator is also exposed to stress arising from situations that impose emotionally demanding pressures, frequently involving intense and open conflict and destructive personal exchanges, particularly in family disputes. In international mediation as well, it is clear that one of the chief tasks of the mediator is to ensure that core concerns (psychological needs, fears, past suffering) must be fully acknowledged and the emotive exchanges surrounding these must be *used* rather than discouraged, if substantive issues are to be adequately addressed (Princen 1992). In addition, working often with limited information and under time constraints is like 'stepping lightly across a minefield. If [the mediator] accidentally steps in the wrong place the entire process can blow up in his face' (Saposnek 1983, p.27). Many factors conspire to impose stress.

The contributors' reflections varied as to the nature and impact of the stress of their work and their approaches to its management. On the one hand, stress is accepted to be a condition of the work of the mediator, part of the job. One contributor sums up this typical view: 'I think anyone who has been in practice as long as I have has to be able to survive stress. But it is not a stress-free occupation. Yesterday's [mediation] was very stressful' (Philip Naughton). On the other hand, though there may be other stresses, conflict alone cannot be assumed to characterise the interaction.

> **Marian Liebmann:** Victim–offender mediation often isn't as full of conflict as you might think. It depends on the situation. It could be but sometimes it isn't. It's about dialogue and understanding. Because sometimes it is people who are not known to each other, and they are not really in conflict. The offender has harmed the victim and dialogue is needed to put this right but there may not be a conflict as such.

Contributors' experiences also challenged stereotypical perspectives about the extent of the emotional content of negotiation in different fields of mediation practice. Mediators from fields other than the family field readily recognised that the subject matter of family mediation in particular, and also the neighbour field, may be more personally distressing than others, because the disputes were between two 'individuals with an intense personal history of problems' (Roy Lewis). That was, however, by no means the whole picture even in the family arena. Costanza Marzotto, a family mediator working also as a psychologist in Italy, described experiencing no more stress in mediation than in other areas of family work, whether with couples in therapy or with violent families requiring social services intervention. In her experience stress arose, not from the conditions of high conflict, but from the mediator's own self-imposed expectation to resolve the conflict themselves. Family mediators claimed no monopoly in having to deal with the effects of emotional stress. The impact of personal conflict was felt in most areas. As one commercial mediator, confirming that his commercial work inevitably involved a greater focus on aspects of principle rather than on the personal, declared, 'I see tears regularly' (Tony Willis). Another commercial mediator also underlined the powerful emotional content of some of his mediations:

> **Philip Naughton:** Sometimes there's a lot at stake even though the money isn't very big... Sometimes very often there is very deep emotion. Whether it be a line manager, or a managing director, or an individual, their livelihood or their self-esteem goes with the outcome.

In the labour field too, mediators experience the impact of individual conflict.

> **Roy Lewis:** [Such conflict] does exist though. Obviously if you've got a party that feels very, very aggrieved and is actually very difficult or, for that matter, an employer who is very difficult, for whatever reason, it is quite wearing. This is why mediation is tougher than arbitration probably. It *is* quite wearing, obviously, to be incredibly patient and professional, try to calm them down, get them to articulate things that could be a way forward as opposed just to restating their position, whatever it may be. And I think it is quite wearing actually. It wouldn't compare with the intense personal wear and tear, I think, of dealing with family problems.

Stress was not necessarily experienced negatively. The demands of the work were described as part of the challenge, strenuous rather than tiring, fun even. Two examples, both from the family field, highlight this positive response to the impact of the stress:

> **Tony Whatling:** I never get tired when I'm working though when I get home I can crash out in front of the television. I'm at an age where I could have retired several years ago. [My wife] occasionally says, 'Do you ever think about it?' Not in a way that she's saying, 'Why don't you?' But [there is] genuine curiosity and I say [I'll retire] when I no longer get that buzz.

For another family mediator, the positive experience of her mediation work is contrasted with her former professional activity. A mediator's trust in the process, derived from a clarity, understanding and experience of the way mediation can serve the negotiation process, can convey an atmosphere of confidence, calm and optimism. This in turn can draw out the competence of those participating. Back-up supervisory and peer support further sustain practice in stressful circumstances.

> **Lorraine Schaffer:** What I think I love about mediation is that I actually look forward to doing the sessions. And whereas as a social worker, sometimes I remember quite dreading going to visit clients or having them come, I never can recall a time when I've actually dreaded mediation; even if I'm very tired, [I] looked forward to mediating. So what I think I *really* trust about it, having

criticised the training, I think the process is actually a very clear one. And I think that is what protects me as a mediator, and clients. Because I think if you are clear about what your role is, the clients are clear about it and I really think that that helps.

People seem to know how to make use of mediation. Whereas as a social worker sometimes the role is very amorphous. When you go to visit people you think, 'What am I here to do really?' I don't feel that with mediation. I do worry obviously when you feel people are not progressing or you can come away from any session thinking about things you could have done differently and that's why having supervision and talking to other mediators is really helpful. What I do like about it is the fact that I can still say I love mediating. I don't find it stressful in a negative way.

The nature and causes of stress

Different kinds of stress were described relating in the main to different kinds of work contexts. In the international arena, special conditions of practice dominate – the distance from home, the uncertainty, the danger. In the Nigeria-Biafra conflict, this mediator, notwithstanding the stress of danger, gained the trust of both sides, allowed each to understand better the perceptions and objectives of the other side. This improved understanding enabled the victor to behave magnanimously ultimately.

Adam Curle: Well I found it, I found Biafra very stressful because very dangerous. And I sort of dreaded going back every time, not so much for myself, partly of course, but for my family, but I knew I sort of had to do it. But there are always stressful aspects. I don't think I suffer from stress very much. But I remember feeling very bad going off to, back to Biafra but then I forgot about it... So then I went back to Gowan (General Gowan of Nigeria) and I told him [about] these awful things [a terrible bombing of a market place in Biafra] and he said that he was very grieved too, genuinely. And he said, 'But you know this is just what happens in war. I can't stop it now because it will only get worse'. But he said, 'I've offered peace to the Biafrans and I've offered them complete restoration of all their position of the country, an amnesty for everybody. And that ought to satisfy them.' But I said, 'Well, it didn't really,' and he said, 'Well, maybe the war may be the only thing that will drive them to give up.' And I said, 'No it won't because they're simply saying that all your promises are empty, they won't accept any of these things and they might as well go on fighting to the end. And possibly there could be a miracle'.

So he said he couldn't believe it and then eventually we argued back and forth and eventually I got him to realise how it was. And then a few weeks later I was in London...and they were very good, they let me go when I had a call from the Secretary General of the Commonwealth early in the morning and he said, 'We've just heard'...We all expected the war would to go on for another four to six months. He said, 'No it's time to end now. There's been a complete breakdown of the Biafran forces; it's absolute chaos.' He said, 'You know the leaders on both sides. Maybe you could do something to prevent a massacre, the victorious soldiers massacring the Biafrans.' So I said, 'All right.' I was very apprehensive. I couldn't imagine what I would do. And when I got over, I found that the war was already over, finished and one of my best friends, Biafran friends, instead of being in chains in the bottom of a dungeon, was walking around in the same hotel as me talking to his friends.

And Gowan had been absolutely right…he said, 'Absolute, complete amnesty for everyone.' He [ensured] anyone who had a previous professorship or, you know, had been an ambassador or something was immediately re-appointed…given full pay. So that was that. Finished. He [Gowan] understood.

Another international mediator conveys a vivid sense of the unique stresses associated with the subject matter of negotiations, most notably its terrible aspects and unremitting intensity.

Diana Francis: I don't like being away a lot. I'm not a born traveller – I really love home. So I find that quite hard and I just accept that as where my life has taken me. The work is very intensive and typically I work right round the clock – you know, I work till going to sleep at 11 at night, often jetlagged, and have to be probably up and preparing at 7 the next morning. I sleep very badly. So how I deal with that is by taking sleeping pills. When I'm away I don't sleep badly out of worry but because I am just thinking workshops, thinking process, all night.

I don't do long stints also for my husband's sake – he prefers me to be away little and often, so that's the work that I do. So it's keeping it relatively short. I find it very tiring because I get very engaged with people. The distress thing is hearing about the dreadful things that people do to each other. I have always been somebody who couldn't bear to hear about torture or killing. And I have to hear about it, it's my job to hear about it. So I have to listen to things that normally speaking I would be closing my ears very tight. And there's no escape. Once you know something you can't not know it. And that I find very hard.

Mediators in the commercial and environmental spheres remark on an intensity of a different kind:

Tony Willis: You do this very intense amount of preparation and…on which you have to get quite skilled at because you have to know what is necessary. Then you have the intense personal interaction with the people involved and sometimes the negotiation carries on, it may settle on the day, some never do and some do.

A lack of preparation can be a source of stress, as it is for another commercial mediator.

David Shapiro: You raised this question about stress. If I know the case, in other words if I've done my homework, it's fun. If I haven't done the homework or only done some, but then don't [feel] totally in command of the facts of the case, and the law of the case, then I feel the stress.

There are also those aspects of stress that can be attributed to the parties themselves as described by this commercial mediator:

Philip Naughton: I told the parties last night that I was going home to kick the cat. He was out! It can be very stressful. It can be stressful because one party can take an entirely unreasonable line as it appears from where I am. Because parties can be very belligerent. One hundred and one different reasons relating to the way in which people deal with each other.

The environment and organisational context of practice generates its own experience of stress and its build up. In this context too, the fact that there are many parties can test to the limit the mediator's patience in dealing with their behaviour. This has to be managed for the job to be done.

Andrew Acland: Yes, I do [find managing other people's conflict stressful] actually. But interestingly it doesn't usually come out at the time. Because if you are in a meeting with quite a few people and there is a high level of conflict in the room, as I said earlier, you can't let it get to you because you will not then be able to do the job they want you to do. But I think there is a cumulative stress around it. And for me it comes out, I find I get increasingly impatient with people who seem wilfully blind or wilfully inflexible or wilfully pig-headed. Or people who are or seem obsessive about trivia, who can't see the wood for the trees. And that is because I think if you do a lot of these situations you get quite good at seeing what really matters and it comes out in impatience with those who can't. Or won't absolutely.

The management of stress

Two main approaches emerge from contributors' reflections on how they deal with the undeniably powerful effect of stress arising from the nature of their work. On the one hand, whatever the field of practice, there is an individual response – of 'switching off', 'locking the door after each case' or just 'getting on with it'.

Another individual response involves a large element of the deliberate taking of care – of careful preparation of the work and of taking care of oneself and one's health. On the other hand, while the individual response can clearly be effective, it is also insufficient. Additional external support appears crucial for many, whether it is the peace of a happy home life; the opportunity to talk to an understanding spouse and friends; the ad hoc and informal support of colleagues, co-workers and trainees in debriefings; or organised supervision or consultancy, required (as one of the primary means of ensuring quality control) for the publicly funded practice of mediation (see Legal Services Commission

2002 Mediation Quality Mark Requirement D4 for family and community mediation).

Individual approaches for dealing with stress

Typical of a common individual approach to dealing with the stressful nature of the work is that of this mediator representing the environmental field of mediation:

> **Andrew Acland:** I deal with it by switching off straight afterwards. I do obviously think about what I've done afterwards and what I would have done differently but I don't obsess over it. And I move on to the next thing fairly rapidly.

This commercial mediator's individual way of coping also, typically, involves informal resort to support:

> **Philip Naughton:** Sometimes it's possible to talk to colleagues; sometimes it's possible to talk about it in a way which I can present the topic, I can talk to my wife. Sometimes I just get on with it.

A similar approach is adopted by another commercial mediator who, in the absence of formal structures of consultation and support, has developed specific personal mechanisms for dealing with the stressful nature of the work. Also typically, the sheer volume of the work impels an inevitable 'moving on'.

> **Tony Willis:** The way I deal with it [stress]? I don't know. I say jokingly, because of my background – I have a pretty strong Protestant work ethic driven into me at an early stage, and I regard myself as someone who works hard to do what they do and that's the right thing to do and so it's never trouble for me. If you've got a job to do, you damn well carry on with the job until it's finished. And so it's part of the job, and it's part of me too... There's nothing organised [in the way of support]. And I do a 'brain dump', quite deliberately. You can ask me about the mediation I did earlier this week on Tuesday and I'd have difficulty. I'd really have to go back into it. It would then start to expand. I'd locked the door. I have to physically open the door... I have to remind myself about the names of the people and then it would start to flood back. But I've moved on... I am doing regularly at least two or three days mediation a week, sometimes four days, even five days, a very heavy mediation workload. I think [for] any professional who does something all the time it is quite difficult not to get better at it.

That perspective is echoed by this family mediator:

> **Fred Gibbons:** I think the sheer volume of work moves the focus on the particular family very quickly into the new case. If I can make a comparison with my work in probation, I lived every case and they kept me awake at night. Sheer

> tiredness would keep me awake at night here. But I think the fact another family is taking the place [of the previous family] means that I'm not involved in any one particular case. The energy that goes into the work is maximum and there's nothing more you can give... I know when I leave, I've done what I can.

Taking care – in respect of the work, its pacing, timing and preparation, was the explicit way one mediator in family disputes addressed the stress of the work.

> **Christoph Paul:** For example I plan very carefully the time when I have the mediations. I take a lot of time before a mediation and after a mediation. So I care for myself. I would never have one mediation after the other. I would always have some stupid office work afterwards. I plan it very carefully. For difficult cases I make [sure I have] supervision.

Taking care in other specific and personal ways was how another contributor, Carl Reynolds, involved in workplace and organisational mediation, approached the problem of stress, highlighting, in particular, the value of self-development both through one's own training and of an understanding of how conflict personally affects oneself. He described too the benefits of a rich resource of physical and other recuperative and enjoyable activities – swimming, cycling, walking, tai chi, and qi kung and others.

External mechanisms of support

All the contributors describe the invaluable support they derive informally from colleagues working in the same field. This example is typical of the collegiate approach to providing back-up debriefing and support in the absence of any formal structure.

> **Andrew Acland:** I do have a very good network of friends and colleagues. And we do meet regularly to talk about things which have happened. And also quite often, particularly in the larger meetings, you may well be working with a team anyway. And certainly I have worked in teams of up to a dozen to deal with really large meetings. And then of course you have the support of the team and you can have very extensive debriefs afterwards.

The terrible circumstances of brutality and suffering that attend much international mediation make heavy demands on those having to address these overwhelming concerns in their daily work.

> **Diana Francis:** I don't find it difficult to talk about my feelings so that's helpful in terms of the kinds of issues that arise. This Committee of Conflict Transformation Support is a very collegial place – you talk about whatever you want to talk about. And that's what we value in each other – that we do talk about things. So I

find that very helpful. I mean I have thought about some kind of supervision – [and] I get this from the group. I think the person who has the hardest deal out of all this is my husband. Sometimes when I come home I just don't want to talk to anybody. I really could do with coming to a home with nobody in it for 24 hours before I became a 'dealable-with' person. I don't want to talk to anybody about it immediately after, or I want to, but on my terms... I'm just reconnecting with daily life. I need a bit of a cushion. And that's hard for him because he has had his life going on and he wants to [talk]. He does know [what's going on] and waits patiently.

A combination of informal and formal networks of support may be available. In the context of labour disputes, for example, the mediator does have recourse to support groups depending on the institutional framework.

Roy Lewis: If you are doing something that's being sponsored by ACAS, for example, you can always talk to ACAS. I've done complete hybrid things where I've been the mediator and I've had an ACAS person playing a role because I've wanted ACAS to be involved as the notetaker, as the person writing the flipcharts, because it's much easier for me not to do that kind of stuff and to concentrate on what the parties are saying and nudge them one way or another. Especially when you come into joint sessions.

Even if you are in caucus, to use the North American phrase, it is quite often handy if you do it double handed, [that is] if you've got an assistant mediator it's no bad thing actually. It's quite common in the commercial field. It's just another pair of hands basically. If the parties are prepared to pay for it it sometimes makes sense to have another person around. Also there is some pressure on mediators actually, there is some obligation to train other people to be mediators. That's encouraged. So in fact it may not work out that expensive because somebody might be doing it for experience. They may not be experienced in mediation as such but they might be highly experienced employment lawyers. And to have someone like that helps a lot.

The assistance of a co-worker in mediation, even a trainee, can have reciprocal benefit not only during the session but in the subsequent debrief exchange, as in commercial mediation: 'What we do is we critique every mediation – me and my trainee. That's what I'm supposed to be doing' (David Shapiro). The responsibility to hand on the expertise of the experienced to new practitioners is also taken seriously as evidenced in the apprenticeship framework that has been established. While this commercial mediator may be a consultant to many, he regrets that he does not have that advantage himself.

David Shapiro: I'm going to be 77. I could drop dead tomorrow. It's my obligation to try to make sure that there's a continuum. We are going to train the senior partner, who is retiring as senior partner, who has got all the qualities of a first-class mediator. Hopefully if we succeed we will have the largest, the most in-depth mediation unit in this country. The point is what I provide is the consulting service for lawyers and mediators. They will come and ask me how do I deal with this? How do I get him to understand where I'm coming from? How do I get him to take up my cause? How do I get him to talk to the other side? And to communicate that I'm trying to be rational? You tell them what you want, let them go get it. But one of my jobs is I know every key mediator in this country and I will tell the people here who are going to be taking a case to mediation how they've got to react to that person.

The value of the peer support provided by a co-worker is well recognised in the way the professional practice and consultancy structures operate in the family and in the community fields of practice.

Marian Liebmann: Working in neighbour mediation, you co-mediate so you have got your co-mediator to debrief with you and that's really essential. So you can let off some steam there. In Bristol we also have an observer at face-to-face meetings (we call them round table meetings) so you've got the observer there as well to give you some feedback. So you've got company to debrief with. I think that makes all the difference. Then you don't have to take the stuff home.

The particular circumstances of elder mediation are mirrored in the way the mediators debrief with one another – seeing the benefits both of admitting their human fallibility frankly and openly, as they do with the parties, and of recognising the necessity for a forgiving approach. In that way learning can be substantial and creative. 'Modelling' should take the form of portraying, not only an ideal to be striven for, but real persons, flawed and genuine (Bowling and Hoffman 2000, citing Kottler 1991).

Yvonne Craig: When I'm working with a co-mediator we always debrief with one another. How do you feel about [this matter]? Anything we can do better? I always try to make it instructive for us. In other words there is a lot of ventilation of the stress that obviously happens in mediation. I try with my co-mediator to find the opportunity for that kind of ventilation. That's the professional way of dealing with the stress.

From the personal point of view I am very fortunate in having a happy life and I swim and I walk and I have my interests and my friends. I'm very fortunate in as much as occasionally, a case where there's been a failure or a problem, or I've done something stupid, that will echo through me. But on the whole, I'm not a perfectionist. One of the things, it's a small thing – when I spoke about this rapport between people who see that I am old and who may notice I have hearing aids, I would very often say quite naturally during the first stage of listening to accounts and when I'm reflecting back, 'Now look,' I will say, 'I am confused about that, or have I understood this correctly?' In other words, I legitimise the fact that we misperceive, we don't understand and we are confused. I help them to realise that it is human to perceive poorly, it is human to misunderstand, because very often then it helps *them* in a situation to see that *I* misunderstood that person. And I take it upon myself to say I misunderstand. And it's also I suppose a way of dealing with my stress, because when we are ventilating perhaps my co-worker isn't so experienced... And I hope it will help people to be kinder to each other. [So] yes, I am not a perfectionist. In our ventilation I always try to focus on what can we learn from this. And learning is about what happened that is destructive and constructive, what happened that we ought to try to avoid creating a similar situation. So it's again about making learning exciting and creative.

The dilemmas of professional regulation

Any process of dispute resolution should be an equitable, efficient and economic process. Whichever process is involved, problems of power differentials arise and certain requirements are necessary if the interests of all the parties are to be served. In mediation there are additional reasons why, it can be argued, professional regulation is so important, not least that it is conducted privately and informally, necessarily without the safeguards of due process. There needs to be frank acknowledgement of the limits, as well as the benefits of the process.

While the central responsibility of mediators is to be clear about what they are doing, how they are doing it and why they are doing it, and the ethical principles that govern such activity, the imperatives of professionalisation demand that the intervention should be subject to standards of quality and accountability. Questions therefore have to be addressed about the distinctive nature of the mediation as an intervention (What *are* the qualities of the good mediator?); about what constitute standards of good practice (What constitutes competent practice?); about issues of fairness and transparency; and most particularly, about how accountability can be achieved. Indeed, whether mediation should be considered a separate *profession* at all, remains an open question particularly in those areas where lawyers carry out both legal and mediation functions.

The following mediator highlights the issue in the context of commercial mediation practice as well as raising another burning question – who should regulate the mediators? European directives on mediation clarify two important issues: first, the importance of separating the functions of standard-setting and accreditation from those of selection, training and the supplying of mediation services (to avoid any risk of a conflict of interest); and second, the recommendation of self-regulation over mandatory public instruments of regulation (Recommendation No. R 98 (1), 1998; EU Green Paper on ADR 2002).

Tony Willis: I think one of the great issues for the field at the moment is the question of whether we are a separate discipline, another profession. And if we are, then we need to start recognising some of the things that come with that. So

> at the moment the main actors tend to be the mediation [training] providers... and they have an interest which is different to the mediator. And this conflict I see as very real... [We don't want] the fights that have gone on between groups of mediators and groups of mediator providers as happened in the USA; I want *mediators* to be the standard-setters.

While it is true to say the 'efficacy of self-regulation is one of the measures by which outsiders judge whether a profession deserves that status' (Abel 1988, p.249), understandings about self-regulation themselves conflict. In any event, the self-regulation of mediators, certainly in the USA, has involved the prior necessity of establishing who has, or ought to have, 'ethical control' over the practice of this multi-disciplinary field (Menkel-Meadow 2001, p.980). This question is, of course, part of the larger enterprise of distinguishing mediation as a discrete and autonomous activity independent of other interventions and of legal process (including attempts to refurbish court process (Roberts 1997)).

In general, whatever theoretical position on the professional project is adopted – whether it is directed towards controlling the market for services, or enhancing professional status or advancing the social good – the professionalisation of mediation does involve official recognition that it is through regulation that the quality of service that is provided can and should be monitored and improved, and that, in turn, can serve the public interest.

In the family mediation field the introduction, in 1996, of public funding for those eligible for legal aid for mediation precipitated an already dynamic trajectory of peer regulation into rapid and far-reaching developments extending both to continuing self-regulation by the profession itself, as well as to external regulation by government (the Legal Services Commission in particular) and other bodies, such as the Law Society.

Overall, contributors considered this topic to be a serious and complicated subject, not easily resolvable. While minority opinion coheres at either end of the perspective spectrum (those strongly in favour of regulation and those strongly opposing it at each end), even so, qualifications were articulated and the requirements of the different fields of practice recognised. The majority view reflected the difficult dilemma in terms of the strong arguments both ways, the 'confusion', not in the sense of muddle or uncertainty but as this mediator put it: 'Confusion is the word. I am really confused because I feel the arguments very strongly both ways. And I don't know how you reconcile them' (Andrew Acland). Some dimensions of the conundrum, ultimately unresolved, are identified in the context of community and victim–offender mediation.

> **Marian Liebmann:** As mediation gets more mainstream, people want to know how we can tell a good mediator from a bad mediator. How we can tell a mediator who has got some skills from somebody who doesn't know anything about anything! But I think issues of accreditation are very fraught really,

because they are in any profession and mediation is no different, but even saying 'profession', there are people who think that mediation should be a profession and people who think that mediation should be something that everybody knows about. So the first lot would argue for professional mediators, the second lot would argue for volunteer mediators.

Even in the victim–offender field you have Norway where all the victim–offender mediators are volunteers and they do about four days of training. And Austria where all the mediators are professionals and they do about a year of training. So it's quite a fraught issue because there are these two quite different understandings. Also, there is [the question of] what process to use? There was a National Vocational Qualification (NVQ) in mediation...and now there's a Mediator's Competence Certificate that Mediation UK provides which I ploughed my way through. But I nearly didn't get it because I thought I'd done a really brilliant case – I'd done some really creative thinking outside the box – but the assessor, because it wasn't a mainstream case – this is the process, this is what we do – they weren't too keen on it. So it was all quite difficult really.

I don't think there's an easy answer to this because you want to have some process that people can do and that people can complete in-service because it's a skill. How to do it in such a way that it is humane, a process that is congruent to what you are actually doing and yet has enough standards about it that people can be sure that this is somebody who knows their stuff. Then in the restorative justice field there has been a working party run by the Home Office, producing some guidelines called 'Best Practice Guidance for Restorative Practitioners' which has been quite useful. Now they are going to make some new occupational standards, a real, hefty chunk of work, which will take about a year. But it will be quite 'over the top' for a volunteer mediator to do and some people are worried whether that this will actually professionalise mediation to the extent that it is no longer open to ordinary people to train and practise. And I think that would be a pity. I'd like to see both, a combination somehow.

Arguments in favour of regulation

That family mediators have a more developed regulatory regime as well as being more comfortable with the notion of professional regulation is, perhaps, not surprising, given the length of practice experience in the UK (nearly 28 years) and the subject matter of family mediation, in particular the special vulnerability of the parties and their children undergoing family breakdown. In addition, certainly in the UK, increased state interest in standards of practice, following the introduction of public funding, has expedited the self-conscious examination of practice standards in terms of the government trend generally towards quality assurance and it components – quality control, assessment and the audit (Power 1994).

The following family mediator's approach to professional regulation is unequivocal.

> **Lorraine Schaffer:** I do believe that all professions should have standards and some kind of accountability so that the public have got some way of redress if they are not happy with the services that they get. So I do think all professions, including mediators, need standards and regulation. It doesn't mean it's not a pain in the neck to have to go through the processes of getting there... A supervisor having a trainee and [it] taking two years to get her through [the competence assessment process]. Family mediation has the most stringent [standards] and I don't think it is too stringent, I think it's right, but it's not universal as you know for all mediators to have this. And it doesn't mean family standards have to apply to all others. But I think if you have *no* standards of practice and *no* codes of conduct and *no* complaints procedures, and *no* equal opportunities policies, then you shouldn't be practising.

A similar affirmative approach to professional regulation is revealed in the practice of family mediation in Italy.

> **Costanza Marzotto:** I think that the regulation of mediators is necessary: the risk in Italy is that any social worker, lawyer or attorney, or psychologist can [set up] practice as a mediator, in the common sense [as a lay mediator], not as a new professional. A lot of people think [that you can] be a mediator without [having] received any special training! Also I and my colleagues, we think that the mediation is a new competence... We need standards of training to protect the clients and the [integrity of] mediation in the world! [That is why] in 1985, we set up the Italian Society of Family Mediators, of which I am one of the founder members and Vice-President.

Yet another family mediator considers the problematic consequences of the proliferation of unregulated mediators, of insufficient specialisation in the work, and of inexperience. In his view, only a sufficient volume of work can sustain the necessary skill and practice should be constantly monitored and appraised.

> **Fred Gibbons:** I think the biggest problem that we have is the continued dilution of the understanding of good practice by watering down and having a mediator on every street corner. I think it really is important that people should specialise in an activity and be constantly evaluated and appraised in terms of their continued learning experience and professional objectives. To intermingle activities as solicitor and mediator, or to claim one is a mediator when it is a small aspect of what you are doing, is very damaging. It will undermine and will probably bring mediation down.
>
> It is very important to recognise that it is a very specialist activity and people do need training and support and evaluation. And not everybody can do it. The problem now is that everybody feels they have this ability to do it. And my experience in court welfare for nearly 20 years is that only one or two people, out of tens of people, really had that ability to do it and manage conflict.

> And I think perhaps one of the most important things, and I've said to people here that you should be able to open the door when somebody's mediating and ask them where they are in the process. They should know exactly what they are doing. I don't think that people are doing enough [work] to be able to understand how to be really effective in what they are doing. I asked the same question of John Haynes [distinguished North American teacher and practitioner]. I said, 'How do you keep sharp, John?' And he said, 'I do at least three a week.' I thought that's a bit like golf really. You've got to keep your hand in. It's four times a week to keep your handicap down.

This endorsement of the need for regulatory standards of practice in order to protect the public is not confined to family mediators. In the labour relations field there are the cost implications of accreditation procedures to be considered and the significant issue of trust in the regulator.

> **Roy Lewis:** I think there's a case for that [accreditation] actually. Because although I think all the different fields are different, there is a core of mediation skills. If someone is going to put themselves forward as a mediator it helps if they've been, as it were, accredited by somebody that you can trust to do this. The downside of that is it makes it all more expensive, I suspect, to the parties. But I'm more comfortable with people having not a professional qualification exactly, but some sort of standard, quality mark.

The issue of trust in the regulator is taken further in the context of commercial mediation.

> **David Shapiro:** The problems are pragmatic. If we had decent regulators who knew what the hell they were doing, and knew something about mediation, and not a bunch of half asses, OK, who pretend they know something about this subject, the answer is I think it [defining quality assurance requirements] would be a great idea. The problem is so-called regulators[2] have no concept of what mediation is all about. I don't know whether it has to be self-regulation. I'm not very much in favour of self-regulation. But if there was formal regulation [it must be] by people who know what the hell they were doing.

This vexed question concerning the nature and proper scope of the regulatory function arouses strong and differing views. There is a broad consensus that regulation should be confined to certain core elements of professional practice – some say training standards only. For example, in the field of family mediation in Germany, this is the view on the limits of regulation:

> **Christoph Paul:** Our idea is that the only regulation should be about good training. And if you have regulation about good training, I think the market will make [the decision].

In the commercial field in the UK the view is that, 'it is absolutely necessary to be trained and absolutely [necessary] for some degree of professional development education' (Tony Willis) .While the necessity for some regulation is recognised, there is strong antipathy to the idea of imposed regulation, by any body other than one composed of mediators themselves.

In community mediation, training and accreditation are seen to be essential requirements for protecting standards of practice. Regulation, perceived as a means of restricting practice, is to be resisted. Much thought needs to be given not only to problematic aspects of the application of regulation generally in community mediation but also in new, less established areas such as elder mediation.

> **Yvonne Craig:** I think that all mediators should be trained and there are stages of training. I think people take each stage as they want it and having completed the stage and are accredited in that stage, are then competent to do the work that that training has fitted them to do. So I do believe in training, I do believe in accreditation. Regulation to me means that no-one can mediate unless they have got bits of paper and if they do, they are subject to some kind of penalty. I think there's a lot of thought to be done; I think one would have to see what is proposed for regulation before one could consider it. I thought I had indicated my idea of regulation is when people are prevented from doing certain things and if they are penalised because they have been asked to do something and they are not trained for it. I think in community mediation at the moment [that] would be difficult. And my sphere of [elder mediation], where would the regulation be there?

Problems associated with regulation

It is difficult to contemplate how the practice of mediation in the international field can be compared with mediation in other contexts in respect of its regulation and the practicability of its implementation. Not only is that work long, slow and painstaking, much of it, as already mentioned 'behind the scenes', but particular third-party interveners may be 'chosen' by political leaders or groups and for reasons that do not necessarily have anything to do with concerns about professional competence – for example, to convey a political message, to ensure a view of 'fairness', even to put pressure on the other side (Princen 1992). There are those mediators, 'principal mediators' (in contrast to 'neutral mediators') who are invited to intervene precisely because they have clout in one respect or another, and are therefore likely to have their own, power-based interests (direct or indirect, partial or otherwise) in the solution (Princen 1992). In this context too, complications for regulation arise not only for structural reasons (for example, a team approach to mediation practice), but also from situational uncertainties and uncertainties of timing, and the kind of mediation that is being attempted – whether 'acute' mediation ('present oriented') to resolve a conflict that has already occurred, or 'preventive' mediation ('future oriented') to prevent disagreements arising (Stenelo 1972).

> **Adam Curle:** I would have thought it [professional regulation] was a very useful thing. But what I have been talking about is something that lasts a long time. [International mediation] is something entirely different.

Doubts about regulation in this arena, and more generally, are further explored. The effectiveness of what has been implemented, an organised forum for peer exchange and support, is considered to be sufficient.

> **Mark Hoffman:** I have to confess I'd be in two minds [on professional regulation] – yes it might be viable to have some notion of knowledge of basic skills set, before getting involved in the work. Yet knowing the process doesn't give anyone the necessary 'feel' for it. What I think actually is valuable, is creating forums for mutual exchange in which people who are doing this kind of work can actually come amongst themselves and talk about and share their experiences and develop a kind of professionalisation through that kind of mutual support and mentoring, whatever it is you want to call it, and possibly focusing on particular kinds of problems, issues and ideas. The Committee for Conflict Transformation Support, chaired by Diana Francis, partly serves this kind of purpose [in] bringing together different people working at different levels and working in different kinds of conflict situations. That's useful and that's a kind of quality control. I think also probably there's also an informal quality control mechanism in terms of people's views about other individuals who are doing the work…people have views about so and so's reputation [and if they have a] reputation they have it for a reason.

Reliance on personal reputation and first-hand experience of an individual's professional *and* personal attributes are the preferred means of assessing quality and competence in the international field.

> **Diana Francis:** I think that is important – that people employing mediators or using them need to be careful that they are fit people to be doing the work. I'm not a great fan of accreditation. There is a dilemma here because it runs contrary to some aspects of equal opportunities. I don't mean in terms of gender or race categories or anything. If I think about who would I work with as a co-facilitator or a fellow mediator, I would do it very largely because somebody I knew, knew them very well, had seen them in action, described them to me in detail, both as a person and as an operator, told me about their approach and I felt, 'That sounds like somebody I could work with.' I certainly wouldn't care about what their qualifications were. I might or might not be impressed by their CV, but mostly it would be about, either I'd met them and had seen them just with people and being a person, or I knew somebody else who had. It would be *direct knowledge* and it would be a bit *ideological*. So I wouldn't be interested in somebody who

> only did Marshall Rosenberg stuff, or somebody who didn't care about justice issues and only about Burton's Needs Theory and never talked about power. But mostly it would be about the person and their personal way of being, really. And it's not that I can't see the dilemmas with that, because I can. And the trouble is it tends to be who you know.

A similar dilemma challenges thinking on this matter in commercial mediation practice and for reasons pertinent to the institutional and judicial framework within which practice occurs.

> **Philip Naughton:** My personal jury [on professional regulation] is still out. There are two very strong competing factors in my mind. On one side is the fact that – really going back to what we were saying a moment ago – if this is a craft which some people are naturally good at, and if it is a process which works, the less it is trammelled by regulation the better. More cases will be settled more incompetently by allowing mediations to happen on the unstructured and unregulated basis as now, is one side of the equation. The other side of the equation is that the courts are putting a lot of pressure upon parties to mediate. And so at least a significant proportion of participants are participating because the state, or the state's judicial system, has said it is a good thing.
>
> Mediation is, at the moment, an entirely unregulated *and* secret process. And it becomes quite difficult to justify, permitting that degree of uncontrolled intervention. Having said that, the third element my jury has to consider is that it works for arbitration. Arbitrators are not required to have any qualification at all. The arbitration *process* is completely regulated but the selection of arbitrators and the entitlement to be appointed as arbitrator, is unregulated. And the best example that I can give is that 100 years ago when I was doing a small boundary dispute…it went to arbitration and was arbitrated by the vicar. That was a small case. But the vicar could be appointed to deal with a multi-million pound international arbitration. The *process* is regulated by the 1996 Arbitration Act or by arbitration rules… Whether or not you exclude [an incompetent mediator] as a result of regulation is a good question isn't it? Do you exclude every incompetent solicitor by requiring solicitors to be regulated?

A strong warning is sounded about the possible harmful consequences of the professionalisation project. As witnessed in the USA a decade earlier when 'legal professionals tumble[d] over each other in their enthusiasm for non-legal dispute resolution alternatives', the dangers of lawyers in the UK dominating the development of alternatives are recognised (Auerbach 1983, p.15). The following mediator regards the lawyer monopolisation of mediation as one of the most worrying consequences of the professional project, a worry in fact shared by the commercial mediator contributors (all lawyers) in their insistence on peer mediator regulation. Other adverse consequences of professionalisation could mean the exclusion of certain contexts of practice, already marginalised in status, and the privileging of paper qualifications over natural talent leading to the restrictive and unequal selection of mediators.

> **Andrew Acland:** One of the first conversations I ever had was with Yvonne Craig. And Yvonne said to me we must always avoid the professionalisation of the field. And I know exactly what she meant. And I think she's right. Because in many ways you are then taking mediation away from something which can be done in the playground or in the community centre and you are formalising it and you are turning it into this business of something which is a legal or a quasi-legal process. That is the downside – that you make it more expensive, less accessible, less normative almost. And you turn it into something which is the people who have letters after their name.
>
> Of course the next stage is that somebody sooner or later will say that only lawyers can be mediators, in which case I shall simply retire and go and do something different. But that does get mooted from time to time. Only people with a professional qualification should be mediators. And I think that's absolute nonsense. In my mediation training I have had barristers and judges who frankly would not make good mediators. And I have had people with very little education who are absolute naturals… And you will also restrict the context in which it is used. And one of the things which saddens me most about the field of mediation and ADR, they are largely talking about the legal and commercial fields. So often I discover that legal mediators are completely unaware of mediation being done in schools or communities or environmental issues outside their remit. And the problem with regulation is this kind of creeping professionalisation, making a very natural human process which has been around for several thousand years into something elitist, professional and restrictive and that would be a disaster.
>
> By all means training, selection processes are terribly important. There is the same problem with [accreditation]. I think the question is always who do you end up excluding. On the other hand, and of course I'm a mediator, I can always see both sides, I think the people who hire mediators have the right to know that they have somebody in whose hands they are safe. But the problem is, and I remember once sitting on one of the bodies which was trying to produce qualifications for mediators, and I remember how much we struggled with those human skills which it is almost impossible to name but which *you know when you see*. How do you actually package up that quality of listening which some people can deliver? How do you actually measure that? You know it when you see it, but some people are naturally good at it.
>
> But also there is another complication with this. That the person who is a good mediator in one situation will be useless in another. And I can think of several examples of very, very skilled mediators who have worked slightly outside their normal context, who have made the most awful messes of the thing. No, [it wasn't because they didn't have substantive knowledge], it was because they didn't fit with the issues and the people. Substantive knowledge is about comfort actually, I think, more than substantive knowledge… [Professionalisation] is inevitable. It's fighting a rising tide. But I think people need to be

aware of what they can lose by over-professionalising. I would just put it like that. Who are you excluding? Are you actually then making it impossible for mediation to happen in certain contexts? You can meet some 12-year-old child who is a brilliant playground mediator. How do you deal with that? How do you deal with the community activist who happens to be very good at dealing with local issues?

Summation

This chapter has considered those aspects of mediation practice that give rise to problems and difficulties as well as challenges and dilemmas, professional and personal. The institutional and political context in which mediation is practised can have a profound influence. This is most apparent, for example, in the way in which the public funding of family mediation has brought benefits, such as a degree of financial security to mediation services, and dangers, for example in the kinds of bureaucratic and financial pressures that threaten the autonomy and independence of practice.

The nature of mediation poses multiple challenges – most notably vital questions about what is the legitimate expression of the mediator's authority and what constitutes the unacceptable exercise of his or her potential power. These questions are part of the larger question of how mediation can find its proper place amongst the range of dispute resolution interventions, so that the various professional roles and functions complement rather than compete with each other.

It emerges too that the practice of mediation is as gruelling as it is creative, demanding the utmost from its practitioners, intellectually, emotionally and imaginatively. It is true to say too that the greatest support and learning comes from mediator colleagues, both through informal and more structured networks of exchange, learning, solidarity and support.

Finally, professional regulation provokes strongly expressed and mixed responses that raise serious and unresolved questions of principle. As mediators, the contributors typically would see both sides of the argument. Most powerful are questions about the nature of the activity – an ancient craft accessible to all with ability, or a discrete, professional discipline with its own hallmarks – a recognised and distinct body of knowledge, mechanisms for the transmission of that knowledge, and mechanisms for self-regulation and evaluation (including complaints and disciplinary procedures). Other fundamental questions concern the qualities of the good mediator, and about how these qualities can be assessed and by whom; and about the nature of the regulatory framework. Some support a limited form of basic regulation, and the value of good selection procedures, quality training and continuing professional development is unanimously endorsed. There is unequivocal support for peer regulation by and for mediators, whether formal (as in family and community mediation) or informal (international and commercial mediation). In all fields, the influence of the context of practice is significant, raising a number of policy, professional and pragmatic concerns – about the nature and scale of the interest of the state in private ordering; about public accountability particularly where legal aid is available; about the relationship of mediation to the public justice system and to the legal profession; and about protecting the creativity, flexibility and integrity of the mediation process.

Notes

1. Support from the judiciary in setting up the first family mediation services was crucial, described as 'visionary' in respect of the SE London Family Mediation Bureau (Fred Gibbons).
2. The Law Society and the European Union initiatives on ADR.

Conclusion

10

The Craft of the Mediator

> Getting something right, even though it may get you nothing, is the spirit of true craftsmanship.
>
> (Sennett 2006, p.196)

This concluding chapter considers practitioners' reflections about the nature of their task – what are its characteristic features and how is it to be defined? Can mediation be perceived as an art, a science, a craft, the skilled exercise of a technique, or as a combination of all these? Over 40 years ago, mediators, proud of their responsiveness to the uniqueness present in every case, highlighted the significance of timing and inspiration in their practice of 'a subtle art' (Douglas 1962, p.108, quoting Meyer 1950, p.6). The concept of the freedom of artistry, where 'timing is everything', was a shared one, certainly amongst labour mediators, and one explicable according to the requirements of each mediation situation, unique because the parties and the particular issues are always different:

> You will not, I trust, gather from what I have said that the task of a labor mediator is an easy one. The sea he sails is only roughly charted and its changing contours are not clearly discernable. Worse still, he has no science of navigation, no fund inherited from the experience of others. He is a solitary artist recognizing, at most, a few guiding stars and depending mainly on his personal power of divination… The only mediation that a mediator really understands is his own… (Douglas 1962)

Even at the time, this view of the mediator's task caused some controversy because, if taken literally, it appeared to preclude any general formulation about the nature of mediation practice except as one of continual improvisation on an ad hoc basis. This definition of the task of the mediator could constitute 'a most convenient public image for a mediator who finds himself in need, for whatever reason, of avoiding too firm a commitment about what he does in dispute cases to bring about settlement' (Douglas 1962, p.109).

More recently, the concept of the artistry of the mediator has taken on a different dimension of meaning compared to that expressed by those labour mediators of the last century. Lang and Taylor (2000) postulate the view that there is an artistry in mediation and that it can be achieved in two ways: first, as a level of practice competence, resourcefulness and effectiveness, resulting in the attainment of an elegant and productive 'effortless flow...[which is] the experience of artistry in mediation practice'; and second, as the summation of professional development, the culmination of a progression from novice, to apprentice, then practitioner, leading finally to the highest stage, that of artist (Lang and Taylor 2000, pp.11, 14).

Different from that earlier conception of the artistry of the mediator, therefore, this later view, both more complex and more grounded, defines artistry in terms of the achievement of professional excellence. A change of thinking is envisaged, from *what* you think to *how* you think about practice, by means both of a new conceptual framework and a practical methodology. Artistry consists of the realisation in practice, over time, of the integration of reflective practice and of 'interactive process'. Three essential elements make up artistry of practice – practice skills, theoretical knowledge, and the ability to make 'useful and appropriate connections between theory and practice' (Lang and Taylor 2000, p.18).According to this analysis, it is not inspiration, therefore, that explains 'artistry' of practice, but rather a sound foundation of theory which establishes 'the ground on which mediators stand, [and] the basis for making choices about timing and implementation of strategies and techniques' (Lang and Taylor 2000, p.20). The next family mediator, in underlining her understanding of what constitutes 'bad practice', influenced directly by the writings of Lang and Taylor (2000), endorses the general need for creativity in practice.

> **Lorraine Schaffer:** Bad practice to me happens when somebody is unaware of what they are doing. Bad practice is [when] mediators who think they know it all, don't want to hear any feedback, don't discuss cases, and practise a model that could be very worrying, like some lawyer mediators who very definitely, from what I hear, are telling clients what they should do. You know I quoted a lot [from Lang and Taylor 2000] although I don't think the book is perfect, it is about developing artistry in practice, whatever that means… I think that all of what I have said before can be summarised: that a mediator who doesn't think or read or reflect on their practice, or try and find new ways of working or having a new understanding, and just does a case in the same way every time, then I would call that not an artistic mediator. You just apply a model pedantically whatever the situation.

Mediating well: the experience of effective practice

> The function of the harp player…is to play on the harp, while the function of the good harp player is to play on it well… A function is performed well when performed in accordance with the excellence proper to it. (Aristotle, *Ethics*, trans. Thomson 1959, pp.38, 39)

Three main themes emerge from the contributors' reflections on the mediation process when it is progressing productively: first, the language that is adopted to describe the experience of effective practice; second, the components of the task; and third, the nature of that effective practice of mediation.

The language of effective practice

The term 'artistry' was not one used by contributors, though several did refer to the experience of aspects of an 'art' particularly when describing effective practice and its less tangible moments of success. The term 'craft' resonated with several contributors who described their task in remarkably consistent terms. This was an activity distinguished both by it primary purpose of achieving party satisfaction over personal satisfaction (compared to the artist's purpose of expressing his/her own ideas, feelings and wishes) and by its core features – the investment of self, of time, of care and of quality in the task:

> Craft – yes a good word…[mediation] is a craft, it underlines the word 'craft'. (Roy Lewis)

> Speaking for myself, I think [mediation] is a craft. (Philip Naughton)

> Mediation practice is a craft at this moment. (Costanza Marzotto)

> I like your term craft, because I think it is a craft. Like in wood sculpture. So I'm attracted to craft rather than art I guess. I think that's right. I think it's the touch and the hold and the use of. It is beauty and use. But I think I have an eye for shape and balance which is also a metaphor. (Andrew Acland)

Something too of the loneliness of the craftsman's[1] lot is conveyed by this mediator describing, in the context of workplace and organisational mediation, that blend of 'learned technology' combined with 'personal sensibility' which contributes to the necessary 'crafting strategy' ('you can't improvise until you know your scales') and the autonomous and disinterested status of the third-party intervener.

> **Carl Reynolds:** Because I think a lot of people who do the kind of work I do, are in the main self-employed, free-lance, there is something of the artisan about it, you know, in the sense that, coming back to sensibility, I think part of that sensibility and self-confidence is connected to the need to be autonomous which then makes it easier to be seen as a neutral third party… So I think a lot of free-lances are autonomous types of people and to a certain extent are like a lone wolf rather than a pack animal.

Unlikely juxtapositions evoke the essence of effective practice in examples from all fields.

Christoph Paul: I wouldn't say mediation is an art. It is not. But it has aspects of an art. It is very helpful to keep an eye on this [aspect] of [there] being something that sometimes has a little bit of an art. Sometimes that has a bit of mystery. I wouldn't say it is a mystery because it is really hard work. But it has something of it.

A recurring theme, expressed here by the next commercial mediator, is that of the combination of elements that need to be integrated together for effective practice.

David Shapiro: All the different things we've been talking about, you can roll them into a taco and bite into it and say, 'Well, that's the art form.' But every single thing we've been talking about goes into the making of a mediator. You don't do this by rote.

There is what has been called a 'magic moment' in mediation when suddenly, even imperceptibly, a shift in orientation occurs, the atmosphere changes, and a collaborative spirit replaces one of competition. Gulliver locates the likely occurrence of this transition at an identifiable phase (Phase 4: Narrowing the Differences) in the negotiation process, a transition that may be gradual but could also be 'quite abrupt' and '[a]lmost suddenly, the parties are coordinating rather than acting separately in open antagonism' (Gulliver 1979, pp.141–2). The next mediator, echoing an earlier reference (see Lang and Taylor 2000, above) to that feeling of 'flow', articulates what mediators commonly experience when there is a successful harnessing of the collaborative endeavour.

Andrew Acland: There are moments, thinking about when you are running a good meeting, and you get moments of flow when actually things start taking on a momentum of their own and you know that to a certain extent you have cracked it and you can surf it. And those are the points at which it does feel like an art, that you have actually pressed the right buttons and something has happened. And you know it is going to be OK. It is all about process.

That wonderful book by Mihaly Csikszentmihalyi called *Flow*. It's actually about those moments when things seem effortless… Very often it feels like everything becomes almost hyper real. [There's] clarity and focus and there's momentum. But there's also a kind of *relaxed attention*. It doesn't happen that often I have to say, but it's wonderful when it does.

But there are particular moments which you can point to and you think 'Yes, this is working. This is OK.' And you can almost step back and reduce the extent of your intervention. I think that's probably right [that it occurs at a particular phase in the process]. Because [with] most of the things I do there is very often no negotiation process *per se*. It is almost, more often, an awareness process when everybody is beginning to get the same conclusions at the same time. Because

> quite often, it depends slightly how you define negotiation. You can take a broad approach and define anything as negotiation, any form of interaction between people. And I guess that's right.
>
> In a model of commercial mediation where people are actually trading, that is more an explicit form of negotiation. A lot of what I do is more about people beginning to move together better… The flow state [achieves] that combination of relaxed attention.

Components of the task

There was unequivocal agreement of contributors in recognising the necessity of *all* of the components necessary for effective practice, with their combination realising a whole that was greater than the sum of its parts. There was agreement too on what those components should be – personal aptitude for the task; taught skills acquired through training and practice apprenticeship; theoretical knowledge; and experience.

Personal aptitude

In the 1990s, a major family mediation organisation, National Family Mediation, with the help of a leading firm of consultant occupational psychologists, devised a sophisticated mandatory selection procedure for recruiting new mediators for its national training programme. The most important criterion of selection was 'aptitude' for mediation. 'Aptitude' was analysed in terms of specific personal attributes relating to four main areas – intellectual attributes; inter-personal attributes; ethical and personal attributes; and motivation attributes. Notwithstanding this ambitious attempt to define the personal qualities of 'the good mediator', those qualities remain as elusive as they are regarded as essential. Contributors' descriptions of these qualities indicate their significance and range and confirm the view 'that understanding what these qualities are and why they work will always be highly personal and situational – a product of the moment and the people in it' (Bowling and Hoffman 2000, p.24). Whether these qualities can be learned or taught and by what means was a more controversial matter.

The following community mediator took the view that these qualities can be learned provided enough time were devoted to the endeavour. Whether or not that investment of time was realistic was another matter.

> **Marian Liebmann:** I think there are certain basic qualities that you would be hard put to teach. If you have somebody who can't listen, if you have somebody who can't empathise with people. If you have somebody who rushed in to make judgments all the time. Somebody who thought that point scoring was a way of getting successful outcomes, somebody with too much ego. If you have people like that you are never going to get anywhere really. You have perhaps to take

someone like that and to say, 'Can you go away and do a basic counselling skills course or listening skills or some other kind of work first?' Because mostly you haven't got time to teach that. I think it can be learned. But I think it would take a long time for some people and if they were children you can have more hope – adults could learn it too but in most mediation services you wouldn't have time to do that. I think people can learn and can change... On the whole I think those things can be learned but for some people it would take a very long time.

Another essential personal quality – the ability to engage with people – was particularly valued by the next family mediator.

Lorraine Schaffer: Sometimes you really do wonder about what mediation is – it is one of the dilemmas really. But I suppose all you can say is that I do think, when we were recruiting for training here, probably the quality I was looking for *as much as anything else*, in terms of knowledge, was the ability to engage with people quite quickly. I think you have to go in a room and start working with people and that very quickly they have to feel they can relax and be comfortable with you. If you are somebody who takes a long time to engage with people, or you come through as very reserved or very formal or whatever the word is, I think they have to engage with people. I think the problem with saying it is about personality is that your personality will suit some people and not everybody. So when you meet other mediators and you know that they are very different from you, I can't then think they can't be good mediators because they are so different from me. So you have to believe that mediators appeal to different people.

Personality is important [but] it is really more about human engagement. You are not there to be a person, you are not there to share personal information. You don't have a relationship as a mediator with people, but I think people have to feel at ease with you. And that is why I think being American is an advantage because I'm not classed as part of the English class system here. I think class is a crucial factor in people feeling comfortable. I think [mediation] is an art as well in the sense of the amount of creativity that you use. Michelle LeBaron's book, *Bridging Troubled Waters*, talks about creativity, using intuition and using your heart. In fact I realise she is a woman writer and...it is too American I think for our taste, but she very much [advocates] mediating from the heart, basically.

Another family mediator takes a different view about the role of intuition in effective practice.

Fred Gibbons: I wouldn't subscribe to that [view that mediation is an intuitive art] at all. If you look at the research, that helps us a great deal to know what are the key qualities and what it is about mediation that is important. I think one of the major pieces of research has pointed out that the capacity of the mediator to interrupt the process when things are getting difficult and knowing *when* to make that judgment, has to be understood. Then to put words over which will help the

> parties to re-engage by changing things around. And then to produce information or to put something to the parties which then takes them back into constructive negotiation. Now to do that, I think you need, first of all, considerable word power... Because the choice of that word is absolutely crucial to whether people move on or not. And I think that the times when I've let hostility run and sometimes it's *very* important that it does run under certain constraints, and [there are] times when you cut in and don't allow another word to be said. And that is not the work of an artist. That is a practised consideration. It's repetition, it's skill and it has to be learned. You make the wrong move and you lose the session. If somebody calls somebody a liar — and this is an obvious example — if you're not in there in a flash, you've lost them.

Precise judgment on the form and the timing of an intervention is clearly viewed as critical for effective practice. The following German family mediator similarly relies primarily not on intuition, but on what he refers to as 'technique' though the subject matter of mediation and the specifics of the situation might mean drawing on different resources.

> **Christoph Paul:** I would say there are situations in my work as a mediator where intuition doesn't help me. When I have high-conflict children mediations, I think intuition sometimes helps and sometimes you really have to know techniques. There are situations where I can't [rely on intuition]. In financial cases also. There are sometimes techniques which are very helpful and you have to have a bunch of techniques where if nothing works, you have to think what kind of technique might be helpful. Maybe people who work with intuition at this [same] moment, [might] just make a joke or open the window or change their tie and it works. But for me, it is very helpful that I rely on *techniques*.

Experience is the critical factor for the next labour mediator, experience of acting in a number of third-party capacities.

> **Roy Lewis:** Craft is a good word — based on doing a great many roles of a third-party kind in labour relations and employment. I do arbitrations, I have the final appeal stage, I chair standing bodies to do with industrial relations. If you add all that experience together then all that adds up to what you bring to the parties in terms of *experience*. It makes you more aware and sensitive to problems. Sometimes, in many of the things I do, there's a mediation within the decision-making process. That is to say I might sit with other people in various roles. For example, I'm a chairman in employment tribunals, part-time; I'm deputy chair of the Central Arbitration Committee. I'm a chairman of a collective body called the Royal Mail National Appeals Panel. For example, all those things involve coming to decisions and the strong preference is for unanimous decisions with people from the two sides of industry as it were, either from the particular industry or at large.

> And so I'm quite accustomed, as it were, to [presiding] over a negotiation process to reach a conclusion. As a chair. And then you can extend that. One of the things I do is a standing procedure in the fire service. I am the independent expert to the technical advisory panel of the national joint council of the local authority fire brigade; I preside over a process by which you try to broker an agreement and if that fails you make recommendations. But the process involves an inner process, first of all, of talking with the other people, two sides of the industry who are doing it with me. And then you see if there is any basis for a unified approach.
>
> Then you have to see whether there is any possibility of agreement between the parties and you try and encourage them, cajole them or whatever means you use to come up with an agreement. It's only if that fails you make a recommendation. Then the question is whether the recommendation will be accepted. Sometimes it will be simply because the parties, for political reasons, can't agree to it but they can accept a third-party recommendation. So there are all those kinds of processes that go into this one end result which you wouldn't necessarily understand just from looking at the constitution of this body. It's a craft, it underlines that word craft... It's a craft, it is patient and not necessarily very fast and you have to be very careful.

The approach – that developing personal qualities involves 'a process of time, intention and discipline, and comes, in our view, not from intellectual inquiry or scholarship but from experience...[that] these qualities can be learned but not taught', was not shared by all (Bowling and Hoffman 2000, p.24). The next international mediator took the view that effective practice of mediation required elements both of training and individual qualities, doubting whether the latter could be acquired.

> **Mark Hoffman:** I don't think you can teach someone to be a facilitator or a mediator if they haven't got certain kinds of qualities...so you can teach certain skills, such as listening, those kinds of things, but if someone doesn't have a certain set of qualities, I'm not sure how far you would get.

In the eyes of another international mediator, effective practice depends on the integration of a broad, flexible and therefore culturally relevant knowledge base, skills, careful advance preparation, practice experience, plus personal aptitude. Her view, held by others as well, is that while some personal *tendencies* could become incorporated into practice skills with experience over time, there were other attributes, 'aptitude' for example, that were less easily acquired.

> **Diana Francis:** The words art and science are not very helpful. I think having a framework of knowledge of possible ways of doing things, of having understood some of the patterns, of having brought into awareness some of the pitfalls *and* named them, of developing some kind of personal but also shared under-

> standing of what it is you are trying to do, and the nuts and bolts of doing it, however provisional those are, however aware one is that in the end they are culturally influenced, I think that is helpful. To do anything without preparation and advance thinking just doesn't make sense. However, I think that's not enough. I think those things are useful and I think they are complementary.
>
> Certain kinds of personal tendencies [can] get built into skills. So I think practice is important but I think there are aptitudes or anti-aptitudes. I can remember when we had people coming for our exploratory day prior to being trained as mediators, we would do a screening process. And people were always very angry when they were screened out, but there were some people you thought, well, this side of eternity they don't have the right aptitude or, as Quakers would say, 'This name would not have occurred to me.' They may be very good as a public speaker or at all kinds [or things]. It doesn't matter. Most of us are not good at everything. And I think there are some people who would take forever to make it.

The following commercial mediator stated, in uncompromising terms, the same view on the scope for acquiring personal aptitude for mediation – that skills may be developed but, by definition, aptitude cannot be acquired.

> **Philip Naughton:** [Mediation] is a craft and so it benefits from training, it benefits from experience, but it is something which either you can do or you can't do. And I think good mediators are good craftsmen – everyone can do the training but not everyone will become a craftsman.

The nature of effective practice

One contributor, a community and workplace mediator, stated that, 'If you practise well, then the parties rarely have a sense of failure' (Carl Reynolds). What does it mean to practise well?

Effective practice reflects the skilled integration of a number of components – theoretical knowledge, attention to process, skills and practice experience, commitment, and above all, the realisation in action of certain essential if elusive personal attributes. Recurrent reference to these attributes by contributors specify the virtues of extraordinary patience; word sensitivity and power; personal maturity and authority; the ability to engage readily with people; dedication; and a curious and enquiring mind. In addition, contributors emphasise that effective practice requires not only the capacity to make delicate judgments relating to the timing of interventions, but emotional awareness, and imaginative thinking that included risk-taking.[2] These formulations correspond remarkably precisely with those 'hallmarks of artistry' identified by Lang and Taylor (2000).

Contributors were of the view that it was experience that could liberate mediators to act in innovative ways that might lead in unpredictable directions, some more successful than others.

> **Tony Willis:** Like any discipline, you start with professional training and like most professionals you leave most of that professional training behind – you use it for the first little while until it becomes implicit and into your DNA somehow. What's left is difficult to define actually... You do things which if you were being trained and tested by CEDR to see whether you'd pass, you'd fail. David Shapiro says that a mediator has to go out on a limb because that's where the fruit is. And we're always doing things which you're not trained to do because they're powerful and your experience suggests that they work because you're sufficiently experienced to make it sufficiently safe for you to do it and it seems the right thing to do. You take risks of course and occasionally you fall out of the boat and start to sink.

The same sense of danger – and excitement – is captured in this description of the spontaneous creativity that some mediators achieve in the international context.

> **Mark Hoffman:** You pick up, as quick as you can, on something from the participants and just run with it. It's very energising; it's really a high-wire act and you have no idea where anything is going.

The ethical implications of this form of risk-taking, especially for the parties, and the necessary attributes required of the mediator, are considered in the same context of international conflict.

> **Diana Francis:** I think tact and courage are both very important. Because I know one ethical problem that I never mentioned was the issue of encouraging people to take risks in process. Because I know you begin carefully in a mediation, but at a certain point, you know that if you don't get beyond this dancing around the edge of the whole, you might as well not have bothered, and actually people start getting scratchy but not naming anything. And at a certain point, I would say, 'I think this is what is happening. I know it's scary but I think you will be able to get further than this.' You know that it's not you who is putting your head on the block and taking these risks. And so that kind of sensitivity has to be there I think. I just think an attention to process and to inner workings is something that you can develop, but that some people are not very prepared for. I think an intuitive empathy enables you to speak in a way that is a listening way, to be able to frame things in ways that are clear but not hurtful, naming but not insulting, inviting but not dragooning.

Mediators recognise the need to draw on both their intellect and their emotions. However elusive, 'emotional intelligence' is acknowledged, in the literature as well as by practitioners, to be essential for effective practice performance – the need for tact, and empathy and to give worth to the capacity for 'hearing the intention beneath another's words' (Sennett 2006, p.120). It is an international mediator too who sums up the overarching requirements that inform what has been called 'artful competence' (Schon 1983, p.19).

> **Adam Curle:** One needs special knowledge about the circumstances. But I think one needs a whole lot of things… Well, it doesn't need any more than human beings need to live satisfactorally. If you think of anybody you know who copes pleasantly, constructively and affectionately with life, then add on top of that the specific conditions, the specific circumstances in which violence occurs. And if one thinks of mediators like Kissinger, well, he was a very bad mediator. He couldn't do it. What he does is to evoke power, force.

Something of the sense of creativity that the following German mediator experiences appears to be bound up with, not just the current developmental phase of mediation in Europe, but more its nature and spirit.

> **Christoph Paul:** I have given lot a of time to mediation. It is my hobby. And of course all this work for these organisations [involving work with mediation professional associations and the Ministry of Justice] is all for free and I spend a lot of time on that. But it gives me a lot. And my wife, for example, always says, 'Christoph, when you come back from any mediation meeting, even if it is the most strenuous congress, you look happy.' The people I meet in mediation, all the other mediators are just delightful. When I meet with lawyers it is not [the same] – [they are] a different kind of person. Mediators are so interested in me, interested in others, *interested in creating something.*
>
> I think the interesting thing about mediation is it is not settled, it is not done, it is not all proved over years and years and generations. It is still flowing. It is flowing, growing, changing. There are so many modifications. For example in my career as a mediator there are so many new things that came up. For example the spirit we got from the Reunite project[3] when we started together. That was a kick for us. Whenever I go to [conferences with] mediators from other countries and see how they are working that is interesting. I always gain so much. I don't get that from my legal work – not at all. You mentioned the word art. I wouldn't say mediation is an art. It is not. But it has aspects of art. It is very helpful to have an eye on this [aspect] of being something that sometimes has a little bit of an art. Sometimes that has a little bit of a mystery. I wouldn't say it is a mystery, because it is really hard work. But it has something of it.

Similarities and differences between different fields of mediation

Cross-cultural studies of negotiation and mediation, supported by empirical data, show that 'patterns of interactive behaviour in negotiations are essentially similar despite marked differences in interests, ideas, values, rules, and assumptions among negotiators in different societies' (Gulliver 1979, p.xv). In theory therefore, although the identification of similarities of process across fields of mediation practice is to be expected, it is acknowledged too that inherent uncertainty and the complexity of variables of 'real-life situations', aspects of which may be unknowable, make any reliable theoretical predictions unlikely (Gulliver 1979, p.xvi).

What do the reflections of the contributors, drawing on their concrete practice experience, reveal about the similarities and differences to be found in their diverse fields? This important question is linked to another about the nature of the commonalities and differences, and the weight that contributors attached to these. Three contributors (each from a separate field of practice) expressed an inability to answer the question because of a lack of sufficient knowledge about other fields (see below) or as the following contributor, a commercial mediator, makes clear, because it may not be possible to make such an assessment:

> **David Shapiro:** I don't know the answer to that [question]. If I was giving you an answer off the top of my head, and it's purely a guess, I would say there are more differences than there are similarities. But that could be a totally incorrect answer. I don't think you can quantify the similarities and the differences. I have given you the best answer I can, which is I don't know. And I can't do any better than that.

The majority view, that there are both commonalities and differences, is complicated by the variety of perspectives on the subject, explored in more detail below.

Commonalities across fields of mediation practice

In the view of the following contributor working in the community, elder and faith mediation fields, the overarching objective of mediation is its central common feature, whatever the arena of application. That is not to say that differences are not important as well.

> **Yvonne Craig:** It is the common aim of all mediation work, whether in high-cost commercial mediation, family or age mediation, that is of bringing people together to reach agreement about improving a situation, relationships or bringing people together to reach an agreement about an outcome. Whatever the framework that is the common aim. A common cause. And the differences arise from a different social or cultural context in which the meetings take place.

A commercial mediator gives greater weight to that commonality by endorsing the similarities over the differences.

> **Tony Willis:** We are all doing exactly the same thing. So the commonality is *vast*. The things that divide us are by comparison, I think, trivial.

On the basis of her teaching of mediators from various fields of practice, the next family mediator recognises the difficulty of being able to make an informed judgment about the issue without having had direct experience herself, through observation or direct practice, of other fields. The important commonalities across fields are affirmed – of values, of process and of understandings about the role of the mediator – as are the differences. She is mindful both of the difficulties involved in the training of practitioners to work in diverse fields and of the dangers of privileging one mode of practice over another.

> **Lorraine Schaffer:** I think unless you actually have met or observed or done other kinds of mediation practice you really can't make judgments, so I don't really profess to know enough. Because I have had to teach people coming in from commercial, from victim–offender, from peer mediation and from community mediation. At least on the courses I have *heard* about the practice and I do think there is a common process to mediation and a common understanding about the role of the mediator. But there are differences… To me that is also a training issue about *how* mediators have the knowledge, competence and ability to get people together, so I don't think you can have one model of mediation practice that is suitable for all. But I do think there is a common thread of values that runs through. I don't think we should think that any one reading of it is better than the other. There are potentially skilled mediators in all fields.

Another mediator, in the environmental field, sees training in different contexts as a valuable opportunity for expanding understanding of differences and of similarities.

> **Andrew Acland:** The similarities [are greater than the differences]. I have always been struck by the transferability of understanding. And that is why I always try to encourage people to work outside any one particular narrow part [of the field]. If I was going to do the ideal training process for all mediators it would include a spell working in very, very different contexts. And I have always said to a lot of legal mediators, for example, there is nothing like barking dogs on a council estate to test your mediation skills.

While noting the similarities across fields of mediation skills, this labour mediator is of the view that what *is* significant, is the specialist knowledge base, substantive as well as procedural and institutional, that differentiates areas of practice.

> **Roy Lewis:** There will be certain skills of the craft that would be doubtless common across different areas where mediation happens. But I go back to my original answer. I don't know how you can operate in those areas without a basic knowledge of the area as well… Simply from my field it would be rather difficult to deal with employment, whether collective or individual issues, without some background knowledge of employment issues…[and] you have to be constantly aware of what ACAS does and the space that ACAS leaves in employment. Because ACAS doesn't cover all the squares. On the other hand you have to be acutely aware of what it does do. You are more likely to do it, without making things worse *and* more effectively, if you've got that knowledge.

Differences across fields of mediation practice

If a common objective, a common thread of values, a core process and core mediator qualities and role, plus a common body of skills and techniques unites the diverse fields of practice, what are the central differences? A specialist knowledge base is one obvious answer as already noted in the labour field.

One significant difference between fields, also highlighted by contributors, is that of the dynamics of conflict that typify different contexts of practice. It is not knowledge about the relevant law or the legal framework, or the substantive subject matter in dispute that is considered crucial for the following commercial mediator contemplating, with extreme reticence, the prospect of mediating in the family or community context. Rather he refers to a lack of understanding of what he calls 'the dynamic of the process'. This, it appears, is less a matter of model of practice (joint or separate meetings; solo or co-mediation), or of competence or context, but rather a matter of having sufficient understanding about the dynamics of family relationships and the nature of family conflict.

> **Philip Naughton:** I wouldn't dream of doing a family mediation, or indeed a community mediation, because I don't believe that I know enough about the process. I believe that the dynamic of the process is pretty different. It is all in open session. Two mediators rather than one. Just a different dynamic. It may be that, to the extent that the ability to be a good mediator is innate, I could pick it up quite quickly. I don't know. But I think there is a big difference between [the fields]. I think that many of the disputes are less clear-cut in family disputes. Family disputes involve relationships which I am going to have difficulty in understanding. I think at the right level of sophistication, I don't know enough about what gets families into trouble.

The following German mediator, working both as a commercial and a family mediator, is perhaps unusually equipped to comment on the question. He draws attention to what he perceives to be both the common aspects and the main differences, in the case of commercial mediation for example, the larger number of parties, the style of practice (more directive) and the involvement of representative lawyers in the process.

> **Christoph Paul:** I would say the similarities are bigger than the differences. And I am always astonished, you know. I came to different fields just by trying, just by doing... And I said this must be somehow different. Of course the more people you have, I think...creates difference. The number of people round the table. And what creates difference, I think, in business mediation, is that it is much more directive. You give much more options. Whereas in family disputes I would never give them options. I would ask *them* to set out the options. [In business mediation] I never mediate between the lawyers. Never. I mediate together with the lawyers. Sometimes they are in the room which I find difficult because of competition [with me as mediator]. I think I have to convince the lawyers more that mediation is a good tool.

In the international sphere, individual style of practice is identified as a relevant difference. In addition the political context determines the conflict dynamic in a major way.

> **Mark Hoffman:** I think there is a *lot* of difference. Part of it is down to individuals. And I think the difference is not in terms of the basic skills sets or even the basic processes that people are trying to do but *how* they go about doing that – so that, you know, the different kinds of qualities or skills that particular mediators and facilitators have, is quite interesting in terms of how they do what they do. But I think, nevertheless, there are variations on themes as opposed to individuals doing wild and dramatically different kinds of processes. Somehow it is got to be down to personalities; it is got to be down to the influence of style... It partly goes back to the other question – can someone in international mediation do family mediation? I think part of that is the context. The integral kind of *conflict situation dynamic* you're dealing with, would be one of those factors that makes a difference. So while there might be certain kinds of commonalities or parallels between what someone's doing in terms of mediating in the Middle East, with someone mediating in family disputes in South East London, the context is also going to be something that has an effect.

The same contributor expands on this difference, explaining that the international mediator is dealing, not with the conflict dynamic of individuals, but with the larger social dynamics of organised violence and acts of political terror. Different qualities, a different mediator disposition even, may be needed, therefore, in international mediation. The capacity for empathy, so essential for dealing with individuals in conflict, might not work in dealing with political injuries at different levels of society.

Another contributor also reflects on the kind of conflict that has to be addressed in international practice, and, in particular, the way in which it is defined and by whom. (Similar preoccupations have emerged in the context of family mediation.[4])

> **Diana Francis:** I'm just thinking that if you are doing inter-personal or inter-family mediation, or within families, you can see that the complexity is there all right. It's a matter of scale. We are not trying to deal with those minute details of inter-personal stuff. We are [dealing] much more [in] broad sweeps. ...But I think it's also very interesting: in relation to inter-group political mediation, at whatever level, the same dilemma applies. I used to be very much in the neighbourhood mediation field of practice. I used to be very much on your side of the debate [about whose definitions of the problem were important], which was ongoing within our mediator group. 'Well, I spotted that the conflict was *really* about this much more deep-seated thing between them and I wanted to confront them with this,' and I always [said], 'No.' Conflict, and we called it 'conflict', we didn't call it 'deep-seated', the conflict is what *they* are presenting it as. *They* get to define the conflict and we deal with that. We don't start digging away, or saying, well, I think you're wrong about what the conflict's [really] about.
>
> You could say the thing that has to be settled is the conflict at the top that is dealt with by the politicians, but actually there is a wider societal inter-group stand off, or volatility, or hostility, or whatever it is that does actually need to be dealt with if the show is to go on in any tolerable sort of way. So it's almost like dealing with the wider conflict. So I still think it is important to know... There may be such a dynamic that people almost forget what the conflict was about in the first place and it becomes about the violence that has been done. And that in itself becomes the cause of the ongoing violence.
>
> So I think there are various levels there that do need to be addressed. So if it is dealing with the past which is the primary focus, you've got a settlement, but still there were crimes committed and there's no trust and there's no justice. So you need reconciliation [processes] for dealing with the past... which is more the equivalent of your underlying relationships in the family. So it's not that easy to separate these things out. Maybe conceptually you need to. Categories are not realities are they? They are groupings of convenience. And challenging those categories at certain points is, I think, important because I often think the leaders who decide things are human beings... and [should] recognise their humanity. Because actually not only is this a human issue as well as a political issue, but their personal motivations will make a big difference.

Another aspect that distinguishes fields of practice, one not confined to the international arena, is that the international mediator is likely to be involved in the facilitation of groups rather than individuals. This requires the mediator to invoke a different theory of practice, address a different dynamic of conflict, introduce more complex time management arrangements, and deploy different, more appropriate methods and skills – as the same contributor examines below.

Diana Francis: My only experience is of inter-personal mediation, organisational mediation, with some row going on at work, disputes between neighbours and with international stuff. I think it's very much the same skills. The theory enlarges and there are more things, like the cultural, structural dynamic. Some of the theory isn't so relevant... You know the stages and processes of conflict transformation, the diagram that I developed and that's in my book. It does actually apply in certain ways to inter-personal stuff as well. But I think the skills are very much the same skills.

One of the differences is that I consider facilitating processes that have root dynamics as well as inter-personal dynamics. In some ways in facilitating groups there are some other things you have to take care of. So that you have got to look after time and fair shares and ground rules and everything between two people or 32 people. But it makes a bit of a difference and time management becomes complicated and I probably use more structured exercises and so on, because that's how you make things work to include people in groups. There is a whole other range of skills which is to do with group process, as against inter-personal conversations, and you may have all kinds of things that you can do, like role plays or using diagrams. The actual handling of the conflict rules are the same, but in group processes you can sculpt or use role play or group work or whatever. So that's another range of workshop skills that you're doing that in a formal mediation wouldn't be acceptable, but [would be] if you are doing a much more informal thing with a larger group.

Specialist knowledge in mediation

There is no disagreement amongst contributors that mediators need to have sufficient knowledge of their specific field if they wish to practise with any degree of self-confidence and if the parties are to have confidence in them. They need to have what contributors referred to variously as a 'knowledge for confidence', 'inner confidence' or an 'easy familiarity' or to feel in their 'comfort zone' about the subject matter being negotiated. For the following environmental mediator's practice, a sense of confidence is essential, confirmed by his experience of mediating in a field where he felt, as a non-lawyer, he lacked adequate knowledge, particularly of legal procedure.

Andrew Acland: This is always fascinating, this question [of specialist knowledge]. One of the reasons I really ducked out of doing legal and commercial mediation was because I felt really very little confidence, so I made a very deliberate decision that I would work on things which I felt I knew about. I have always been fascinated by political issues and environmental issues and I've always followed them closely. Having said that, if I'm working on undersea carbon sequestration, now quite clearly I don't entirely understand all the chemistry of the climate cycle, but I think you need to know enough to be able to spell the words and to understand the basic concepts. Because if you don't, people will not have confidence in you. You have to know something about the issues which you are working on, but you do not need to be an expert in them. I like to understand what people are talking about, so there's a certain amount of personal choice, of what actually gives you confidence. I think it's not so much knowledge. It's about feeling comfortable with the issues and the people with whom you are working. And also being interested in it.

I find environmental and sustainability issues fascinating and have done since I was about 15. Whereas frankly the nitty gritty of insurance procedures really doesn't do it for me. Then, I think, if only to have the confidence of the parties, having a real specialist knowledge and a real reputation in the field is probably incredibly helpful.

Some contributors regarded specialist knowledge as essential for working in their field. A background in child psychology and understanding about child development is regarded certainly as helpful to an understanding of the subject matter of family disputes. For this Italian mediator, an indispensable psycho-social theoretical and methodological framework of reference informs her approach to family mediation.

Costanza Marzotto: Family mediation is very different because of both the actors on the scene and the nature of their affective and ethical relationships, which pre-existed the conflict and which need to be maintained also after the break of the conjugal pact. It is different in terms of the issues in question and in terms of what is at stake. The inheritance and the children are issues with a highly symbolic content and for them the negotiation acquires a very special significance. It is not about goods and entities in themselves, but each issue in mediation has a high symbolic value which needs to be discovered and named for the individual and for the family group as part of a multi-generational set. These issues of mediation are material and ethical at the same time as are the ties between the generations and the ancestral goods (money, the house, the children, etc.) which need to be protected for the survival of family relationships.

Thus mediation is different because of the competences required of the mediator who is expected to have specific knowledge of the needs within the family group, depending on the individual member's age, gender and life stage, and depending on the stage of the process of separation/divorce. The family mediator is required to explore deeply within him/herself in order to figure out the best way to assist the family's health and well-being; in this way the mediator will prepare him or herself to help, free from any prejudice, couples that are in the process of separation or divorce but are still looking for help in their negotiation. [On the other hand] what family mediation has in common with mediation in other contexts are the negotiation techniques such as exploring the needs beneath the positions; dealing with one question at a time; and exploring the options fully before the choice of the final decision.

Other areas of mediation practice are also seen to require specialist knowledge – whether of employment matters (see above), of inter-cultural work including religious culture, or of the elderly. *Within* specialist fields of practice there is continuing debate as to what expertise is necessary as illustrated by the current debate in the victim–offender field.

> **Marian Liebmann:** I think there are some issues that people either need extra training on or indeed to be a professional from that field [and] people are still arguing about that. I'm a member of Mediation UK's Mediation and Reparation Committee and there are two of us who are also community mediators. We see community mediation skills as really very relevant to victim–offender mediation. And the rest of the Committee, people who don't have community mediation skills, see community mediation and victim–offender mediation as totally different things and not relevant to each other, and that to be a victim–offender mediator you really need to be completely immersed in the criminal justice system. And that unless you've been immersed in the criminal justice system for a long time you can't possibly undertake victim–offender mediation. It comes up from time to time when people are debating who should be accredited. People express worry that community mediation services are dabbling in victim–offender work when they don't think they're competent. I think a lot of the skills are common ones but I think you do need some background knowledge of context – whether it's family, whether it's community, whether it's victim–offender.

For commercial mediation (though not for any other area of practice) one view is that 'basically a decent commercial lawyer mediator who spends his time getting prepared for a case, does not need any specialist knowledge' (David Shapiro). Another commercial mediator distinguishes between two kinds of specialist knowledge, that relating to the legal issues and that relating to the legal system and other dispute resolution processes.

> **Tony Willis:** You don't have to be a specialist in legal issues though, but a specialist in the process by which they're trying to resolve the dispute is certainly a very great help. Experience of legal process. Experience of the resolution process, of the dispute resolution process. So a really detailed experience of the adversarial and non-adversarial dispute resolution systems that are involved. You need to know the way the courts work. You need to know how arbitrators work. You need to know how the legal advice is going to be structured. Why they're taking the step that they're taking. It is terribly important that as a legally qualified mediator you do deliberately take that attitude.
> There is [the possibility of transferability of skills. But] I'm doubtful about family because the discipline has developed in such a different way...and because I think dealing with families does require additional skills which lots of lawyer mediators who are terribly good lawyer mediators, mediators who

happen to be lawyers, would find very difficult to deal with – I just think it is an absolute reflection of the importance of the field and that you're messing about with children's lives and so on in a way which I would not feel comfortable contemplating.

The importance of specific knowledge (professional, social and of context rather than technical) is upheld too by this contributor practising in both the fields of commercial and family mediation in Germany. The main difference is that in the family field, there are unknowable aspects associated with the uniqueness of every family.

Christoph Paul: I think special knowledge is helpful. John Haynes [the late North American mediator trainer and practitioner] said you don't have to know anything about [the subject], you can mediate everything. Probably it has been true with him. For me it is very helpful knowing a little bit about it. But for example, I remember I did a mediation within a firm, there were technical things involved which I did not know anything about. I think I did a successful mediation without knowing anything about it. I think what is much more helpful is to know something about the social background the people live in. For example, if you do a business mediation, you have to have the possibility of getting to the people there. You have managers. You have to have somehow the possibilities of knowing how they are in their field – [the professional and social context], absolutely. But beside that, I think the family situations that are offered within family mediation are so different. *You don't know it anyway.* Sometimes I say, 'That's really interesting – the kind of family life they live.' I never heard that it's possible but it works. It worked at least for a couple of years and they have children together and whatever. And I look at it and if I would have read it in a book they'd say what a crazy writer.

Another contributor, citing the advantage, in many commercial mediation cases, of specialist knowledge *and* mediator expertise ideally combined in the one practitioner,[5] points to the practical difficulty of finding a mediator who will be perceived by both parties as non-aligned in a small specialist field. Of course this can be an occupational hazard for any practitioner working in more than one professional capacity, the lawyer mediator in particular.

Philip Naughton: I'm sure that I have done cases in fields which I don't profess any specialisation, like wet shipping cases where I miss easy familiarity with the subject matter and I think it makes it much more difficult for me and I know others disagree… I think the position goes really like this. That if you are a specialist in a field *and* you're a good mediator, then you start with the benefit or advantage which in most cases will have an effect upon the effectiveness of the mediation process. Having said that, there is no doubt that sometimes parties will select a mediator because they're *not* a specialist in that particular field but they are a very good mediator, often because the whole club is too small, if you see

> what I mean, so people tend always to have fixed ideas about how disputes should resolve, or alternatively people are known to always be on one side of the dispute or the other side of the dispute, or always acting for the insurer or always acting for the insured.

Finally, some of the advantages of *not* having specialist knowledge are explored in the international context. What is critical is knowing enough, without one having to be an expert, and knowing what one does not know.

> **Diana Francis:** I think a degree of ignorance can be very helpful, but then you have to know how ignorant you are. If you have to be behaving with humility [you] will then have a right to ask, in a genuine way, questions which need to be asked and which you couldn't ask with any sincerity if you already knew the answers. So there is a utility to that. If you just irritate people with your ignorance… I think in any case people have to not be irritated by your ignorance but equally there is a tendency, for people who know an awful lot, to think they know the answers, and then that kind of runs counter to mediatory energies, if you like.
> So certainly I don't think you need to feel you're the expert. I think you have to know enough to hear what is significant, and sometimes background knowledge will tell you, 'This isn't a passing remark, this has a certain load.' My skills are most to do with process… If I'm being asked to be an expert, it tends to be in terms of broad experience, a range of different viewpoints, anecdotes and so on, and just having some kind of meta [view] that you, little by little, build a knowledge of, the dynamics of, or ingredients of, just by having met a lot of people. So being a generalist has its own strength. It clearly has its weaknesses as well. I think for a mediator, it is much less important [to have specialist knowledge] than it is for somebody who is a technical adviser, or certainly an adjudicator or somebody who comes up with solutions. It's a bit like any other mediation. You might say, 'Have you ever explored anything along the lines of…?' So something *very* gentle and open.

The craft of mediation

> The craftsman has to learn how to make things, but he learns in the process of making them. (Aristotle, *Ethics*, trans. Thomson 1959, p.56)

The revival of alternative approaches to conflict and dispute in the USA, and the community justice movement in particular, was one manifestation, arising from the social movement of the 1960s, of the 'new consciousness' that challenged traditional attitudes and values in the context of dispute resolution (a process memorably observed by Reich in *The Greening of America*, 1970). The values of mediation exemplified the spirit of the time – the importance of respect, dignity, fairness, justice, reciprocity, individual participation, consensus and party control. The resurrection of these values countered a dominant, prevailing value system characterised by adversarial processes, impersonality, lawyer control and rule-centred authoritarian command.

This movement of the late 20th century reiterates, in some curious and reminiscent respects, the origin and rise of another humanising movement in the late 19th century, the Arts and Crafts Movement. This was a movement also born of ideals that grew out of a concern for the disastrous effects of mechanisation, industrialisation and unregulated trade. It celebrated craftsmanship and new approaches to design and the decorative arts with value being placed on the individualised response, the natural beauty of materials and an approach that embodied the principles of simplicity, usefulness and honesty. Greatly influenced by the theorist and critic, John Ruskin, and the activist and practitioner, William Morris, as well as others, mainly architects, designers and artists, this movement ushered in the revival of an ancient tradition of workshop practice and individual creativity in the making of things and of craftsmanship.

In the 21st century too, the values and achievements of craftsmanship are being newly affirmed, this time in contrast to a prevailing work ethic characterising the 'new capitalism' of global labour supply and automation where the experiential base of talent counts for less and less, where the focus is on knowledge that is short-term and flexible, and where it is cheaper to have turnover than to retrain (Sennett 2006). In such a fluid, mobile and present-oriented world of work, 'skill' is defined as the ability to do something new, rather than draw on what one has already learned to do, and mental superficiality is privileged over accumulated knowledge and experience (Sennett 2006).

Consistent with the reflections of the overwhelming majority of contributors there emerges a view of mediation practice, its essential common elements and its rich diversity, as a form of craftsmanship. There is, of course, nothing new in conceiving of mediation as 'a time when people can make something together' (Davis, in Kolb 1994). The singular facets (mental, social and practical) of craftsmanship and the manner in which the mediator can be conceived of as a contemporary practitioner of this ancient and universal craft, correspond with those same core values and ideal elements of practice identified in contributors' reflections – the importance of self; disinterested commitment; the necessity for taking care; the value of accumulated experience over time; engaging with problems; the endeavour toward fashioning something useful; the representation of an appreciation of the beauty of an everyday activity; and the pursuit of quality. Together these general attributes cohere in what Sennett (2006, p.104) describes as 'an embracing definition of craftsmanship' that is 'doing something well for its own sake' and at the same time contributing something that matters to other people. What makes mediation the craft it is, as contributors testify, are those distinguishing features that are summarised below.

- *Thinking like the craftsman* represents the way in which the task of the mediator is perceived by mediators themselves – as persons curious about their work, dedicated, fascinated, loving and even obsessed by what they are doing. There is an explicit assumption that the more one understands how to do something well, the more one cares about it. That requires commitment, self-discipline and self-criticism in the pursuit of quality.

- The focus on getting something right for its own sake, obsessive in some respects, can lead to 'a kind of ungenerous possessiveness' too (Sennett 2006, p.195). 'Competition is no stranger to craftsmanship, and good craftsmen, be they computer programmers, musicians, or carpenters, can be highly intolerant of those who are incompetent or simply not as good' (Sennett 2006, p.195).

- The expertise of mediation is gained largely from others working in the field in the guildhall mode – mediator trainers, the deployment of the apprenticeship model for acquiring skills and experience, and continuing educational development and support provided by informal networks of peers, foster exchanges in a spirit of collegiality. 'Craftsmanship fits easily within the mediaeval guild frame in that the apprentice as much as the master could seek to make something well for its own sake' (Sennett 2006, p.108). The notion of the guildhall inspires too a model for quality, assuring mediation practice that emphasises the value of regular exposure to peer practitioners as a source of the most effective learning, rather than relying on certification or the procedures of formal regulation (Coletta and DiDomenico 2000).

- Learning how to get things right through trial and error and the making of mistakes is key to the pursuit of knowledge and practice skills. 'Craftsmanship requires mastering and owning a particular domain of knowledge' (Sennett 2006, p.115).

- The value base of mediation, in placing the parties first, aspires to contribute something that matters to others. Respect for the parties and their decision-making authority is paramount. Trust in the process and earned by the mediators and the parties is considered essential for effective practice.

- The role of the self is the main tool in a mediator's practice. Individual charisma – in contrast to the promotion of the ego – may be significant in some situations, quiet unobtrusiveness in others. Motivation for choosing to do this work (a belief in its objective value) and emotional intelligence, calm objectivity and reasonableness, as well as the power of creative thinking are essential attributes.

- The experiential knowledge base is one that requires extensive practice skill, refined and deepened over time. Experience gives mediators the opportunity to develop their understanding of what they are doing, gradually expanding knowledge and skill. That experience enables practitioners to respond to the objectively difficult circumstances that characterise situations of conflict with 'the intuitive judgments of a skilled craftsman' (Schon 1983, p.276).

- Universal characteristics inherent in the activity are discernable in all mediations (the informing principles, objectives and the staged process). At the same time 'the situations of practice are characterised by unique events' calling for unique responses sometimes called 'an art of practice' (Schon 1983, p.17).

- Notwithstanding institutional and funding constraints in some contexts, mediators have the capacity for autonomy in the practice of their craft. This gives them control over professional decisions and self-direction in their own work which can lead to a sense of identity and achievement.

- Finally, while pride in one's work is to be encouraged, and '[w]hile it's important not to romanticise the balm of craftsmanship, it matters equally to understand the consequences of doing something well for its own sake. Ability counts for something, by a measure which is both concrete and impersonal' (Sennett 2006).

Whither mediation?

> The varieties of dispute settlement, and the socially sanctioned choices in any culture, communicate the ideals people cherish, their perceptions of themselves, and the quality of their relationships with others. They indicate whether people wish to avoid or encourage conflict, suppress it, or resolve it amicably. Ultimately the most basic values of society are revealed in its dispute-settlement procedures. (Auerbach 1983, p.304)

Radical ideological and institutional changes have transformed, in a remarkably short period since the 1980s, civil disputing arrangements across the common law and civilian worlds of the west (charted by Roberts and Palmer 2005). The growth of a body of mediators (establishing professional status in certain fields), the legal profession's embrace of ADR, and court sponsorship of settlement (through judicial encouragement and the introduction of novel litigation procedures that require early-stage negotiation on pain of cost sanctions) reflect the cultural shift of approach to dispute resolution that has taken place – negotiation and consensual decision-making challenging the dominance of third-party decision-making (Roberts and Palmer 2005).

In domains other than civil justice, equivalent developments reflect innovative alternative dispute resolution approaches in the sphere of criminal and restorative justice, the environment, the workplace, the community, education and other specialist areas such as disability and medical negligence. Of course, in the international arena and in labour relations (since the Conciliation Act, 1896), mediation, conciliation and facilitative interventions have been long endorsed and practised.

Some contributors reflected generally on the future direction of mediation. Notwithstanding acknowledgement of the ethical significance that the affirmation of human values in mediation's recent discovery represents, a questioning approach to future possibilities for mediation is adopted by the following commercial mediator.

> **Philip Naughton:** I think the only thing I can think of is to reflect upon where it [mediation] is going to go. It *is* a very new process and what I'm not entirely satisfied about in my own mind is whether or not it is the right model, the only model, the fashionable model. And whether in another 10 or 20 years, we will be saying, 'Well, once upon a time we used to mediate.' Thinking [of] an example, the Summary Jury Trial was all the thing in the States in the late 80s and it was completely eclipsed by mediation. And Early Neutral Evaluation in the northern districts of California was bound to go places and it really hasn't caught on at all. And so if I knew what was coming next I'm sure I could corner the market, but I don't. But I do wonder whether or not it's the last word. It could be said, well, what we've done is gone back to a reliance upon human values and human relationships which has a long history. But we moved away from that when the litigation process was formalised. Presumably we moved away for a reason. I wonder whether the best example I can give is whether or not you may see in the next few years a reaction by those responsible for the formal dispute resolution process, improving its efficiency, reducing its cost, which will swing the pendulum in a different direction.

These thoughts raise important questions about the extent to which specific innovative procedures, such as the 'mini-trial' and early neutral evaluation (ENE), introduced into the legal process ostensibly to enhance client participation in decision-making and to promote settlement, do, in fact, fulfil those objectives or are 'simply crisis management measures, designed to allay mounting consumer anxiety and dissatisfaction' (Roberts and Palmer 2005, p.361). Whether that ethical dimension at the heart of mediation ('Are you treated as a human being or are those qualities not considered?') can be incorporated into the formal justice system poses other imponderable questions about the future (Davis 1984, p.54).

One of the several, and conflicting, influences (political, institutional and legal) that stimulated the early growth, in the USA and in the UK, of alternative dispute resolution processes, and of mediation in particular, was the idealism of its early pioneers. This idealism embodied that hope that consensual and participatory dispute resolution processes, more attuned to human values and needs (compared to the traditional adversarial, hierarchical formal justice system), would transform not only disputing individuals but also 'nudge society in the same direction' (Chase 2005, p.135). That hope still burns with a fire fuelled by a conviction, even in its most tentative form, about the future importance, if not necessity, of more widespread understanding about and deployment of mediation: 'I believe from my own experience that the type of mediation I have tried to define represents a short wavering step in the right direction' (Curle 1986, p.53).

This is the view not only of those who mediate in the international arena with direct experience of the violence of political conflict but also the perspective of someone who, in the context of workplace conflict, describes his motivation in becoming a mediator.

Carl Reynolds: I would certainly say that part of my motivation for doing this work is because I think that what I do, and what I'm using, and what other people are doing as well, is very important for human development.

A heavy responsibility is seen to lie on those who do know about mediation and who work in the domain of conflict resolution. If the potential of mediation for addressing wider conflict in human affairs, now and in the future, is to be realised, there is no time to lose. Not surprisingly perhaps, it is an environmental mediator who recognises the extreme urgency for greater understanding and education in society and for change in the way people deal with each other, not only individually, but in their social, economic and political relationships.

Andrew Acland: Again I have mixed feelings about everything and I certainly always had very mixed feelings about Bush and Folger and their transformative approach,[6] but I do think that people in this field do need to have at least some sense of the wider process of which they have become a part. That ultimately mediation is not just about settling the case which is in front of you, it is about changing the way in which people deal with each other much more generally. I am also aware of the difficulties it throws up. But I originally came into mediation in the political field with the belief that conflict between human beings is really the great plague. It is the thing that we have to learn to deal with or we will obliterate ourselves. Not only will we end up having a global nuclear war or something eventually, it will actually happen if we don't learn to deal with conflict.

But one of the things that working in the environmental field has really brought home to me is that our chances of actually getting through this century

> are not actually that great because the stresses which will come through population, through water resource, through the effect of climate change on geography, will put human populations in confrontation with each other in a way in which we have never known in human history.
>
> Unless we can deal with those confrontations we are actually going to end up in an awful mess. If we cannot learn to spread an almost institutionalised non-violent conflict resolution process, things are really going to get very nasty. I think the mediation and conflict resolution world as a whole has not been anything like forward enough in actually teaching governments and groups of people how to do this. I think it behoves all of us to try to take this forward. At the first whiff of serious conflict we all tend to run for the hills. We will happily deal with these immediate situations but we won't, we don't really engage with the bigger picture. And I think that there is a lot we can do to actually teach the world about this. This is sounding awfully pious and solemn. There is a bigger picture here. And I think people who do this work by virtue of doing it take some responsibility for making it work in a bigger picture.

The sense of urgency of the need for more rational and constructive approaches to dealing with future conflict is shared by this commercial mediator.

> **Tony Willis:** If there's one thing I'm really concerned about, [it] is global competition for resources... What underpins mediation seems to me to be critical, if I'm not to be too pompous about it, to the survival of civilisation as it is at the moment. And yet *and yet* we exist in a little, tiny self-important bubble and the realisation, if I'm right about what I've just said, we don't seem to be able to be getting out of there. And that seems to me to be a really serious issue. It is translating the essential ingredients of what mediation is into day-to-day life. I would wish that the lessons to be learned from mediators and the skills to be deployed were more widely recognised *and* implemented...working out mechanisms which were not regulatory and law-driven but which encouraged people to agree.

The reflexive relationship between disputing processes and the wider culture is one upheld by scholars as well as practitioners notwithstanding the paradoxical paradigm:

> If disputing practice is locked in a pas-de-deux with culture, destined to follow its greater partner's lead, how can the process partner possibly effect a change that departs from what is already choreographed? (Chase 2005, p.138)

The solution to this paradox lies in the recognition that culture is always subject to change and that just as ways of disputing reflect the culture in which they are found, so too will changes in disputing have cultural reverberations (Chase

2005). The perspectives of individuals can and do contribute to changes of culture.

Indeed the radical changes in disputing processes that occurred in the 1980s (and which are now an established and expanding feature of the world of ADR in the West) are testimony to the contribution of those pioneering early mediators whose idealism still informs the best of contemporary mediation thinking and practice. It is hoped that this work, in providing a forum for the present generation of mediators to reflect on their practice in all its rich variety and across disparate fields, will stimulate further exchange, improve understanding and contribute to a continuing refinement of our craft.

Notes

1. In using this term, there is obviously no intention to privilege either gender; the alternatives, craftswoman or craftsperson, would seem contrived.
2. Indeed, in 1992, the Society of Professionals in Dispute Resolution (SPIDR), encouraged by the distinguished community mediator, Albie Davis, introduced an annual Mary Parker Follett Award (in memory of Follett's uncelebrated contribution in the 1920s to thinking on power and constructive conflict resolution) which was designed to honour a person or organisation who 'in the spirit of risk-taking' and collaboration, makes a significant contribution to the field of conflict resolution (Merry, in Kolb et al. 1994, p.260).
3. A joint collaboration as part of the Reunite pilot on mediation in child abduction cases.
4. For example, a controversial subject in the 1980s centred on the tendency to regard the parties' definition of the issues as the 'presenting' problem, symptom of more 'real' underlying conflict. This approach, imported into family mediation from family therapy, threatened to transform the intervener's role from one of facilitating mediator, intent on affirming the value *of the parties'* meanings, to that of leader and knowing expert, privileging the intervener's psychological interpretations. The controversial issue of the extent to which it is useful to explore the past is a recurring one amongst family mediators. (See Grillo 1991 and Chapter 4).
5. Of course, all the necessary expertise need not reside in the same person, and, in some fields, the option of bringing in a co-worker with the relevant complementary expertise is common practice.
6. According to Bush and Folger (1994), the unique promise of mediation is its capacity to transform not only the character of individual disputants but society as a whole.

Appendix: Topic Guide

In the making of this book, each contributor was interviewed individually once, and there was no exchange between the contributors. All were asked the questions listed below, in that order. Further clarification was requested when necessary. Each interview was audiotaped and the tape recording transcribed into print. Contributors were given the opportunity to check their quoted material.

- What brought you into mediation?
- What particular personal qualities do you think you bring to this work?
- What are your attitudes to conflict – personal and professional?
- Do any particular principles inform your mediation practice?
- Do you draw on theoretical sources in your mediation practice?
- What do you perceive to be the main problems of practice?
- How do you deal with any stresses arising in work that involves disputes and conflict?
- How would you describe your style of practice?
- What is your model of practice?
- Do you consider mediation an autonomous, discrete form of intervention or a generic tool, used among others in the course of another professional practice?
- What do you consider to be the purpose of mediation? To settle a dispute? To solve a problem? To transform relationships? Other objectives?
- Does a mediator require specialist knowledge of the substantive issue being mediated or is generic mediator competence sufficient within and/or across fields of practice?
- How important is a sound grasp of theory for effective practice?
- To what extent, if any, has research influenced or changed your practice?
- How much of good mediation practice is an art? Or a craft? Or a skill? Or a technique?

- Is mediation a practical tool for settling disputes efficiently, quickly and economically or is it a qualitatively 'better' way of addressing disputes?
- What contextual factors – political, legal, professional, funding, etc. – affect mediation practice?
- What are your views on professional regulation?
- How diverse or how similar is mediation practice across fields?
- What additional comments or observations would you like to make?

Bibliography

Abel, R.L. (1982) 'The Contradictions of Informal Justice.' In R.L. Abel (ed.) *The Politics of Informal Justice*, Volume 1. New York: Academic Press.

Abel, R.L. (1988) *The Legal Profession in England and Wales*. Oxford: Blackwell.

ACAS (Advisory, Conciliation and Arbitration Service) (n.d.) *The ACAS Role in Conciliation, Arbitration and Mediation*. London: ACAS Reports and Publications.

ACLEC Report (Advisory Committee on Legal Education and Conflict) (1999) *Mediation in Family Disputes: Education and Conduct Standards for Mediators*. London: Lord Chancellor's Department.

Aristotle (1959) *The Ethics of Aristotle*. (Trans. J.A.K. Thomson) London: Penguin Boks.

Astor, H. and Chinkin C. (2002) *Dispute Resolution in Australia*, 2nd edn. Chatswood, Australia: Butterworths.

Auerbach, J.S. (1983) *Justice Without Law?* New York: Oxford University Press.

Bar Tal, D. (1998) 'Societal beliefs in times of intractable conflict: The Israeli case.' *International Journal of Conflict Management 9*, 1, 22–50.

Beal, S. and Saul, J.A. (2001) 'Examining Assumptions: Training Mediators for Transformative Practice', in J.P. Folger and R.A.B. Bush (eds) *Designing Mediation: Approaches to Training and Practice within a Transformative Framework*. New York: Institute for the Study of Conflict Transformation Inc.

Bottomley, A. (1984) 'Resolving Family Disputes: A Critical View.' In M.D.A. Freeman (ed.) *State. Law and the Family*. London: Tavistock.

Bottomley, A. (1985) 'What is Happening to Family Law? A Feminist Critique of Conciliation.' In J. Brophy and C. Smart (eds) *Women in Law*. London: Routledge and Kegan Paul.

Bowling, D. and Hoffman, D. (2000) 'In theory: Bringing peace into the room: The personal qualities of the mediator and their impact on the mediation.' *Negotiation Journal 16*, 5, 5–27.

Bush, R.A.B. and Folger, J.P. (1994) *The Promise of Mediation: Reponding to Conflict through Empowerment and Recognition*. San Francisco: Jossey-Bass.

Bush, R.A.B. and Folger, J.P. (2005) *The Promise of Mediation: The Transformative Approach to Conflict*, 2nd edn. San Francisco: Jossey-Bass.

Caplan, P. (1995) 'Anthropology and the Study of Disputes.' In P. Caplan (ed.) *Understanding Disputes: The Politics of Argument*. Oxford: Berg Publishers.

Charbonneau, P. (2001) 'How Practical is Theory.' In J.P. Folger and R.A.B. Bush (eds) *Designing Mediation: Approaches to Training and Practice within a Transformative Framework*. New York: Institute for the Study of Conflict Transformation.

Chase, O.F. (2005) *Law, Culture and Ritual: Disputing Systems in Cross-Cultural Context*. New York and London: New York University Press.

Cobb, S. and Rifkin, J. (1991) 'Practice and paradox: Deconstructing neutrality in mediation.' *Law and Social Inquiry 16*, 1, 35–62.

Coletta, C. and DiDomenico, A. (2000) 'Thoughts on mediators as craftspeople'. *Alternative Dispute Resolution Reporter 4*, 17.

Conneely, S. (2002) *Family Mediation in Ireland*. England: Ashgate.

Coogler, O.J. (1978) *Structured Mediation in Divorce Settlement*. Lexington, MA: Lexington Books/D.C. Heath.

Corbin, J. (1994) *Gaza First: The Secret Norway Channel to Peach between Israel and the PLO*. London: Bloomsbury Publishing.

Cormick, G.W. (1977) 'The Ethics of Mediation: Some Unexplored Territory.' October. Unpublished paper prepared for the Society of Professionals in Dispute Resolution, Fifth Annual Meeting.

Cormick, G.W. (1981) 'Environmental Mediation in the US. Experience and Future Directions I.' Unpublished paper presented to the American Association for Advancement of Science. (Annual meeting, Toronto, Canada.)

Cormick, G.W. (1982) 'Intervention and self-determination in environmental disputes: a mediator's perspective.' *Resolve* Winter.

Council of Europe (1998) *Recommendation No. R (98) 1 of the Committee of Ministers to Member States on Family Mediation*. Strasbourg.

Coyne, W.F. Jr. (1999) 'The case for settlement counsel.' *14 Ohio St. J. on Dispute Resolution* 367, 375–90.

Curle, A. (1986) *In the Middle: Non Official Mediation in Violent Situations*. Leamington Spa: Berg.

Curle, A. (1990a) *Reflections on the Co-ordinating Committe for Conflict Resolution Training in Europe*. Newsletter. Committee for Conflict Transformation Support (CCTS).

Curle, A. (1990b) *Tools for Transformation: A Personal Study*. London: Hawthorn Press.

Davis, A.M. (1984) 'Comment.' In *A Study of Barriers to the Use of Alternative Methods of Dispute Resolution*. Sponsored by the Vermont Law School Dispute Resolution Project, South Royalton. Moderator: John P. McCory.

Davis, A.M. and Gadlin, H. (1988) 'Mediators gain trust, the old fashioned way – we earn it!' *Negotiation Journal 4*, 1, 55–62.

Davis, G. and Bader, K. (1985) 'In-court mediation: The consumer view.' Parts I and II. *Family Law 15*, 3, 42–49; 4, 82–86.

Davis, G. and Roberts, M. (1988) *Access to Agreement: A Consumer Study of Mediation in Family Disputes*. Milton Keynes: Open University Press.

Davis, G. *et al.* (2000) 'Monitoring Publicly Funded Family Mediation.' Final Report to the Legal Services Commission, July. London: Legal Services Commission.

Della Noce, D.J., Bush, R.A.B. and Folger, J.P. (2001) 'Myths and Misconceptions about the Transformative Orientation.' In J.P. Folger and R.A.B. Bush (eds) *Designing Mediation: Approaches to Training and Practice within a Transformative Framework*. New York: Institute for the Study of Conflict Transformation.

Deutsch, M. (1973) *The Resolution of Conflict: Constructive and Destructive Processes*. New Haven, CT: Yale University Press.

Dingwall, R. (1988) 'Empowerment or Enforcement? Some Questions about Power and Control in Divorce Mediation.' In R. Dingwall and J. Eekelaar (eds) *Divorce Mediation and the Legal Process*. Oxford: Oxford University Press.

Dingwall, R. and Greatbatch, D. (1993) 'Who is in charge? Rhetoric and evidence in the study of mediation.' *Journal of Social Welfare and Family Law 15*, 367–85.

Dingwall, R. and Greatbatch, D. (1995) 'Family mediation researchers and practitioners in the shadow of the green paper: A rejoinder to Marian Roberts.' *Journal of Social Welfare and Family Law 17*, 2, 199–206.

Douglas, A. (1957) 'The peaceful settlement of industrial and intergroup disputes.' *Journal of Conflict Resolution 1*, 1, 69–81.

Douglas, A. (1962) *Industrial Peacemaking*. New York: Columbia University Press.

Eckhoff, T. (1969) 'The Mediator and the Judge.' In V. Aubert (ed.) *Sociology of Law*. Harmondsworth: Penguin.

Emery, R.E. (1994) *Renegotiating Family Relationships: Divorce, Child Custody and Mediation*. New York: The Guilford Press.

Emery, R.E., Matthews, S. and Wyer, M. (1991) 'Child custody mediation and litigation: Further evidence on the differing views of mothers and fathers.' *Journal of Consulting and Clinical Psychology 59*, 3, 410–18.

Emery, R.E. *et al.* (2001) 'Child custody mediation and litigation: Custody, contact and coparenting twelve years after initial dispute resolution.' *Journal of Consulting and Clinical Psychology 69*, 323–32.

Emery, R.E., Sbarra, D. and Grover, T. (2005) 'Divorce mediation: Research and reflections.' *Mediation in Practice*, May, 7–18.

Felstiner, W.L.F., Abel, R.L. and Sarat, A. (1980–81) 'The emergence and transformation of disputes: Naming, blaming, claiming…'. *Law and Society Review 15*, 3, 631–54.

Felstiner, W.L.F. and Sarat, A. (1992) 'Enactments of power: Negotiating reality and responsibility in lawyer–client interactions.' *Cornell Law Review 77*, 1447–1498.

Felstiner, W.L.F. and Williams, L. (1985) 'Community Mediation in Dorchester, Mass.' In S.B. Goldberg, E.D. Green and F.E.A. Sander (eds) *Dispute Resolution*. Boston and Toronto: Little, Brown.

Fisher, R. and Ury, W. (1981) *Getting to Yes*. Boston: Houghton Mifflin.

Fiss, O.M. (1984) 'Against settlement.' *93 Yale Law Journal*, 1073–90.

Folberg, J. (1984) 'Divorce Mediation – The Emerging American Model.' In J.M. Eekelaar and S.N. Katz (eds) *The Resolution of Family Conflict, Comparative Legal Perspectives*. Toronto: Butterworths.

Folberg, J. and Milne, A. (eds) (1988) *Divorce Mediation: Theory and Practice*. New York: Guilford Press.

Folberg, J. and Taylor, A. (1984) *Mediation: A Comprehensive Guide to Resolving Conflicts without Litigation*. San Francisco: Jossey-Bass.

Folger, J.P. and Bush, R.A.B. (2001) 'Transformative Mediation and Third Party Intervention: Ten Hallmarks of Transformative Mediation Practice.' In J.P. Folger and R.A.B Bush (eds) *Designing Mediation: Approaches to Training and Practice within a Transformative Framework*. New York: Institute for the Study of Conflict Transformation.

Francis, D. (2002) *People, Peace and Power: Conflict Transformation in Action*. London: Pluto Press.

Freeman, M.D.A. (1984) 'Questioning the Delegalization Movement in Family Law: Do We Really Want a Family Court?' In J.M. Eekelaar and S.N. Katz (eds) *The Resolution of Family Conflict: Comparative Legal Perspectives*. Toronto: Butterworths.

Fuller, L.L. (1971) 'Mediation – its forms and functions.' *Southern California Law Review 44*, 305–39.

Galanter, M. (1984) 'What Else is New? The Emergence of the Judge as Mediator in Civil Cases 1930–1980.' Working paper, Disputes Processing Research Programme. Madison: University of Wisconsin.

Gaynier, L.P. (2005) 'Transformative mediation: In search of a theory of practice.' *Conflict Resolution Quarterly 22*, 3, 397–408.

Gilligan, C. (1982) *In a Different Voice*. Cambridge, MA: Harvard University Press.

Glasser, C. (1994) 'Solving the Litigation Crisis.' *The Litigator 1*, 14.

Goethe, J.W. von (1809, trans. 1971) *Elective Affinities*. Harmondsworth: Penguin.

Golan, D. (2000) 'Variations in mediation: How – and why – legal mediatiors change styles in the course of a case.' *Journal of Dispute Resolution*, 1, 41–61.

Golann, D. (2002) 'Is legal mediation a process of repair – or separation? An empirical study, and its implications.' *Harvard Negotiation Law Review 7*, 301–36.

Grillo, T. (1991) 'The mediation alternative: Process dangers for women.' *Yale Law Journal 100*, 6, 1545–640.

Gulliver, P.H. (1977) 'On Mediators.' In I. Hamnett (ed.) *Social Anthropology and Law*. London: Academic Press.

Gulliver, P.H. (1979) *Disputes and Negotiations: A Cross-Cultural Perspective*. New York: Academic Press.

Hamnett, I. (1977) (ed.) *Social Anthropology and Law*. London: Academic Press.

Hampshire, S. (2000) *Conflict is Justice*. Princeton, NJ: Princeton University Press.

Haynes, J.M. (1981) *Divorce Mediation*. New York: Springer.

Haynes, J.M. (1985) 'Matching readiness and willingness to the mediator's strategies.' *Negotiation Journal*, January, 79–92.

Haynes, J.M. (1992) 'Mediation and therapy: An alternative view.' *Mediation Quarterly 10*, 1, 21–34.

Haynes, J.M. (1993) *The Fundamentals of Family Mediation*. London: Old Bailey Press.

Jones, T.S. (2001) 'Editors' Introduction.' *Conflict Resolution Quarterly 19*, 2, 131–134.

Kelly, J.B. (1995) 'Power imbalances in divorce and interpersonal mediation assessment and intervention.' *Mediation Quarterly 13*, 2, 85–98.

Kelly, J.B. (2004) 'Family mediation research: Is there empirical support for the field?' *Conflict Resolution Quarterly 22*, 1–2, 3–35.

Kelly, J.B. and Duryee, M.A. (1992) 'Women's and men's views of mediation in voluntary and mandatory mediation settings.' *Family and Conciliation Courts Review 30*, 1, 34–49.

Kolb, D.M. *et al.* (1994) *When Talk Works: Profiles of Mediators*. San Francisco: Jossey-Bass.

Kressel, K. (1985) *The Process of Divorce*. New York: Basic Books.

Kressel, K. and Pruitt, D.G. (1985) 'Themes in the mediation of social conflict.' *Journal of Social Issues 41*, 2, 179–198.

Landsberger, H.A. (1956) 'Final report on a research project in mediation.' *Labour Law Journal 7*, 501–10, August.

Lang, M.D. and Taylor, A. (2000) *The Making of a Mediator: Developing Artistry in Practice*. San Francisco: Jossey-Bass.

Legal Services Commission (2002) *Quality Mark Standard for Mediation*. London.

Lord Chancellor's Advisory Committee on Legal Education and Conduct (ACLEC) (1999). 'Mediating Family Disputes: Education and Conduct Standards for Mediators. Report.' London: Lord Chancellor's Department.

Lukes, S. (1973) *Individualism*. Oxford: Basil Blackwell.

Lukes, S. (1974) *Power: A Radical View*. Basingstoke: Macmillan Education.

Mackay, Lord (1995) *Looking to the Future: Mediation and the Ground for Divorce*. Cm. 2799. London.

Matthews, R. (ed.) (1988) *Informal Justice?* London: Sage.

McCarthy, P. and Walker, J. (1996) 'Involvement of lawyers in the mediation process.' *Family Law 26*, 154–8.

McCrory, J.P. (1981) 'Environmental mediation – another piece for the puzzle.' *Vermont Law Review* 6, 1, 49–84.

McCrory, J.P. (1988) 'Confidentiality in mediation (conciliation) of matrimonial disputes.' *Modern Law Review 51*, 4, 442–66.

McDermott, E.P. (2005) 'Summary of research on Mediation Program of US Equal Employment Opportunity Commission.' *Alternative Resolutions 14*, 3, 4–6.

McDermott, E.P and Obar, R. (2004) '"What's going on" in mediation: An empirical analysis of the influence of the mediator's style on party satisfaction and monetary benefit.' *Harvard Negotiation Law Review 9*, 75–114.

McGuigan, R. and McMechan, S. (2005) 'Integral conflict analysis: A comprehensive quadrant analysis of an organizational conflict.' *Conflict Resolution Quarterly 22*, 3, 349–63.

Menkel-Meadow, C.J. (1985) 'Portia in a different voice: Speculation on a women's lawyering process.' *Berkeley Women's Law Journal 1*, 1, 39–63.

Menkel-Meadow, C.J. (1993) 'Lawyer negotiations: Theories and realities – what we learn from mediation.' *Modern Law Review 56*, 3, 361–379. (Special Issue: *Dispute Resolution: Civil Justice and its Alternatives.*)

Menkel-Meadow, C.J. (ed.) (1995) *Mediation: Theory, Policy and Practice.* Dartmouth, Aldershot: Ashgate.

Menkel-Meadow, C.J. (2001) 'Ethics in ADR: The many C's of professional responsibility and dispute resolution.' *Fordham Urban Law Journal 28*, 4, 979–90.

Menkel-Meadow, C.J., Love, L.P., Schneider, A.K. and Sternlight, J.R. (2005) *Dispute Resolution: Beyond the Adversarial Model.* New York: Aspen Publishers.

Meyer, A.S. (1950) 'Some thoughts about mediation.' Mimeographed paper.

Meyer, A.S. (1960) 'Functions of the mediator in collective bargaining.' *Industrial and Labor Relations Review 13*, 159–65.

Mnookin, R.H. and Kornhauser, L. (1979) 'Bargaining in the shadow of the law: The case of divorce.' *Yale Law Journal 88*, 950–997.

National Institute for Dispute Resolution (NIDR) (1993) *Interim Guidelines for Selecting Mediators.* Washington, DC.

National Organisation for Education, Training and Standards Setting in Advice, Advocacy Counselling, Guidance, Mediation and Psychotherapy (CAMPAG) (1998) *Mediation Standards.* London: CAMPAG.

Ogus, A. (1998) 'Rethinking Self-Regulation.' In R. Baldwin, C. Scott and C. Hood (eds) *A Reader in Regulation.* Oxford: Oxford University Press.

O'Neill, O. (2002) 'A Question of Trust.' *Reith Lectures*, BBC, Radio 4.

Pearson, J. and Thoennes, N. (1989) 'Divorce Mediation: Reflections on a Decade of Research.' In K. Kressel, D.G. Pruitt and Associates. (eds) *Mediation Research: The Process and Effectiveness of Third Party Intervention.* San Francisco: Jossey-Bass.

Pou, C. (2003) '"Embracing limbo": Thinking about rethinking dispute resolution ethics.' *Penn State Law Review 108*, 1, 199–226.

Power, M. (1994) *The Audit Explosion.* London: Demos.

Princen, T. (1992) *Intermediaries in International Conflict.* Princeton, NJ: Princeton University Press.

Pruitt, D.G. (1981) *Negotiation Behaviour.* New York: Academic Press.

Raiffa, H. (1982) *The Art and Science of Negotiation.* Cambridge, MA: Belknap, Harvard University Press.

Reich, C.A. (1970) *The Greening of America: How the Youth Revolution is Trying to Make America Livable.* New York: Random House.

Rifkin, J. (1994) 'The Practitioner's Dilemma.' In J.P. Folger and T.S. Jones, (eds) *New Directions in Mediation*. London: Sage Publications.

Riskin, L.L. (1984) 'Towards new standards for the neutral lawyer in mediation.' *Arizona Law Review 26*, 330–62.

Riskin, L.L. (1994) 'Mediator orientations, strategies and techniques.' *Alternatives to High Cost Litigation 12*, 9, 111–114.

Riskin, L.L. (2003) 'Decsion-making in mediation: The new old grid and the new new grid system.' *Notre Dame Law Review 79*, 1, 1–54.

Roberts, M. (1992a) 'Systems or selves? Some ethical issues in family mediation.' *Mediation Quarterly 10*, 1.

Roberts, M. (1992b) 'Who is in charge? Reflections on recent research on the role of the mediator.' *Journal of Social Welfare and Family Law 5*, 372–87.

Roberts, M. (1994) 'Who is in charge? Effecting a productive exchange between researchers and practitioners in the field of family mediation.' *Journal of Social Welfare and Family Law 4*, 439–54.

Roberts, M. (1996) Family mediation and the interests of women – facts and fears.' *Family Law 26*, April, 239–41.

Roberts, M. (1997) *Mediation in Family Disputes: Principles of Practice*, 2nd edn. Aldershot, Hampshire: Ashgate.

Roberts, M. (2005) 'Hearing both sides: Structural safeguards for protecting fairness in family mediation.' *Mediation in Practice*, May, 23–32.

Roberts, M. (2006) 'Voluntary participation in family mediation.' *Family Law 36*, 57–62.

Roberts, M. (2007) *Mediation and Family Disputes: Principles of Practice*, 3rd edn. (forthcoming).

Roberts, S.A. (1979) *Order and Dispute: An Introduction to Legal Anthropology*. Harmondsworth: Penguin.

Roberts, S.A. (1983) 'The Study of Dispute: Anthropological Perspectives.' In J.A. Bossy (ed.) *Disputes and Settlements: Law and Human Relations in the West*. Cambridge: Cambridge University Press.

Roberts, S.A. (1986) 'Towards a Minimal Form of Alternative Intervention.' *Mediation Quarterly 11*, 25–41.

Roberts, S.A. (2002) 'Institutionalized settlement in England: A contemporary panorama.' *Willamette Journal of International Law and Dispute Resolution 10*, 17–35.

Roberts, S.A. and Palmer, M. (2005) *Dispute Processes: ADR and the Primary Forms of Decision-Making*. Cambridge: Cambridge University Press.

Rubin, J.Z. and Brown, B.R. (1975) *The Social Psychology of Bargaining and Negotiation*. New York: Academic Press.

Saposnek, D.T. (1983) *Mediating Child Custody Disputes*. San Francisco: Jossey-Bass.

Sarat, A. and Felstiner, W.L.F. (1995) *Divorce Lawyers and their Clients: Power and Meaning in the Legal Process*. Oxford: Oxford University Press.

Schelling, T.C. (1960) *The Strategy of Conflict*. Cambridge, MA: Harvard University Press.

Schon, D.A. (1983) *The Reflective Practitioner: How Professionals Think in Action*. New York: Basic Books.

Schuck, P.H. (1987) *Agent Orange on Trial: Mass Toxic Disasters in the Courts*. Cambridge, MA: Belknap Press of Harvard University Press.

Sennett, R. (2003) *Respect: The Formation of Character in an Age of Inequality*. London: Penguin/Allen Lane.

Sennett, R. (2006) *The Culture of the New Capitalism*. New Haven and London: Yale University Press.

Shah-Kazemi, S.N. (2000) 'Cross-cultural mediation: A critical view of the dynamics of culture in family disputes.' *International Journal of Law, Policy and the Family 14*, 302–25.

Silbey, S.S. and Merry, S.E. (1986) 'Mediator settlement strategies.' *Law and Policy 8*, 1, 7–32.

Simmel, G. (1908a) *The Sociology of Georg Simmel*. Trans. K.H. Wolff 1955. New York: Free Press.

Simmel, G. (1908b) *On Individuality and Social Forms*. D.N. Levine (ed.) (1971) Chicago: University of Chicago Press.

Society of Professionals in Dispute Resolution (SPIDR) Commission (1989) *Qualifying Neutrals: The Basic Principles*. Washington, DC: National Institute for Dispute Regulation.

Stenelo, L.-G. (1972) *Mediation in International Negotiations*. Malmö, Sweden: Nordens Boktryckeri.

Stevens, C.M. (1963) *Strategy and Collective Bargaining Negotiation*. New York: McGraw Hill.

Stulberg, J. (1981) 'The Theory and Practice of Mediation: A Reply to Professor Susskind.' 6 Vermont Law Review 85, reprinted in S.B. Goldberg, E.D. Green and F.E.A. Sander (eds) *Dispute Resolution*. Boston and Toronto: Little, Brown and Company.

Stulberg, J. (1987) *Taking Charge/Managing Conflict*. Lexington, MA: Lexington Books.

Sutton, A. (1981) 'Science in Court.' In M. King (ed.) *Childhood, Welfare and Justice*. London: B.T. Batsford.

Thoennes, N.A. and Pearson, J. (1985) 'Predicting outcomes in divorce mediation: The influence of people and process.' *Journal of Social Issues 41*, 2, 115–26.

UK College of Family Mediators (2000) *Domestic Abuse Screening Policy*. London.

UK College of Family Mediators (2002) *Children, Young People and Family Mediation: Policy and Practice Guidelines*. London.

Walker, J., McCarthy, P. and Timms, N. (1994) *Mediation: The Making and Remaking of Cooperative Relationship: An Evaluation of the Effectiveness of Comprehensive Mediation*. Newcastle-upon-Tyne: Relate Centre for Family Studies.

Walker, J., McCarthy, P., Stark, C. and Laing, K. (2004) *Picking Up The Pieces: Marriage and Divorce Two Years After Information Provision*. London: Department for Constitutional Affairs.

Wallerstein, J. and Kelly, J.R. (1980) *Surviving the Break Up*. London: Grant McIntyre.

Watson, L.M. Jr. (2002) *Effective Advocacy in Mediation: A Planning Guide to Prepare for a Civil Trial Mediation*. Upchurch Watson White and Max Mediation Group. Online at www.uww-adr.com/2004/pdfs/effectivadvocacy.pdf, accessed 29 January 2007.

Woolf, Lord (1996) *Access to Justice: Final Report to the Lord Chancellor on the Civil Justice System of England and Wales*. London: HMSO.

Further Reading Recommended by the Contributors

Acland, A.F. (1990) *A Sudden Outbreak of Common Sense: Managing Conflict Through Mediation.* London: Hutchinson Business Books.

Acland, A.F. (1995) *Resolving Disputes Without Going to Court.* London: Random Century.

Avruch, K. (1998) *Culture and Conflict Resolution.* Washington, DC: Institute of Peace Press.

Bagshaw, D. (2001) 'The three M's – mediation, postmodernism, and the new Millennium.' *Mediation Quarterly 18*, 3, 205–20.

Bagshaw, D. (2003) 'Contested Truths: Disclosing Domestic Violence in Family Law Mediation.' In W.J. Pammer and J. Killian (eds) *Handbook of Conflict Management.* New York: Marcel Dekker.

Banks, M. (1984) *Conflict in World Society: A New Perspective on International Relations.* Brighton: Harvester Press.

Banks, M. and Mitchell, C. (1995) *Handbook of Conflict Resolution: The Analytical Problem-Solving Approach.* London: Pinter.

Beer, J.E. (1997) *The Mediator's Handbook.* Philadelphia, PA: Friends Suburban Project.

Bennis, W., Benne, K. and Chin, R. (eds) (1984) *The Planning of Change.* New York: Holt, Reinhart and Winston.

Burton, J. (1987) *Resolving Deep-Rooted Conflicts: A Handbook.* Lanham, MD: University Press of America.

Burton, J. (1990) (ed.) *Conflict: Human Needs Theory.* London: Macmillan.

Coogler, O.J. (1978) *Structured Mediation in Divorce Settlement.* Lexington, MA: Lexington Books/D.C. Heath.

Cornelius, H. and Faire, S. (1989) *Everyone Can Win: How to Resolve Conflict.* New South Wales: Simon and Schuster.

Csikszentmihalyi, M. (1991) *Flow: The Psychology of Optimal Experience.* New York: HarperCollins.

Curle, A. (1971) *Making Peace.* London: Tavistock Publications.

Duffy-Toft, M. (2003) *The Geography of Ethnic Violence: Identity, Interests and the Indivisibility of Territory.* Princeton, NJ: Princeton University Press.

Francis, D. (2000) 'Culture, Power Asymmetries and Gender in Conflict Transformation.' *The Berghof Handbook for Conflict Transformation.* Berlin: Berghof Research Center for Constructive Conflict Management. www.berghof-handbook.net, accessed 29 January 2007.

Galtung, J. (1990) 'Cultural violence.' *Journal of Peace Research 27*, 3, 291–305.

Goss-Mayr, J. and Goss-Mayr, H. (1990) *The Gospel and the Struggle for Peace.* Alkmaar, The Netherlands: International Fellowship of Reconciliation.

Habermas, J. (1987) *The Theory of Communicative Action.* Trans. T. McCarthy. Cambridge, MA: Harvard University Press.

Jung, C.G. and Storr, A. (1983) *The Essential Jung*. Princeton, NJ: Princeton University Press.

Kahn-Freund, O. (1954) 'Intergroup conflicts and their settlement.' *British Journal of Sociology 5*, 193.

Keen, D. (1998) *The Economic Functions of Violence in Civil Wars*. Adelphi Paper 320. IISS/Oxford University Press.

LeBaron, M. (1998) 'Mediation and multicultural reality.' *Peace and Conflict Studies 5*, 1, 41–56.

LeBaron, M. (2005) *Bridging Troubled Waters – Conflict Resolution From the Heart*. New York: Jossey-Bass.

LeBaron, M. and Zumeta, Z.D. (2003) 'Lawyers, culture and mediation practice.' *Conflict Resolution Quarterly 20*, 4, 463–72.

Lederach, J.P. (1995) *Preparing for Peace: Conflict Transformation Across Cultures*. New York: Syracuse University Press.

Lederach, J.P. (2003) *The Little Book of Conflict Transformation*. Intercourse, PA: Good Books.

Marshall, T.F. (1985) *Alternatives to Criminal Courts*. Aldershot: Gower.

Marzotto, C. and Tamanza, G. (2004) 'The evaluation of family mediation: An empirical process research.' *Family Mediation 2004 – Back to the Future*. Conference paper. Edinburgh, Scotland.

Maslow, A. (1962) *Toward a Psychology of Being*. Princeton, NJ: Van Nostrand.

Mayer, B. (2000) *The Dynamics of Conflict Resolution: A Practitioners' Guide*. San Francisco: Jossey-Bass.

Mediation UK (1995) *Training Manual in Community Mediation*. Bristol: Mediation UK.

Mindell, A. (1993) *The Leader as Martial Artist: An Introduction to Deep Democracy*. San Francisco: HarperCollins.

Mintzberg, H. (1983) *Structures in Fives: Designing Effective Organizations*. Englewood Cliffs, NJ: Prentice Hall.

Moore, C.W. (1996) *The Mediation Process: Practical Strategies for Resolving Conflict*. San Francisco: Jossey-Bass.

Naughton, P. (2003) 'Mediators are Magicians: A Modern Myth.' Talk given to the Society of Construction Law.

Roberts, S.A. (1979) *Order and Dispute: An Introduction to Legal Anthropology*. Harmondsworth: Penguin.

Rogers, C. (1968) *Freedom to Learn*. Columbus, OH: Charles E. Merrill.

Rogers, C. (1977) *On Personal Power*. New York: Delacorte.

Rosenberg, M.B. (2005) *Nonviolent Communication: A Language of Life*. Encinitas, CA: PuddleDancer Press.

Shapiro, D. (2000) 'Pushing the envelope – selective techniques in tough mediations.' *The Arbitration and Dispute Resolution Law Journal*. (2000), 117–142.

Shapiro, D. (2001) 'Tough talking.' *The Arbitration and Dispute Resolution Law Journal*, (2001), 2–4.

Tannen, D. (1990) *You Just Don't Understand. Women and Men in Conversation*. New York: Morrow.

Tidwell, A. (1998) *Conflict Resolved? A Critical Assessment of Conflict Resolution*. London: Continuum.

Winslade, S. and Monk, G. (2000) *Narrative Mediation: A New Approach to Conflict Resolution*. San Fransico: Jossey-Bass.

Wood, E. and Kestner, P. (1989) *The Coming of Age*. Washington, DC: American Bar Association.

Woodhouse, T. and Ramsbotham, O. (2000) *Peacekeeping and Conflict Resolution*. London: Frank Cass.

Wright, M. (1991) *Justice for Victims and Offenders*. Philadelphia, PA: Open University Press.

Zehr, H. and Toews, B. (eds) (2004) *Critical Issues in Restorative Justice*. Monsey, NY: Criminal Justice Press.

Subject Index

Abkhasia 41
abuse 99, 111, 150–1, 156, 178
Acland, Andrew 9, 24–5, 44, 49, 58, 63–4, 73, 128, 140, 194
   commonalities across fields 219
   flow 210–1
   future development 232
   impartiality 100–1
   mediation as intervention 81–2
   party control 104
   party motivation 91–2
   power and responsibility 180
   practice styles 143
   preparation 151–2
   professional regulation 201–2
   specialist knowledge 223–4
   stress 188
   stress management 189
   sui generis mediation 162–3
   support 190
   theory and practice 112, 117, 121
   voluntary participation 103
adjudication 27, 29, 72–3, 86, 87, 103
ADR 18, 23, 29, 110, 111, 166, 172, 201, 230, 231, 232, 234
   EU Green Paper 193, 203
adversariality 165, 166–7, 172, 173, 228, 232
Advisory, Conciliation and Arbitration Service (ACAS) 29–30, 40, 52, 103, 191, 220

Africa 119, 177
age 175
Age Concern 75, 149
Agent Orange 28, 52
agreement 134
Albania 82, 169
Algeria 24
Ali, Mohammed 31
alternative dispute resolution *see* ADR
anger 79, 96, 159
Anti-Social Behaviour Orders 170
apartheid 25
approachability 46
arbitration 27, 29–30, 51–2, 65–6, 139, 200
Arbitration Act 1996 200
artistry 207–8
Arts and Crafts Movement 228
Asia 160
Austria 195

Bagshaw, Dale 99
Balkans 31, 159, 177
Biafra 23, 31, 154, 186–7
bitterness 178–9
Bristol Mediation 32
Britain *see* UK
Bromley model 151, 164
Buddhism 30, 31
Burton, J. 106, 108

calmness 49, 54, 183, 229
Cambridge Mediation Service 38
Camden Mediation Service 115
Campaign for Nuclear Disarmament (CND) 36
Canterbury, Archbishop of 24–5

Carroll, Eileen 26
Carter, Jimmy 30
Catholic University, Milan 34
caucus 147, 155–6, 158, 191
CEDR (Centre for Dispute Resolution) 26, 216
Central Arbitration Committee 213
Centre for Action Research in Professional Practice (CARPP) 126
Centre for Mediation Studies and Conflict Resolution 39
Centre for Peace, Nonviolence and Human Rights 93
children 33, 87, 114, 123, 224
   child abduction 18, 234
   child protection 18
   family conflict 59–60, 111, 157, 169, 171, 181–2
Christianity 30, 31–2
civil justice 18, 231
civil liberties 61
class 96, 175
co-mediation 159–62, 192
co-workers 191–2, 234
coercion 18, 99, 103, 134
Cold War 36
commercial mediation 18, 24, 28, 36–7, 50–1, 106–7, 114, 148
   adversariality 167–8
   co-mediation 161
   documentation 163
   emotional content 184–5
   future development 231, 233
   limitations of theory 116

Subject Index

negotiated settlements
  76–7
party exploitation and
  manipulation 175–7
plenary or joint meetings
  152–4, 163
practice styles 135, 141
preparation 151–2
professional regulation
  197, 198, 200
purpose 73–4
specialist knowledge
  225–6, 226–7
stress 187–8
Committee of Conflict
  Transformation Support
  32, 190–1, 199
communication 78, 79, 80, 85,
  179
community mediation 18, 29,
  45, 46–7, 86, 135–6,
  167, 192, 231
  housing issues 170
  Ismailis 157–8
  personal aptitude 211–12
  practice styles 140
  preparation 149
  professional regulation 198
  purpose 74
  voluntary participation 101
compassion 95
Conciliation Act 1896 29, 231
conferences 147
conflict 49, 54–6, 184, 196
  conflict resolution 32–3,
    50, 80
  dealing with conflict 62–6
  dimensions and responses
    56–61
  intractable conflict 64, 66
constructive management 63
contributors 9–15
  questionnaire 235–6
Coogler Model of Structured
  Mediation 164
Council of Europe 93
counselling 85, 169
Court Reporting Officers 80
courts 73, 80, 86, 165, 166
craft 207–8, 227–30
  components 211–15
  language 209–11

Craig, Yvonne 9, 29, 34, 45,
  61, 63, 75, 79, 96, 201
  aims of mediation 218
  co-mediation 192–3
  elderly people 178–9
  justice and fairness 167
  limitations of theory 115
  multi-disciplinary workers
    85–6
  party control 107–8
  practice styles 136
  preparation 149
  professional regulation 198
  victim-offender mediation
    120–1
  voluntary participation 101
criminal justice system 27, 56,
  58, 167, 225, 231
Croatia 72, 93
cultural issues 100, 111, 115,
  147, 157–8, 162, 225,
  233–4
curiosity 45, 46
Curle, Adam 9–10, 16, 23, 31,
  34, 56, 71, 72, 106, 232
  effective practice 217
  limitations of theory 115
  professional regulation 199
  shuttle mediation 154–5
  stress 186–7
Cyprus 40

danger 148, 154, 186
Davis, Albie 234
directive behaviour 145
disability 231
discernment 86, 91
disputes 17, 80
  neighbour disputes 47, 60,
    74, 78, 150, 153, 192
distress 17, 55, 183, 187
divorce 33, 77, 102, 123, 169,
  171, 172
doctors 85
Dutch Reformed Church 25

Early Neutral Evaluation (ENE)
education 231, 232
effectiveness 18, 76, 172,
  208–11, 211–15,
  215–17
Egypt 30, 66

elder mediation 18, 45, 74–5,
  79, 101, 107–8, 135–6,
  167, 192–3, 225
  parties capacity to
    participate 178–9
  preparation 149
  professional regulation 198
emotions 65–6, 184
  commercial mediation
    184–5
empathy 96, 217
environmental mediation 18,
  100, 103, 104, 112,
  173, 180, 231
  future development 232–3
  specialist knowledge
    223–4
  stress 187, 188
equality 96
equity 17
ethics 231
ethnic issues 100, 137, 162,
  166
Europe 19, 71, 85, 134
evil 91

facilitation 49, 50, 78, 106,
  231
fairness 17, 95, 156, 165,
  166–9, 193, 227
family conflict 33–4, 34–5,
  36–7, 64–5, 85
  children 59–60, 111, 169,
    171, 181–2
  parents 59–60, 157, 181
  purpose of mediation 75,
    77–9
family loss 37–8
family mediation 18, 24, 28,
  93, 111, 112, 122–3,
  148, 153, 173
  differences across fields
    222, 234
  eclectic mediation models
    157
  funding 170–1, 194
  impartiality 98
  judgmental stance 182
  personal aptitude 212–13
  practice styles 137, 138,
    139
  preparation 151

family mediation *cont.*
  professional regulation
    195–6, 196–7
  respect 95–6
  separate structuring 163–4
  specialist knowledge 224,
    226
  stress 184, 185–6
  voluntary participation
    101–2
family therapy 38, 181
family welfare interventions 27
fear 96, 184
Fellowship of Reconciliation
  32
finance 111
FIRM (Forum for Initiatives in
  Restoration and
  Mediation) 29
Follett, Mary Parker 234
Francis, Diana 10, 31–3, 47–8,
  58–9, 72, 126, 128,
  199
  advantages of mediation 88
  co-mediation 160–1, 192
  differences across fields
    222, 223
  effective practice 216
  gender 182–3
  international mediation
    119, 120
  justice and fairness 168–9
  limitations of theory
    115–16
  mediation as intervention
    82–3
  personal aptitude 214–15
  practice styles 141–2
  professional regulation
    199–200
  remuneration 183
  respect 95
  specialist knowledge 227
  stress 187
  support 190–1
  theory and practice 113
Friends Suburban Project,
  Philadelphia 27, 118
funding 76, 170–2, 188–9

Gandhi, Indira 31

Gandhi, Mahatma 32, 119,
  128
gender 89, 96, 100, 137, 145,
  147, 158, 160, 175
  international mediation
    182–3
genogrammes 122–3
Georgia 41, 48, 183
Germany 19, 77–8, 84, 97,
  102, 116, 117, 143–4,
  148, 157, 197, 213,
  217, 220, 226
  mandatory mediation
    102–3
Gibbons, Fred 10–11, 24,
  27–8, 37–8, 44, 45
  family mediation 119–20
  non-judgmental approach
    182
  personal aptitude 212–13
  professional regulation
    196–7
  stress management 189–90
good faith 91, 92
Goss-Mayr, Jean and
  Hildegarde 119
Gowan, President 115, 186–7
group mediation 222–3
Guardian, The 182

Harvard Negotiation Model
  114, 127
hatred 54, 63, 71, 179
Haynes, John 99, 128, 137,
  197, 226
Hoffman, Mark 11, 40, 50,
  60–1, 71–2, 76, 105,
  108, 142
  advantages of mediation 87
  differences across fields
    221
  effective practice 216
  international mediation
    172
  party control 106
  personal aptitude 214
  professional regulation 199
  theory and practice
    113–14
  violence 177
Home Office 195
Hopgood, William 139

hostages 24–5
hostility 62, 213
housing issues 18, 170
  sheltered housing 75, 107
humour 43, 45, 138, 143
Hungary 159

impartiality 41, 97–101
India 31, 115, 154, 160
industrial relations 24, 29,
  51–2, 65–6, 156
industrialisation 228
inheritance 77
Institute of Family Therapy
  Mediation Service 40
insurers 77
intelligence 44, 216–17
international conflict 24, 54,
  55, 82, 83, 177, 221–2
  purpose of mediation 71
International Fellowship of
  Reconciliation 32, 119
international mediation 18, 23,
  105–6, 113–14, 148,
  231
  co-mediation 160–1
  differences across fields
    221–2
  eclectic mediation models
    158–9
  effective practice 216
  funding 171–2
  gender 182–3
  limitations of theory
    115–16
  personal aptitude 214–15
  power 168–9
  practice styles 141–2
  professional regulation
    199–200
  respect 955
  specialist knowledge 227
  stress 186–7, 190
interpreters 48
intuition 121, 213
Iran 24
Ismailis 157–8
Israel 30, 64, 66, 97
Italian Society of Family
  Mediators 196
Italy 19, 95, 122, 143, 164,
  184, 196, 224

Subject Index

Japan 162
Jordan 66
judgmental stance 96, 134, 182
justice 18, 31–2, 95, 165, 166–9, 227
    restorative justice 167, 195, 231

King, Martin Luther 32
Kissinger, Henry 217
Kosovo 64, 82, 169

labour relations 18, 24, 29, 59, 88–9, 103, 104–5, 112–13, 231
    eclectic mediation models 156–7
    personal aptitude 213–14
    personal conflict 185
    practice styles 138
    professional regulation 197
    reluctance to participate 175
    support 191
Landlord and Tenant Courts 166
Law Society 172, 194, 203
lawyers 18, 25–6, 55, 56, 83–4, 86, 109, 136, 141, 152, 170, 228
    as mediators 172–3, 193, 196, 200, 225–6, 230
    commercial mediation 176
    consulting service 192
    employment lawyers 191
    negotiations 90
Lederach, John-Paul 32, 95
legal aid 172
legal profession 80, 109, 172–3
Legal Services Commission (LSC) 76, 194
legal system 165, 166, 167–8, 194, 232
Lewis, Roy 11, 29–30, 51–2, 59, 65–6, 77, 184, 209
    advantages of mediation 89
    commonalities across fields 220
    craft 213–14

eclectic mediation models 156–7
impartiality 98
party control 105
party reluctance 175
personal conflict 185
practice styles 138
professional regulation 197
support 191
theory and practice 113, 118, 125–6
voluntary participation 103
libel 89
Libya 25
Liebmann, Marian 12, 27, 46–7, 57, 64, 74
    advantages of mediation 88
    housing issues 170
    impartiality 99
    limitations of theory 114
    literature 118–19
    mediation as intervention 86
    party control 107
    personal aptitude 211–12
    practice styles 136
    preparation 149–50
    professional regulation 194–5
    support 192
    theory and practice 122
    victim-offender mediation 184
listening 44, 45, 48, 143
literature 18, 109, 113, 117–29
litigation 26, 27, 52, 72–3, 86, 88, 103, 230

Mackie, Karl 26
magistrates 29, 120–1
Mandela, Nelson 25
Marcos, President 119
Marshall Plan 71
Marshall, Tony 167
Mary Parker Follett Award 234
Marzotto, Costanza 12, 33–4, 46, 63, 209
    family mediation 95–6, 122–3
    practice styles 143
    professional regulation 196

specialist knowledge 224
theory and practice 122–3
Mediation 29
mediation 17–19, 69–70, 109, 165
    advantages 86–92
    autonomy and external intervention 169–72
    caucus 147, 155–6, 158
    co-mediation 159–62, 192
    commonalities across fields 217–18, 218–27
    craft 207–8, 227–30
    development 166
    differences across fields 220–3
    eclectic models 156–7
    effective practice 208–11, 211–15, 215–17
    funding 76, 170–2, 188–9
    future development 230–4
    impartiality 97–101
    intervention 80–6, 133–4
    justice and fairness 166–9
    legal framework 172–3
    limitations of theory 114–17
    mandatory mediation 101–3, 108
    mediator authority 104–8
    negotiated settlements 76–9
    party control 73–6, 86–7, 88, 104–8
    party responsibility 91
    plenary or joint meetings 147, 152–4, 158, 163
    practice models 146–8, 163–4
    practice styles 132–5, 135–7, 139–42, 143–4, 144–6
    practice styles and negotiations 138–9
    practice styles and parties 137–8
    practice styles and personality 142–3
    principles 94, 108
    professional practice 173–4

mediation *cont.*
  professional regulation
    193–5, 195–8,
    198–202
  purpose 70–9, 92–3
  respect 95–7, 108
  specialist knowledge
    223–7
  sui generis mediation 147,
    162–3
  theory and practice
    110–11, 111–14,
    117–28
  voluntary participation
    101–4
Mediation UK 225
  Mediation UK Manual
    118–19
Mediators Competence
  Certificate 195
mediators 19–20, 42–4,
  131–2
  discernment 86, 91
  experience of conflict 23–5
  family mediation 169–70
  fortuitous influences 38–40
  intellectual curiosity 25–6
  mediator authority 104–8
  patience 50–3
  personal experience 34–8,
    56, 57
  personal qualities 43–4,
    44–9, 211–15,
    229–30
  power and responsibility
    179–80
  practice styles 132–5,
    135–7, 139–42,
    143–4, 144–6
  practice styles and
    negotiations 138–9
  practice styles and parties
    137–8
  practice styles and
    personality 142–3
  professional innovation
    27–30
  professional practice 85,
    93, 110–11, 173–4
  stress 183–6, 186–9
  stress management 188–93

support 190–3
trust of parties 175–7
values and ideology 30–8
medical negligence 18, 231
meetings 147
  plenary or joint meetings
    152–4, 158, 163
men 89, 159, 182–3
mental health 178
mercy 95
Middle East 66, 169
Miles, David 26
mini-trials 231
Ministry of Justice 217
modelling 192
Moldova 40, 41, 76, 142, 172
Morris, William 228

National Family Mediation
  211
National Vocational
  Qualification (NVQ)
  195
Naughton, Philip 12, 26, 46,
  57–8, 76–7, 184, 209
  advantages of mediation 90
  caucus 155
  craft 215
  differences across fields
    220
  future development 231
  lawyers 83–4
  limitations of theory 117
  personal conflict 185
  practice styles 135
  professional regulation 200
  specialist knowledge
    226–7
  stress 188
  stress management 189
  trust of parties 175
negotiation 80, 90, 103, 133,
  217–18
  Harvard Negotiation Model
    114, 127
  negotiated settlements
    76–9
  practice styles 138–9
  second track negotiation 41
neighbour disputes 47, 60, 74,
  78, 150, 153, 192

Nepal 40
neutrality 18, 41, 80, 98–9
NGO 41
Nigeria 31, 115, 154, 186–7
noise 78
North America 18, 19, 110,
  120, 134, 135, 144,
  164, 167, 191, 226
Northern Ireland 40, 64
Norway 195
nuclear war 36
nurses 85

offender–victim mediation 18,
  27, 66, 103, 120–1,
  122, 167, 184
  preparation 149–50
  professional training 195
  specialist knowledge 225
Organisation for Security and
  Co-operation in Europe
  76, 172
organisational mediation 103,
  112, 163
  practice styles 140
  stress 188
Osijek, Croatia 72, 93

pacifism 30, 31–2, 34
pain 60, 63
Pakistan 31, 115, 154, 158
Palestine 64
parents 33, 93, 123
  family conflict 59–60, 157,
    181
parties 92, 136, 147, 174
  capacity to participate
    178–9
  exploitation and
    manipulation of
    process 175–7
  party control 73–9, 86–7,
    88, 104–8, 227
  party motivation 91–2
  party responsibility 91
  practice styles 137–8
  reluctance to participate
    175
  voluntary participation
    101–4
  patience 43, 44, 45, 47, 50–3

Paul, Christoph 12–13, 25, 45, 56–7, 64–5, 78
  advantages of mediation 88
  differences across fields 221
  eclectic mediation models 157
  effective practice 217
  intuition 213
  lawyers 84, 173
  mediation 210
  practice styles 144
  preparation 148
  respect 97
  specialist knowledge 226
  stress management 190
  theory and practice 116, 117
  voluntary participation 102–3
peace 72, 95, 158
people, concern for 45, 46, 47
personal conflict 17, 184–5
personal development 63
Philippines 32, 119
political conflict 17, 60–1, 177, 221–2
poverty 166
power 18, 162, 165, 166, 217
practice 18, 109, 131–2, 164, 207–8
  effective practice 208–11, 211–15, 215–17
  practice models 146–8, 163–4
  practice styles 132–5, 135–7, 139–42, 143–4, 144–6
    negotiations 138–9
    parties 137–8
    personality 142–3
  professional practice 85, 93, 110–11, 173–4
  theory and practice 110–11, 111–14, 117–28
preparation 147, 148–52
probation service 27–8
professional regulation 76, 193–5, 202–3
  arguments in favour 195–8
  problems 198–202

property 111
psychology 48
public policy fields 18

Quakers 30, 31, 119, 215
quarrels 17, 92

race 96, 100, 115, 175
RAF 36
regulation 76, 193–5, 202–3
  arguments in favour 195–8
  problems 198–202
  self-regulation 194
relationships 54, 63, 75, 85, 232
research 18, 110, 117–27
respect 17, 32, 45, 95–7, 227, 229
restorative justice 167, 195, 231
Reunite 217, 234
Reynolds, Carl 13, 35–6, 39, 46, 48–9, 190
  free-lances 209
  impartiality 100
  importance of mediation 232
  party control 105
  practice styles 140
  respect 96
  voluntary participation 101
Rogers, Carl 46
Royal Mail National Appeals Panel 213
Ruskin, John 228
Rwanda 154

sadness 96
safety 147, 149, 151
Schaffer, Lorraine 13, 39, 45, 49, 59–60, 78–9
  bad practice 208
  commonalities across fields 219
  impartiality 98
  mediation as intervention 85
  personal aptitude 212
  practice styles 138, 139
  preparation 151
  professional regulation 196
  research 126

stress 185–6
theory and practice 112, 124–5
truth 99–100
voluntary participation 102
second track negotiation 41
self-knowledge 48–9
self-regulation 194
separation 33, 78, 169, 172
Serbia 64, 82, 169
settlement 134
  negotiated settlements 76–9
sexuality 96
Shapiro, David 14, 28, 36, 52, 53, 61, 77, 118, 218, 225
  advantages of mediation 89
  commercial mediation 106–7, 116
  consulting service 191–2
  lawyers 83, 152, 176–7
  mediators 210
  party control 106
  practice styles 142–3
  professional regulation 197
  stress 187–8
  trust of parties 176
sheltered housing 75, 107
shuttle mediation 64, 65, 100, 122, 147, 154–5, 156, 158
Sierra Leone 177
Small Claims Courts 166
social change 63
social conflict 17
social work 38, 39, 49, 85, 86, 96, 181, 185, 186
Society of Professionals in Dispute Resolution (SPIDR) 234
sociopaths 91
South Africa 25
South East London Family Mediation Bureau 164, 203
Soviet Union 32
specialist knowledge 223–7
Sri Lanka 31, 40, 154–5, 182
stress 17, 55, 183–6
  management 188–93
  nature and causes 186–9

suffering 17, 63, 184, 190
sui generis mediation 147, 162–3
Summary Jury Trial 231
suspicion 71

tact 217
talking 80
Tbilisi 41, 161
teachers 85, 86
telephone industry 28
Thames barges 24, 27
theory 109
    limitations of theory 114–17
    theory and practice 110–11, 111–14, 117–28
therapy 85, 86, 169
tolerance 45
toughness 46, 50, 51
Trade Union and Labour Relations (Consolidation) Act 1992 29
trade unions 29, 39
Transformative Mediation Framework 132–3, 134
translators 48
trust 175–7, 229

UK 18, 26, 33, 74, 77, 85, 134, 164, 195, 198
    ADR 232
    industrial relations legislation 29
UK College of Family Mediators 93
USA 18, 19, 26, 28, 40, 52, 74, 92, 119, 172, 194, 200, 227, 231
    ADR 232
    Iran hostage crisis 24
    practice styles 132–3, 133–4

victim–offender mediation 18, 27, 66, 103, 120–1, 122, 167, 184
    preparation 149–50
    professional training 195
    specialist knowledge 225

violence 35–6, 54, 60–1, 87, 115–16, 177, 221, 222

Waite, Terry 25
waiting rooms 147, 151
war 23, 186–7
Warwick University 30
wealth 166
Whatling, Tony 14, 34–5, 38, 63, 75, 88
    divorce proceedings 171
    Ismailis 157–8
    practice styles 137
    respect 96
    stress 185
    theory and practice 112, 123–4, 125
Willis, Tony 15, 24, 26, 36–7, 44, 51, 57, 73–4, 185, 198, 219
    advantages of mediation 90–1
    children 181–2, 226
    co-mediation 161
    commercial mediation 153–4
    effective practice 216
    future development 233
    justice and fairness 167–8
    lawyers 84, 141
    practice styles 141
    professional regulation 193–4
    respect 97
    specialist knowledge 225–6
    stress 187, 189
    stress management 189
    theory and practice 114
Winston, Jack 28
women 89, 159, 166, 183
work ethic 228
workplace 18, 231
Wright, Martin 167

Zimbabwe 154

Author Index

Abel, R.L. 55, 166, 194
ACAS (Advisory, Conciliation and Arbitration Service) 152
ACLEC 172
Aristotle 208, 227
Astor, H. 23
Auerbach, J.S. 165, 166, 200, 230

Bader, K. 166
Banks, M. 40
Bar Tal, D. 55, 66
Beal, S. 134
Bottomley 166
Bowling, D. 42, 44, 192, 211, 214
Brown, B.R. 17, 42
Burton, J. 40, 50, 55, 60, 71, 72, 108, 200
Bush, R.A.B. 70, 125, 132, 133, 134

Caplan, P. 55
Charbonneau, P. 132
Chase, O.F. 232, 233, 234
Chinkin, C. 23
Cobb, S. 127
Coletta, C. 229
Conneely, S. 42, 131
Coogler, O.J. 119, 128, 147, 164
Corbin, J. 131
Cornelius, H. 120
Council of Europe 93
Coyne, W.F. Jr. 152
Csikszentmihalyi, M. 210
Curle, A. 30, 31, 50, 71, 232

Davis, A.M. 17, 94, 166, 175, 231

Davis, G. 93, 99, 166, 170, 181
Della Noce, D.J. 134
Deutsch, M. 42
DiDomenico, A. 229
Dingwall, R. 110, 160
Douglas, A. 51, 62, 66, 174, 207, 208
Duffy, M. 177
Duryee, M.A. 127

Emery, R.E. 87, 138

Faire, S. 120
Felstiner, W.L.F. 55, 170
Fisher, R. 123, 134
Fiss, O.M. 166
Folberg, J. 147, 154, 155, 165
Folger, J.P. 70, 125, 132, 133, 234
Francis, D. 158
Freeman, M.D.A. 166
Friends Suburban Project 118
Fuller, L.L. 17, 69, 93, 132, 146, 181

Gadlin, H. 175
Galanter, M. 172
Galtung, J. 120
Gaynier 70
Gilligan, C. 168
Glasser, C. 87
Golann, D. 152
Goss-Mayr, J. and Goss-Mayr, H. 119
Greatbatch, D. 110
Grillo, T. 62, 127, 234
Gulliver, P.H. 20, 42, 62, 69, 122, 127, 133, 136, 137, 174, 210, 218

Habermas, J. 40
Hamnett, I. 90
Hampshire, S. 54, 146
Haynes, J.M. 62, 86, 99, 123, 124, 147
Hoffman, D. 42, 44, 192, 211, 214

Jones, T.S. 111

Kahn-Freund, O. 125
Keen, D. 177
Kelly, J.R. 125, 126, 127
Kolb, D.M. 20, 131, 139, 140, 228, 234
Kornhauser, L. 90, 103
Kressel, K. 54, 55, 134, 169, 174, 183

Landsberger, H.A. 43
Lang, M.D. 134, 207, 208, 210, 215
LeBaron, M. 212
Lederach, J.P. 32, 95, 119, 142
Legal Services Commission 188–9
Lukes, S. 17

Mackay, Lord 108, 172
Marshall, T.F. 121, 167
Marzotto, C. 41
Maslow, A. 124
Matthews, R. 166
Mayer, B. 124
McCarthy, P. 87
McCrory, J.P. 94
McDermott, E.P. 145
McGuigan, R. 109
McMechan, S. 109
Mediation UK 118–19

Menkel-Meadow, C.J. 23, 50, 89, 90, 109, 111, 131, 134, 135, 152, 155, 164, 166, 176, 194
Merry, S.E. 132, 139, 179, 234
Meyer, A.S. 42, 51, 69, 207
Milne, A. 155
Mitchell, C. 158
Mnookin, R.H. 90, 103
Moore, C.W. 119

Naughton, P. 93

O'Neill, O. 76
Ogus, A. 127

Palmer, M. 23, 55, 69, 80, 103, 166, 172, 230, 231
Pearson, J. 146
Pou, C. 127, 132
Power, M. 195
Princen, T. 30, 41, 54, 71, 184, 198
Pruitt, D.G. 42, 134

Raiffa, H. 43
Reich, C.A. 227
Rifkin, J. 127
Rifkin, J. 18, 110
Riskin, L.L. 132, 136
Roberts, M. 86, 89, 93, 99, 102, 154, 160, 181, 194
Roberts, S.A. 23, 55, 69, 80, 103, 120, 146, 148, 156, 163, 166, 172, 230, 231
Rosenberg, M.B. 200
Rubin, J.Z. 17, 42

Saposnek, D.T. 133, 184
Sarat, A. 55
Saul, J.A. 134
Schon, D.A. 111, 162, 217, 230
Schuck, P.H. 52, 53
Sennett, R. 17, 96, 207, 217, 228, 229
Shah-Kazemi, S.N. 108

Silbey, S.S. 132, 139, 179
Simmel, G. 18, 42, 43, 54, 55, 62, 69, 72, 93, 98, 183
Stenelo, L-G. 88, 199
Stevens, C.M. 109
Stulberg, J. 42, 43, 155

Tannen, D. 123
Taylor, A. 134, 207, 208, 210, 215
Taylor, A. 147, 154, 165
Thoennes, N. 146
Timms, N. 87
Tutu, D. 165

UK College of Family Mediators 93, 150, 151, 181
Ury, W. 123, 134

Walker, J. 87, 138
Wallerstein, J. 125
Watson, L.M. Jr. 135
Williams, L. 170
Winslade, J. 125
Woolf, Lord 108, 172
Wright, M. 121, 167